INTO THE EYES

M000219249

Leila Kulpas is a psychiatrist specialized in treating adults with childhood trauma using psychotherapy and minimal medications. She has a B.A. (Honours Class I) degree in English for her original research on the influence of Virginia Wolf's Childhood trauma on her writing. Her prose has appeared in The Vancouver Psychoanalytic Psychotherapy Review, A National Voices anthology, The Pacific Rim Review of Books, and daily newspapers, and her poetry has been published in chapbooks edited by Patrick Lane, an Ascent Aspirations Magazine anthology and on the internet by Pandora's Collective.

ISBN 978-1-9995703-0-9
First Edition, February, 2019

This work of creative non-fiction reflects, to the best of my ability, what actually happened in my first seventeen years, although doubtless there are inaccuracies due to the fallibility of memory and, of course, many of the conversations are partly approximations. In addition, some identities and names have been altered to protect privacy.

This book is dedicated to Aileen Outram, William Carlyle Wright, Polly Stephens, Laurence Richard Wright and Arthur Newell Smith.

Contents

List of Figures

ACKNOWLEDGEMENTS

I am grateful to many people for their assistance with this manuscript. My husband Newell Smith has been unfailing in his support, and has spent countless hours upgrading old photographs, as well as formatting. Dennis Kulpas was encouraging from the beginning. Roberta Jackson was very generous in her encouragement, and made helpful suggestions. Margaret Keane has been faithfully supportive. Naomi Pauls and Philip Sherwood made valuable editing suggestions. Robin Laurence commented on the memoir, made many invaluable suggestions and has been generously supportive over the years. Beverly Cramp has been very encouraging and has made useful comments. Heather Stephens made many helpful suggestions. Andrea Lawson read the work and her comments were of considerable assistance. Robyn Outram gave her permission to include her photograph of my father milking a cow. Laurence Wright listened patiently as I read much of the memoir aloud, and made helpful comments. Julie Ann Salisbury provided excellent advice. Gail Harwood generously gave useful information about publishing. And, over the years, Gary Ladd and Ulrich Lanius have deepened my understanding of the nature of Posttraumatic Stress Disorder.

Preface

I spent most of my first seventeen years some two hundred miles, or three hundred and twenty kilometres, north of Sydney, on a high mountain plateau known as Barrington Tops, which is part of the Great Dividing Range of New South Wales.

When I was six or so, my siblings and I felt so negative about the cold and rainy climate there and the atmosphere within the family, that we used to sing the following parody:

> "Home, home on the range,
>   Where the deer and the antelope play,
>   Where never is heard
>   An encouraging word,
>   And the skies are cloudy all day."

Nevertheless, I now see myself as having been, in many respects, a very lucky young person. Although my first six years were without toys or celebrations of Christmas or birthdays, and I received too little attention from my hard-working parents, their interactions with me at that time were kind and gentle, and I was content. And, even though a great deal of negativity entered my life after we settled on our Barrington Tops property when I was five, my parents awakened in me a passion for the exquisitely beautiful natural world around us and its creatures, and my food was home-grown and free of pesticides. And, despite the fact that, most of the time after I was six or so, I felt either unseen or despised by my overworked mother, many other people were loving towards me. When I was six, after my mother gave me the worst thrashing of my life—from which I still have physical scars—Auntie Charlotte, one of my father's siblings, who was staying with us at the time, comforted me, told me my mother was treating me unfairly, and that she herself loved me. It was she who gave me the idea of escaping to the city when I was old enough, and dreaming of this became a major part of my survival. And I knew I was loved by my father, my sister, Amelia, four years my senior, Uncle Bill, another of my father's siblings, Polly, who was married to my mother's cousin, my maternal grandmother, Nan, Violet Rose, a family friend, as well as by several other people at various times during my growing up years. And I loved, and felt love from, certain of our animals, including

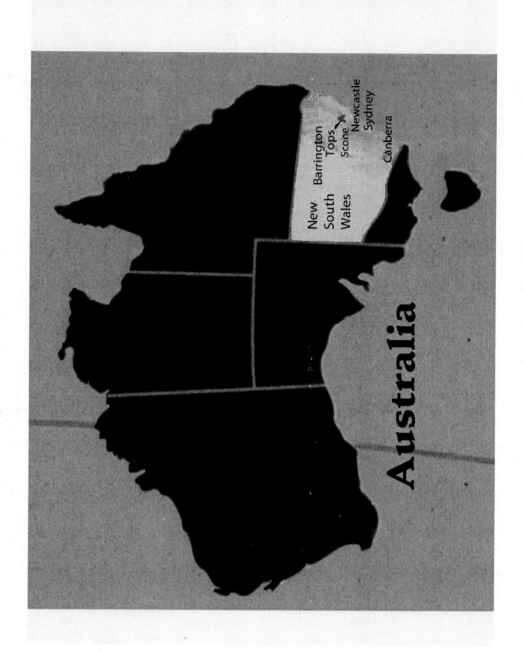

Figure 0.1: The location of Barrington Tops in relation to Scone, Newcastle, and Sydney, NSW.

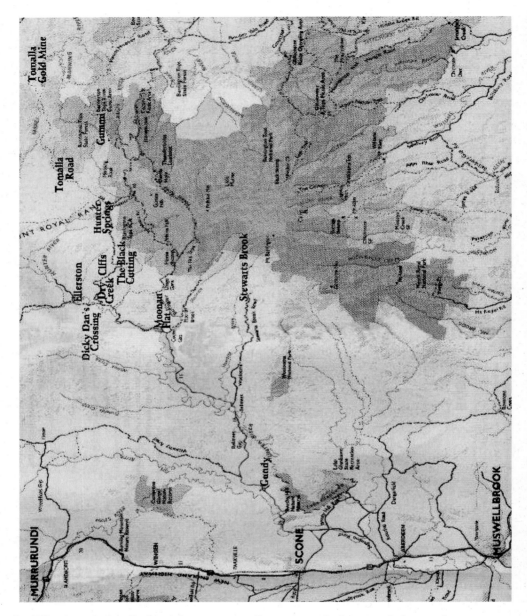

Figure 0.2: Left side, centre, Scone, and the road from there through Gundy, Moonan Flat, Dicky Dan's Crossing (now bypassed) and Dry Creek to Hunter's Springs, where the family property is located. Tomalla Gold mine, the site of the reef my father found, is on the far right near the top of the map. The large, pale grey area is Barrington Tops National Park.

my father's part-draft gelding, Hungry, our pet kangaroo, Toots, and my mare Rahnee.

Quirky human characters and frequent hilarious, strange or curious incidents distracted me and enriched my life, as well.

I ended up believing in myself enough to spend, in my twenties, some two years part-time while I worked, and two years after this full-time, up-grading my initial poor education, matriculating with marks high enough to secure a place in medical school, some time after which I become a psychiatrist.

The memoir begins with the predominantly positive memory of my mother telling stories from her life as she, Amelia and I, seven at the time, examine the objects in an old iron trunk—something we did repeatedly after we settled on our property. The work then takes the reader back to my first memories from 1947, when I was three, and we lived with Pod Taylor—who took me for walks and of whom I was fond—a landowner on the plateau some distance from where we eventually settled, and for whom both my parents worked at the time. Following this, the memoir continues sequentially, starting with the two years my family spent off the mountain, in the Upper Hunter Valley, while my parents continued to save to buy their own land—a project begun after they'd married over a decade previously.

There, initially, they both trapped rabbits for their skins—a grisly but lucrative occupation—and for the first six months or so, our family of five, then, lived in tents. We subsequently resided in two other locations in the valley, one because my mother was pregnant with my younger brother, Laurence, and the other to be close enough to my father's next job, felling trees for a large landholder, so that he could visit frequently.

My mother had led us to believe that living on our own land would be like being in a kind of paradise, but after we settled on our seven hundred acres on Barrington Tops, in 1949, managing the farm and paying the mortgage put my parents under more stress than ever. My father began to binge drink—though, for the most part, he remained kind and loving— and my mother to rage and beat, with me as her main target.

Being only some one hundred miles, or one hundred and sixty-one kilometres, from the city of Newcastle, we were not isolated compared with those who live in Australia's vast inland regions, but at the time, the fifty-four mile, or eighty-seven kilometre, journey to Scone, the nearest town with restaurants and a hospital, took four hours. The road was mostly a dirt track that became slippery or boggy after rain, and the streams crossing it often flooded. In addition, our farm was situated at an elevation of four-thousand, five hundred feet, or one-thousand, three-hundred and seventy-two metres, above sea level and the high rainfall, as well as occasional winter snowfalls, added to our difficulties traveling.

Ironically, our nearest neighbours, who were only a couple of hundred yards away in the small valley where we lived, almost totally ignored us: according to my parents, they saw us as belonging to an inferior class. However, we knew, and had amiable relationships with, the six or so other families scattered over the plateau, as well as many of the people who lived farther away in the same Scone district.

The nearest bush school was fourteen miles, or twenty-three kilometres, away, and my siblings and I were schooled through what we called "correspondence"—our lessons coming in the mail from Blackfriars Correspondence School in Sydney, with my mother as supervisor, and the completed work being returned by the same means.

Like my parents, most of the people in the district had little formal education, and were of English or Celtic descent, but whereas most of them saw themselves as belonging to a Christian religion, and attended church at least occasionally, my parents were Atheists and Communists. I wasn't aware of their beliefs isolating us, but I learned when I was a teenager that they sometimes made us the subject of gossip—a major form of local entertainment.

The memoir is in the present tense, and in my voice, which matures as I do. The world of the child is limited by experience, but my own memories, and those of the patients I have treated in my psychiatric practice, have taught me that intelligent children are, from an early age, capable of sophisticated thought not limited nearly as much as most people think by vocabulary. Stephen Pinker in The Language Instinct[1] states that thinking takes place through what he calls "mentalese," which uses symbols or images rather than words, and I see this as especially relevant in early childhood. In addition, bright children remember experiences beyond their comprehension, but which awaken their curiosity, to repeatedly re-examine these, sometimes over many decades, in the light of newly-acquired knowledge.

Footnotes, as well as a glossary at the end of the work, define words and expressions idiosyncratic to Australia.

---

[1] Pinker, Stephen, The Language Instinct, William Morrow & Co., 1994

Part I

THE EARLY YEARS

Chapter One

THE BROKEN DOLL (1951)

When I dream of going through the old iron trunk with my elder sister, Amelia, and my mother, time flows like honey. After my family settled on our seven-hundred acres of bushland on the high, wild plateau of Barrington Tops in New South Wales when I was five, we stored our woolens in there during the summers to keep them safe from moths. One afternoon in late spring, Mum would notice the warmth and brightness of the sun streaming through a western window, and tell us that summer was almost here, and it was time to put our woolens away. And, curiously, in autumn, the temporary return of a similar brightness and warmth, which would have been usual only a few weeks previously, would surprise us into realizing that it had become cool so gradually that we hadn't noticed, and that it was time to take them out again.

But at any time of year, Amelia or I had only to mention wanting to see something in the trunk for Mum to drop whatever she was doing and hurry to it. We always looked at everything inside, and said more or less the same things at the same times, as if we were following a script.

***

Her blond hair pinned into rolls around her head, Mum stands looking at the trunk, which is rather like a brown boulder, and sits in a dark corner of the bedroom she shares with Dad. "This used to belong to my poor old father," she says, as always, before she opens it. "I'm afraid it's badly rusted."

She creaks the lid open, removes something, and, with us following, carries it to the other side of the room. There, in the bright light from the window, she examines a brown jacket at arms' length. "That's a *good English* tweed," she says, nodding, then lays it on the bedspread. "I used

2

to wear that when I rode Dolly." She pauses, and, a warble of sadness in her voice, continues, "She was the sweetest little thing! She had this way of moving—"ambling," it's called. I've never known another horse that did that. So easy... like dancing."

I stare at the jacket till the orange and green specks in its brown float above it, as I remember riding bareback, and in a dress, the homely mare called Dolly we have now, legs snuggling into the warmth of her woolly sides. But *Ugh!* I feel her backbone cutting up into me. I know she's not talking about this Dolly, but I say, "Dolly?" as if I think she is.

She clucks. "Oh, not the Dolly you know—*my* Dolly! A mare I had before you were born." She goes to the wardrobe, brings back the family album, and shows us a photograph of herself as a young woman riding a dark mare with a long forelock.

"Oh." My eyes continue staring at the jacket, and the green and orange shift into a landscape... *the hills around Gundy, where I walked with Mum when I was four, the day she told me she was going to the hospital to get a baby for me to play with...*

Gradually, I become aware of silence, and force my eyes to look around the room. Only Amelia, who's eleven, four years older than I am, fair hair pinned back from her broad face, and her hands clasped before her. She smiles, and my mouth smiles back, but my eyes are searching the dark.

Maybe Mum's gone for good... Maybe she was never here?

Don't be silly! She'll be back any second.

But maybe she won't.

Then, from the darkness, bumping, and I know Mum is "rooting in the trunk," as Amelia calls it.

She walks into the light slowly, carrying a bundle of letters bound together by a strip of shiny blue material. Her voice is scratchy. "These are from your father. He wrote them a long time ago." She clears her throat. "Before we were married." A forefinger taps the blue strip. "This material's from a dress I used to wear when I first got to know him." She places the bundle on the bed and sighs. "I'd still be wearing blue all the time, if he had his way!" She pauses. "I used to wear that dress to the dances in the woolshed."

An image comes of the huge room in which they shore the sheep long ago, on a property not far from ours.

"People rode for miles to dances in those days. Some even came from down below."

Down below—the gently rolling countryside of the Upper Hunter valley that spreads out from the bottom of the mountain...

She describes how the men made the room ready for a dance. "They strung a rope across one corner, and hung blankets over it so that the women could change in private. They even set up a full-length mirror. It was nice to be able to make sure your dress wasn't tucked up or anything." She pauses. "They'd mop the floor and then polish it with kerosene and sawdust. There wasn't much they could do about the cracks between the floorboards, though. Inches wide, some of them."

One night as she was dressing, her blue rhinestone necklace slipped from her hand and disappeared through one of them. "Under the floor was manure, feet deep—the sheep waiting to be shorn had been penned there for God knows how many years," Mum says. "I never expected to see that necklace again. But one of the men tied a handkerchief over his nose and mouth and found it for me." She looks at us. "Your father."

"Read us some of the letters, Mum," Amelia says.

A peculiar look comes over her face. "No."

"Please," we both say.

"No."

"Why not?"

"Because."

She takes the letters with her instead of leaving them on the bed when she makes her next trip to the trunk, and reappears with a doll resting on her forearm as if it's a real baby. But seeing that the head nestled in the crook of her arm is bandaged, my eyes begin to ache. *The towel twisted around my head so I can't breathe... The dress I'm taking off tight over my eyes... I have to get it off! Right away! The sound of stitches breaking... Mum stomping down the hallway to the sewing machine, one of my dresses over her arm. "I wish you could think of other people just once in a while!"*

She sits on the bed, lays the doll next to her, and starts unwinding the bandage. As the last of it comes away, pieces of china clink into a heap, and I see that only part of the head is attached to the body. She begins arranging the pieces, starting with those with nylon hair stuck to them, then turns a piece over to show two white teeth between dark red lips, and puts this in place. Next, she picks up what looks like a matchstick with a ball the size of a marble at each end. "All sleeping dolls have the same ugly eye mechanism," she says, turning the piece over to show, on the balls, what look like pale blue targets. "The eyes," she says.

Figure 1.1: My parents when they were courting.

Cold and blue like hers when she grabs me to beat me.

She fits the balls, which have eyelashes above, behind two holes with eyelashes below in another piece of china, and puts the result above the mouth piece, and, suddenly, the face comes alive.

She speaks slowly. "My Auntie... gave her... to me, when... I was... five." Her next words come in a rush, "I'd never even *seen* a doll like her before. Oh, Mum had helped me make those stupid flat ones you cut out of magazines and glue onto cardboard. Useless damn things!" She pauses. "My Auntie sat her on a chair. 'She's yours,' she said. *Mine?* I could hardly believe it." She takes a breath and lowers her eyes. "I couldn't wait to play with her. I picked her up, and went to run outside." She looks down.

Amelia breaks the silence, "What happened?"

Hunched over now, her head droops. "I tripped on the mat."

After a while, her fingers find an envelope, feel inside it, and emerge with a wad of yellowed newspaper. "The postmistress at Moonan saved this for me. It's an advertisement for a dolls' hospital in Sydney." She sighs, and drags out, "I suppose a person ought to write to them. They might be able to do something for her."

"Why didn't you get it fixed when it happened?" Amelia asks.

"Oh, we didn't have money for things like that! Dad worked as hard as he could, but there was nothing to spare." She sits thinking for awhile, and then says, "He managed the station.[1]"

"The station?" I ask, though I know the place she means.

"The property around the road. They used to call a lot of places 'stations' in those days. And, he ran the mail as well. He'd ride down to the end of the Black Cutting,[2] leave his horse there and walk the rest of the way down the mountain to Ellerston—eight miles there, and eight back—carrying the mailbag. He reckoned it was too hard on the horse to climb that mountain. Rain, sleet or snow, he delivered that mail three times every week." She shakes her head. "Those useless so-and-sos that run the mail now have a *Landrover*, and they can only manage twice a week!"

She shakes her head. "Dad worked *hard*." She looks around fiercely. "But there were times when we didn't even have meat. We had to shoot a wombat once."

---

[1] The Australian word for a large landholding used for livestock production, and equivalent to a North American ranch, though the word originally referred to the homestead and outbuildings only. The owner is called a "grazier" or "pastoralist," rather than a rancher.

[2] "Cutting" is the word Australians use for a road cut around the side of a hill or mountain.

Amelia screws up her face. "You ate a wombat?"

"You'll eat anything if you're hungry enough, my girl." She laughs. "But it *was* awful! No taste at all. And talk about tough! Must've been an old one. A young wombat would probably have been alright." She pauses.

The wombat emerging from its burrow with mud on its coarse fur, pausing to peer at the man with the stick-thing in his hand. And then—

"We tried all kinds of animals. Porcupine[3] is good—just like chicken. Course, you don't like killing the poor things.

"Dad did his best, but it still wasn't enough. Mum wasn't... much help. She—she was from *the city*. Sick a lot of the time. She was away in Sydney for months the year I was twelve. Dad had to do everything. I helped him as much as I could. Mum had been running the telephone exchange, so now *I* had to do that. And there was my schoolwork—it came in the mail like yours—and I had to supervise your Uncle Geoff's as well; he was a couple of years behind me."

But I want her to get the doll fixed. "You could still write to the dolls' hospital."

Amelia pushes the ad on the bed towards her. "Yeah, Mum. You should."

Smiling and her eyes bright, Mum looks from her to me, and says, "Well... I spose I could..." She starts to get up, as if she's going to do it right away, and excitement rises in me. But, a moment later, she sits back down so hard that the doll's face cracks apart. Staring ahead, she doesn't seem to notice.

Maybe if we push her a bit more... "The dolls' hospital would probably be able to fix her," I say.

"Yeah, I bet they could," Amelia chimes in.

Mum frowns and hunches over again. "Well..." She wriggles. "Their address has probably changed by now. A person wouldn't know what they'd charge, either." She quickly gathers up the pieces, and holding them against the attached part of the head with one hand, winds the bandage around them again, and lays the doll on the bed before going to get something else.

She reappears, sits on the bed, and places a parcel wrapped in torn, buff coloured tissue paper on her lap. Unwrapping it carefully, she lifts

---

[3]An Echidna, or spiny anteater, which belongs to the family Tachyglossidae in the monotreme order of egg-laying mammals—the platypus being the only other mammal that lays eggs. These animals eat ants and termites but are not closely related to the true anteaters of the Americas.

out a crinkled white baby's dress with an embroidered bodice, gives it a shake, and holds it up. "I know it's hard to believe, but this was Claude's dress." She laughs. "Imagine your big fourteen-year-old brother this tiny." She lays the dress on the bed, and leans over it, smiling as she moves a forefinger back and forth over the places where, now, only embroidery bridges holes. "That's the dress he wore in the hospital."

An image comes, of her with him in her arms, a look of adoration on her face. Then she shows us Amelia's and Laurence's baby dresses, and, as always, I wonder where mine is, but don't ask.

***

One day when Mum has gone riding, and Amelia and I are alone in the house, we go to my parents' bedroom, and take the bundle of letters from the trunk. Slipping one out, Amelia unfolds it and starts reading.

"Tell me what it says."

She looks up.

"Come on. Read it to me."

Still she doesn't answer, and I'm readying myself to make more of a fuss when she says, "This one's a poem."

A poem? One of those towers of pretty-sounding words?"

"It's—it's to Mum."

"Read it to me. Come on."

"Well—I'm not sure I should."

"You're reading it."

Her chin goes in the air. "I'm eleven." She hesitates and then says, "It's—it's a love poem."

"Oh! Come on."

"Well—promise you won't tell anyone."

"Course I won't."

She clears her throat, and reads,

"'Sweet-scented orchid, my love for you
Is vast as a forest, pure as a crystal stream.'"

"Dad couldn't have written that!"

"Well, it's his writing. And it says, "To my Darling Gwen."

Dad wrote these things?

We hear a noise outside, and Amelia quickly pushes the letter into the bundle, and shoves it back in the trunk. The screech of the lid closing makes us jump, and we hurry to the loungeroom, where we listen for the sound of Mum's riding boots on the back veranda. But all we hear is the whoosh and squeak of shrubs being blown against the tin outside of the house.

Chapter Two

A FOREST OF HORSES' LEGS (1947)

Three years old, I'm sitting on the floor of the verandah[1] at Pod's place, where we live. It's hot, but the boards are cool on the backs of my bare legs. In front of me, steps lead down to a dirt yard, where hens in shallow depressions ruffle their feathers and chatter to one another. They're "dust bathing," the Pale One has told me, and the air around them is golden with dust.

On one side of me is the wire netting that's around the edge of the verandah, its shadow patterning that side with a net. I move the unpatterned hand into its shadow, and it gets patterned, too, and, as I move it away again, the net slips off. I do this over and over.

Sssssss! A spiked, black creature towers above me, eyes burning, jagged teeth, black lips. A fur-spiked thing flashes to my arm. Pain. Screams rip out of me. Footsteps, coming fast. The Pale One steps through the door, pocket flaps of her dress flapping.

"Monty! You jealous bugger of a thing!"

Spikes shrink down, smooth into cat lumpiness. The Pale One's brown boot slides under the cat's belly, lifts. The cat arches through the air, stretching, shrinking, stretching. Lands. The hens scatter, cackling.

She squats near me, turns my arm gently, and brings her face close to my elbow. Her blue eyes look into mine. "I know it hurts. Bugger of a thing scratched you. See?" Tracks of tiny, shiny red beads. She touches the place. Beads smudge red on her finger. "Blood," she says. I touch, and my finger gets smudged, too.

---

[1] Open to the air but protected from sun and rain by the main roof of the house, a pleasant place to sit, work, play or sleep in hot climates; frequently seen in houses in rural Australia.

"I'll be back in a minute," she says. Fast footsteps fade, stop and start again, getting louder till she's beside me. She unscrews the cap of a bottle, tips yellow liquid onto something white. Scent tickles my nose. "Solyptol[2] will make it better." The yellowed white also gets smudged with red as she dabs it on my arm. "Hurts," I say, crying some more.

"You'll be alright." She stands up and goes back inside, muttering, "Who'd ever have thought it? A cat jealous like that!"

***

In the late afternoon, I'm watching the Pale One cook when Pod, shorter than she is, comes into the shadowy kitchen and stands, a thumb hooked over his belt.

"Would you like me to take the little girl for a walk, Gwen?"

Her voice wavers upwards. "Yeah? Well, that'd be good—if you're sure you want to."

He squats, brings his face close enough to mine for me to see the branching red lines on his nose, and smiles. "Want to come out into the paddock[3] with me?"

I feel my face smiling, and nod. "Yeah!"

"Climb up, then," he says, turning around.

With my legs on either side of his neck, I hold onto his head, and he stands up. I shift my hands to get more comfortable, but he moves them. "Mustn't put your hands over me eyes. Horsey's got to be able to see where he's going, alright?"

Brightness bursts into my eyes as Pod clomps onto the verandah. The hens are gone from the depressions where they spend their days, but orange feathers drift through the air. I try to catch one, but it floats away.

Beyond the wooden gate up ahead, bright green. We go through it, and follow a brown track through green scattered with black and grey logs and stumps. "Hang on," Pod says as we come to a log across the track. His hands keep me steady as he climbs over it.

"I know what!" His head half turns and I wish I could see all of his face. "Let's go for a run. Hold on tight now!"

Down on the track, one brown boot, and then the other, comes out and disappears, green and fences and bushes and silver dead trees rush by, and cool swirls over my face till giggles come out of me. He stops and

---

[2]The brand name of a disinfectant with eucalyptus oil as its main ingredient.

[3]In country Australia, to go "out in the paddock or paddocks" usually means to go outside somewhere on one's own property, but it can also refer to a space enclosed by a fence, and designated by an adjective such as "potato," or "back," can refer to anybody's property.'

Figure 2.1: Me at three on our mare Dolly with ringbarked eucalyptus trees in the background.

squats, puffing. "Get down for a while, now, and give the poor old horsey a rest."

We stand side by side in front of a cluster of small trees with thin brown trunks. I walk over and rub my hand on one, and then another, and look at Pod.

"Nice and smooth, aren't they? It's a little forest. See? This one, and this, and this, and those—a forest."

I look around at them. "Fowest."

"Yes, a little forest."

"A wittle fowest." I clap my hands together, pleased to learn a new word.

His arm suddenly shoots out. "Look. A bunny rabbit."

With a white flash, something small and grey disappears in a patch of dark green. I run to the green and look for it, Pod following.

"It's hiding in the ferns," he says. He looks around. "Well, I guess it's time to go home." He squats so I can climb up. Now great big orange feathers float far away in the pale sky. At the gate, the dark house looms. As we step onto the verandah, I ask Pod to let me down, and run into the kitchen, his voice following me.

"Here she is Gwen, safe and sound."

"How was she?"

Pod laughs. "We saw a bunny rabbit. Pretty exciting, eh? Naah, she was good." He turns to go outside. "Well, I'd best go and lock up the chooks.[4]"

At the far end of the room, Amelia and Claude, just out of the tin tub, rub at their shining skins with towels. Then behind me and far above my head, the lovely voice. "And how are you poppin' up, young lady?"

I turn, and the Tall One with the red hair is leaning down, big hands on his knees. His eyes gaze into mine.

The Pale One's voice is high. "Pod took her for a walk."

He straightens up. "Well, that's good. For you, I mean. Gives you a bit of a break."

She sighs. "I need it after I've had her all day."

A break? From me?

***

One day when I'm alone on the verandah, I make my way slowly down the steps, and the feet slap across the warm ground. The hens stop ruffling

---

[4]Fowls, or what North Americans call "chickens."

their feathers, cock their heads on one side, and make quark-quark-quark noises as if they're trying to tell me something.

Slabs of splintery wood stop me. Through one of the big gaps between them I see what look like the brown, black, cream and orange trunks of trees in a forest. But then a squeal comes from somewhere high among them, two of the "trunks" lift into the air, bend, and stamp back down again, and I know that I'm looking at horses' legs in a dirt yard, and not a forest. Pod has told me that horses squeal like that when they bite one another. Pressing my face against the splinters, I see, a little way away, the big brown shape of Hungry, the Tall One's horse. I squeeze through the space between the slabs and stand up, and the feet wind me round the horses till I'm in front of him.

Hungry rumbles hello, the long, soft-looking things on the top of his head swivelling towards me. His head dips, and he sighs, gazing at me through strands of black hair, his huge brown eyes full of warmth and caring. Wanting somehow to be inside what I see in those eyes, I move closer, until the feed-bag that covers his nose is resting on my head, soft crunching sounds sliding my hair back and forth with delicious silky sensations.

Then other sounds slowly separate into words. "Leila!" called over and over. I lean out and look up. On the verandah, the Tall One in his hat, the Pale One, shorter, and Pod, shorter still, all looking down at me. *But what's wrong?*

There are sharps in the Tall One's voice. "Stay where you are! Don't move! I'm coming to get you."

"Don't go near his hooves!" the Pale One yells. "Stay where you are." And, in a low voice, "For God's sake. Surely to God... she... Hungry... those great hooves... cranky bugger when he's eating... She... Why on earth... She... She..."

I'm happy and safe in this space close to Hungry... and the lovely rubbing...

The Tall One's hat bobs down the steps, and in moments he's above me, his big arms lifting me onto his shoulder. I glide over horses' backs—brown and black and cream and orange—out the gate, and up the steps. He deposits me on the verandah.

The Pale One squats next to me. A glimpse of blue eyes before I look down. Her hand warming my back. The pretty voice. "You mustn't go into the yard with the horses by yourself. I know you like Hungry, but when he's eating, he can get awfully cranky, and he stamps his feet. And if one of those great big hooves landed on you, that'd be the end of you,"

Figure 2.2: Hungry, my father's part-draft gelding.

she says, shaking her head. "He wouldn't mean to hurt you, but he could, by accident. He's an awful pig!"

She gives me a gentle shake. "Look at me." Blue eyes stare into mine, and her voice becomes hard. "Do you understand what I just told you? You must *never* go into the horse yard by yourself *ever* again. Promise me now. Understand? Promise?"

I nod my head. "Yeah." *But I know I was safe there.*

Chapter Three

GREY GOLD

Rain loud on the roof, we're all on the verandah, the grown-ups drinking tea out of Pod's flowered cups. In the yard below, water slithers around the overflowing hens' baths. Claude puts his hand on his top on the floor and stops it spinning. He looks at the Tall One. "We're going to leave here?"

"We have to, son. But not right away."

Leave Pod? I look at him next to me, sipping his tea, his little finger sticking out like it always does.

Pod smiles. "Don't worry. I'll still come and take you for walks."

"Well, anyway," the Tall One continues, "I've taken a rabbiting contract down below. It starts in a few months."

Claude sets his top skidding across the boards again. "Down below?"

"In the Hunter Valley, down off the mountain. They want the rabbits cleaned up on a big property in the hills behind Belltrees." The Tall One looks at Pod. "Cecil Rossington's already there. Plenty to go round, he reckons."

The Pale One sighs. "I wish we could stay up here. I hate it there! I can't stand the heat, to start with."

The Tall One says, "Well, I'd rather stay up here, meself." He looks at Pod. "But you won't be needing me in a few months, eh, Pod?"

Pod puts his cup down and stuffs his pipe with tobacco. "I'd like to be able to keep you on, Joe—you know that. At least I've got a house to live in now—you did a great job building this place. And all your hard work since... And you, too, Gwen. It's been so nice having you to cook and look after the house." He clamps the pipe between his teeth, lights it, and starts puffing.

Figure 3.1: My mother and me in front of Dolly, on my grandparents' property, which my parents later bought.

"Well, nothing lasts forever. And a man can earn more money rabbiting than doing just about anything else. It'll bring us a lot closer to getting our own place." He looks at Claude. "Do you know what they use rabbit skins for?" Claude shakes his head, and the Tall One points to his hat sitting on a chair. "Felt hats." He pauses. "Well, in some places, they sell the rabbits for meat, too—but we're not getting into that." He clears his throat and looks at the Pale One. "A house goes with the job."

"A house?" The Pale One sits up. She glances at Pod. "Oh—it's been good being in your place, Pod. But, well, we've lived in four different bark huts since we were married—if we count the one we were in here till Joe built this place. We've never had a house to ourselves... eleven years."

Pod takes the pipe out of his mouth and it clinks onto the ashtray.

Figure 3.2: My parents just married.

"Four bark huts! That must be some kind of record. Four... That's quite something."

The Pale One gazes at the Tall One. "Course bark huts can be very nice. The one Joe built at Kangaroo Creek when we were gold panning was wonderful."

The Tall One glances at the Pale One, looks down, and folds his arms. "Well, as I was saying, there is a house. Only thing is... it won't... be vacant when the job starts—not right away, that is."

The Pale One frowns. "Not vacant?"

"It will be. Later." He coughs. "I thought—well, I thought... you and the kids could stay at your parents' place for a while, since they're no longer there." He glances at Pod. "Gwen's parents have bought a place down near Sydney." Looking back at the Pale One, he says, "Well, as I was saying, just till the house is available. We'd have to ask them, of course."

"When will the house be available?" the Pale one asks sharply.

"A—a few months after the contract starts. "Once Cecil and his wife move out of it when his contract ends." He pauses. "You and the kids could come down then."

"And just exactly how much longer will that be?"

He studies his fingers. "A few months, I understand."

"How many months?"

"Well, er—s-s-six months I think he said, from the time my contract starts. I'll have to camp[1] there till then."

Nobody says anything for a while. The Pale One gets out her hankie and sniffles into it, and Pod shifts in his seat, picks up a newspaper from beside his chair, glances at the front page, then mutters something about having to fix the shed door, and leaves.

The Pale One gets up, walks to the edge of the verandah and stands looking down into the yard with her back to us. After a few minutes, she blows her nose, comes back, and lies in her chair, staring up at the ceiling. "I wish you'd tell me things straight away!"

"Well, anyway, how about staying at your mother and father's?"

She looks at him. "I suppose we could. But I'd rather we were all together."

"Maybe you could build a hut. Like at Kangaroo Creek," Claude says.

The Pale One looks at him. "He made it from stringy bark. It had a great big fireplace across one end. Do you remember?"

"Yeah. Why can't we go back to Kangaroo Creek, Dad?" Claude asks. "You could get some more gold."

"That's all very well, son, but you don't know what back-breaking work panning for gold is. I'd be that exhausted of a night, I'd be in a dead sleep the second me head hit the pillow. We got a cradle[2] set up, eventually, but it still wasn't much fun."

"A cradle?"

"A contraption you put in the stream that lets the water do the work for you. Gold panning's a tough way to make a living. And we had to look after you and Amelia, who was only tiny."

---

[1] As a verb, to stay in makeshift accommodation—usually a tent. Labourers formerly lived in such accommodation while they were working on the land. When used as a noun, it means such accommodation.

[2] A contraption used in the old gold panning days, which used the water pressure in a stream to trap gold.

"And me," I say.

"You hadn't even crossed our minds at that stage," the Pale one says, and she and the Tall One laugh.

"What did you do with all the gold you found?" Amelia asks.

"All *what* gold?" the Pale One says. "I wish we'd found half as much as you kids seem to think we did."

The Tall One says, "Most of the time, we just about made wages. And in the end the hut caught on fire."

The Pale One looks at Claude. "Remember that?"

"Yeah, I remember you and Dad and Harold filling buckets from the creek. And the flames."

The Pale One says, "Yes, cousin Harold was with us, then. It was a terrible thing to see that hut alight. Even with all the water, and bashing at it with wet cornbags,[3] the fire still did a lot of damage."

"That stringybark[4] burns like tinder," the Tall One says.

"None of the bark huts we lived in after that was as nice, the Pale One says. "And Kangaroo Creek was such a beautiful place. All kinds of birds. And at night we used to watch the flying possums[5] She looks at Claude and Amelia. "They have a flap of skin between their front and back legs so they can fly." She pauses.

"The next hut we had was horrible. I don't know who built it, but for some reason, they'd stuffed crumpled newspaper in all the cracks, and I used to lie there in the dark listening to spiders and God knows what else rattling around on it." She's silent for a while. "It was a terrible time with the war and everything. Harold and some of my other cousins had joined the army and gone to fight overseas by then. Everyone was terrified the Nazis were going to take over the world. Then the Japanese bombed Darwin and attacked Sydney Harbour with midget-subs. They even shelled Newcastle. Some people up here reckoned they saw the flashes. So, once I did get to sleep, I'd have nightmares about Japanese soldiers breaking in."

"What are Nasties?" Amelia asks.

The Pale One laughs. "They were *Nasties* alright. But they were called *Nart-sees*. Bad people in Germany who wanted to rule the world."

---

[3]Large bags, about two by three feet, made of heavy string.

[4]A type of eucalyptus, the very thick bark of which was traditionally used for building huts in the bush.

[5]Also called "sugar gliders," because of their taste for sweet substances, Petaurus breviceps are small, omnivorous, arboreal, and nocturnal gliding possums belonging to the marsupial infraclass."

Figure 3.3: My father in a buggy drawn by Hungry, with Claude and Amelia as small children standing, in the bush near Kangaroo Creek.

Claude looks at the Tall One. "Well, I still think we should go back to Kangaroo Creek."

"We can't, son." He pauses. "No—we're going after grey gold this time."

Amelia frowns, and the Pale One explains, "Your father means rabbit skins. People call them grey gold because they're worth so much."

The Tall One clears his throat. "In the Depression, a lot of people

Figure 3.4: My mother and Claude, about seven, on horses near Kangaroo Creek.

made their fortunes trapping rabbits. And not just blokes[6] like me—out-of-work professionals like lawyers, and businessmen. And you can still make a lot of money at it."

Claude stands up and looks at the Tall One. "Why don't you build a

---

[6]Australian slang for "men."

Figure 3.5: Me, three, on the front steps of my grandparents'—
and later our—tin and tarpaper house.

bark hut at the rabbiting place?"

He gives a dry laugh. "You have to have stringybark trees to build
one, and there aren't any down there, for a start. There's hardly a tree
of any kind left. That land was cleared years ago. A few jimmyburns[7]
are about all there is. Hardly any dead trees, even. And the rabbits have
eaten everything down to the roots. You can hardly find a blade of grass,
let alone a tree."

"No trees," The Pale One almost sobs. "Oh, I wish we could just stay
up here!"

"Jimmyburns?" Amelia asks.

"Damn bushes that sting you if you touch them," the Pale One explains.

---

[7]Native Australian bushes with thorns that cause a painful burning sensation.

The Tall One looks at her. "Well, staying up here for a while would probably be the best thing for you and the kids. You could come down once the house is empty."

***

My grandparents' house is a lovely orange colour, and all around it are great big dead trees. There are chooks, a cow, and fat white pigs that snort and squeal and live in a muddy sty. But they keep getting out, and the Pale One has to find them and chase them back in.

"Living with your father in a tent would be a damn side better than this," she says.

When the Tall One comes back from the rabbiting place for a few days, she tells him about the pigs. "I'm totally fed up with the things. What if we all come down to where you are? Being in a tent would be better."

Claude's voice is as loud as a grown-up's. "We can't all fit in a tent."

"You haven't seen the tents your father puts up," the Pale One says. "We lived in one down at Kangaroo Creek while he was building the hut."

The Tall One smiles. "We could have two tents. Oh, it'd be no trouble at all to build an extra one. It's not me I've been worried about—it's you fullahs.[8] I've lived in tents off and on since I was eight."

Claude stares at him. "Eight?"

"When me poor old Dad took me out of school to work with him and me brothers on the roads."

"Didn't you have to do schoolwork?"

"I should've been in school. But nobody worried much about things like that in those days. Dad told the teacher he needed me to help him, and that was that. 'Course Mum didn't like me leaving, but there wasn't much she could do about it—she knew Dad couldn't afford to pay anyone."

The Pale One breaks in. "Listen, Joe, how about us coming down there?"

"Well, yeah, we can do that. We'll have to get rid of the pigs and chooks and things, or let someone keep them till we've saved up enough to come back up here. I think Cecil has a tarp[9] he could loan me."

Claude glares. "I don't want to live in a tent."

"There's nothing wrong with living in a tent," the Pale One says. "Don't worry, it'll be alright. Actually, it'll be fun."

---

[8]The way "fellows" is often pronounced in Australia; in the plural, it was probably originally used to mean just males, but, like "guys" in North America, it's now used for both males or females.

[9]Tarpaulin.

Figure 3.6: Claude, ten, my mother, me, three and Amelia, seven, on my grandparents' property.

The Tall One looks at her. "There is one bit of good news I forgot to tell you. There's a school not far away, and a bus Claude and Amelia can catch. So you won't have to teach them while we're there."

"I don't mind supervising them. Correspondence[10] school's good. But if they can go to school, I'll be able to have my own trapline.[11]"

---

[10]Many children who lived in remote regions received their lessons by post from Blackfriars Correspondence School in Sydney, and returned them by the same means; usually, a parent acted as "supervisor."

[11]A line of rabbit traps.

Chapter Four

RABBITS AS FAR AS THE EYE CAN SEE

After Daddy goes back to the rabbiting camp, a man in a hat with a wide brim curled up at the edges, comes to get us in his car. He, Mummy, Claude and Amelia fill the boot[1] with our things, and then we pile inside. The engine grinds as we go down a steep hill, and then there are low, pale yellow hills all around. It's sunny, I get warmer and warmer, and then my eyes close.

I wake when we bump to a stop alongside of another car, and in front of us is a cliff. When we get out, the grass on the land all around is as pale as Mummy's hair. She points to two white structures with sticks poking out of their ends on a flat below us. "Our tents," she says. Beside them, their heads drooping, are Hungry, and our other horse, Dolly. Not far away are several tall live trees and a house like Pod's, with a ridged, silver roof and a verandah. *I wish Pod was here.*

Bent over, Daddy backs out of one of the tents, stands up, and waves. And then his hat is bobbing up a little track to where we are. He shakes hands with the man who brought us and says, "Thanks, mate," and then hugs each of us. The grown-ups empty the boot, loading themselves up with stuff, and they give Amelia and Claude things to carry, too. There are still things there on the ground, and I ask if I can carry some, but they say I'm too little. We follow Daddy down the track, and I see the car we came in drive away. They put the things on the bags on the ground inside one of the tents, and go back to get the rest.

The sky is streaked with red when Mummy asks me to come for a walk with her. We climb back up the little track, through columns of

---

[1] The storage space in a car, known as the "trunk" in North America.

Figure 4.1: The rabbiting place: on the left, the house we eventually moved into, and, on the right, the tents we lived in for six months.

orange dirt I hadn't noticed before, as tall as Mummy, wide, then thin, then wide again, and dotted with dark little stones. I point. "Look, Mummy—pretty."

"Pretty? That's not pretty! That's soil erosion. It's a terrible thing. Bloody rabbits eat everything down to the ground so there's nothing to keep the soil in place when it rains. Everything except the hard clay gets washed away. Pretty? That's not pretty! That's a crime!"

When we get to the place where the car we came in stopped, the other one is still there. "Cecil's car," Mummy says. But the ground all around it is strangely soft-looking. Then I notice that the soft is lumpy, and then that the lumps are moving, slowly.

"Rabbits," Mummy says through clenched teeth. "As far as the eye can see."

Figure 4.2: A rabbit plague photographed in 1961. According to my memory, there were even more where we were rabbiting.

That's what the lumps are! They're like the ones at Pod's, except that, as well as grey, there are black, white and spotted ones. And on the tops of their heads are things like the long leaves of plants, moving this way and that. The rabbits don't run from us, but slowly move away on their long feet. I try to catch one, but my fingers only touch fur.

When we get back, Daddy is squatting beside a fire near the tents, and holding a frying pan over it, and there's a lovely aroma. He looks up. "Incredible, isn't it? Told you! Just one moving mass."

Mummy laughs. "Leila was quite delighted with them. Tried to catch one."

"Did she? They'd look like nice pets to her. Kids! What a terrible plague. Miles and miles of good country ruined." Shaking his head, he lifts the pan off the fire and sets it on a flat stone. "A man won't feel bad killing them." He stands up, grabs Mummy in his arms, and smacks a kiss on her lips. "They'll make us our fortune, me dear. We'll be able to buy your parents' place before you know it."

He scoops a handful of tea from a jar, and throws it into a black billycan[2] of boiling water hanging from a wire above the flames, making the water in it froth up, then hooks a stick under the can's handle, lifts it off, and stands it on the ground.

***

My bed is on the floor of one of the tents and I wake while it's still dark. Daddy is there, bent over, with a lantern. "Go back to sleep," he whispers. "Me and Cecil are leaving to collect our rabbits." Then he slips out.

When I wake again, it's daylight. Mummy dresses me, and after we've eaten breakfast, Claude and Amelia go to catch the school bus, and she takes me to where Daddy is sitting on a log. "He'll look after you now," she says. "I have to go round the traps he's set for me." She walks past the tents, up the little path through the orange columns, and disappears.

Daddy takes a furry wad from a bag, turns it so the fur is inside, and puts a big hand with a piece of wire bent double inside where the fur is. When he pulls his hand out, there's a snap, and the skin becomes flat and shiny with pink slivers, fur poking from its edges. "This is a rabbit skin," he says. He taps the ends of the wire that are sticking out. "And this is a bow. I'm stretching the skins on bows and hanging them in the sun so they'll dry." Standing up, he walks in a cloud of flies to a fence nearby, and hooks the bow onto the netting next to the skins already there. As soon as he lets the skin go, it becomes black with flies, like the others at that end. The ones at the opposite end have almost no flies on them and shine in the sun.

The feet keep taking me where they want to, till suddenly, one hurts and lifts off the ground. I stand there, crying. Daddy comes over. "What've you done to yourself now? Lean against me, and let me see." He looks under my foot, then points a big finger the flies keep landing on to a spiky black lump stuck there.

"That's what's hurting. I'd pull it out, but me hands are too dirty. You'll have to do it yourself." He takes a breath. "Like this." He pinches his thumb and forefinger together and makes picking movements in the

---

[2] A tin can about six inches across and ten deep, with a handle, used for boiling water over a campfire and for making tea; also called a "billy."

air above where the black thing is. Leaning against him, I manage to get hold of it and pull it out after a couple of tries. "That's called a cat's head,[3]" he says. "Remember Monty?"

Monty! Spiked fur. Beaded red tracks. I stare at him.

"It's shaped like his head, but it's a seed. Other name's bindi." He glances at me. "Do you know what it was trying to do? It was trying to catch a ride on that foot of yours so it could find some nice dirt to grow in. Its sharp spikes make it stick. That's nature. If you had a hard hoof—like Hungry or a sheep—you wouldn't notice it. It doesn't care whether it sticks onto a sheep's hoof, or its wool—or the foot of a little girl, for that matter. Anyhow, your foot feels better now, doesn't it?"

I nod.

He stands up, stretches, and makes "Errr" noises. Then he goes back to sitting on the log. "Your mother'll be back soon. We'll have a bit of tucker[4] then."

It gets hotter and hotter as the feet float me back and forth over the hard dirt, and then I hear strange sounds... CLINK... clink... CLINK... clink... Daddy nods towards the hill that rises next to us. "That's your mother resetting her traps. Banging in the pegs."

I search the cliff for her, but the corners of my eyes hurt.

Daddy says, "Wave your arms to chase the flies away." He shows me how. "You'd better get back into one of the tents before they eat you alive."

I can't seem to move.

"Did you hear me? Go on!"

Slowly, the feet turn and begin floating me back to the tent. CLINK... clink... CLINK... clink... CLINK... clink... The feet stop, and I search for her again, but can't see her.

"Go on. Go back to the tent."

As the feet take me there, I pass the green meat safe[5] with our food in it hanging from the branch of a small tree, and in its shade. In the tent, I sit down hard on my bottom. There, among the boxes and tins and bottles and bags, I wriggle into a space that fits me, and my eyes close, and open, and close.

---

[3] The common name for the seed, shaped roughly like a cat's head, of a low-growing plant, *Emex Australis*

[4] Australian slang for food.

[5] A small metal cupboard perforated all over with tiny holes to allow air to circulate through it while keeping flies out; hung in a shady, cool place, it was used, when refrigeration was not available, to store corned meat and other food.

When I wake, Mummy is back. Her white arm reaches into the meat safe and brings out a cloth bag. She unties its string, pulls a second bag out of the first, unties it, and slides the red meat onto an enamel plate. Then, out of another bag, she gets the gluey, floury damper.[6]

After we've eaten, Cecil arrives, he and Daddy again leave on their horses—Mummy says to collect other rabbits. She tells me they "poison" them, which means they leave stuff called poison on food they eat and they go to sleep and never wake up.

Then she starts stretching her skins on bows, like Daddy did, and the feet take me wandering through the low, dry bushes nearby. They prick and scratch more and more as I push through them till they're so thick they stop me; then the feet take me back out again, and over to where she is, and I stand there crying.

She gives me a long look while her hands wave through the cloud of flies around her face, then gets up and comes over to me. She peers at my arms and legs, sighs, and gets me to turn around so she can see my back. "Thorns, all over you! Those feet of yours have taken you into the bushes again." Another deep sigh. "I can't do anything about them right now—my hands are too filthy. Go and wait outside the tent, and when I've finished here, I'll come and dig them out for you."

I squat in the shade of the tent I sleep in, watching her. After a long time, she stands up and goes to a dish sitting on a flat rock, pours water into it from a drum, soaps her hands, scrubs them with a brush till they're red, then rinses and dries them. She comes to where I am, takes me into the tent, and lays a towel on my bed on the ground.

I lie on the towel, waiting. Floating. She whirrs the cap off a bottle. "Solyptol will kill the germs," she says. She tips the bottle till it glugs yellow liquid a white thing like a rabbit's tail, and, scent strong in the air, uses this to wipe a needle and tweezers. Then her lovely face moves just above my skin all over the front of my body, the bottle glugging, and the white thing sopping. The breeze of her breath cools the little pools on my skin, and tiny creeks run down my sides, and under me. Then her fingers trail all over me, stopping at each thorn, pricking with the needle and lifting the skin, then squeezing with her fingers, or pinching with the tweezers, and sopping again. Then she gets me to roll over and does the same thing on my back.

---

[6] Australian bush "bread," formerly made from flour, baking powder, fat and water, but now made with butter, or sometimes cream, and this version uses beer instead of water. In former times, it was cooked in a cast iron casserole called a "camp oven" over the fire.

She whirrs the cap back on the bottle, and everything stops. "You can get up, now—the thorns are all gone." I don't move.

"Come on. They're all gone."

I sit up and grab my foot. "It hurts, Mummy. Torns," I say.

She shakes her head. "That's enough. I've dug every one of them out. Hurry and get up!"

Every now and then the feet take me into those bushes again. "That kid's so good when I have to dig thorns out of her," Mummy tells Daddy. "She keeps absolutely still, and she doesn't cry or anything It's as if she can't even feel the needle."

Chapter Five

GOING ROUND THE TRAPS

I wake in the dark as Mummy lights the lantern. She reminds me that Cecil and Daddy have gone to town to sell their skins, and she's taking us kids round her trapline today. "Your father and Cecil can ride around and pick up their rabbits, but I catch mine in traps," she says, as she helps me into a thick cardigan.

It's light by the time we set off, Mummy with a cornbag[1] over one shoulder, and, over the other, a small white bag with things in it. Claude carries a digging tool called a setter,[2] and Amelia a sieve. Everything around us is white with what Mummy calls frost, except for black stones and logs, the grass crunches under my boots, and my face hurts—from the cold, Amelia says.

In the jaws of the first trap is something long and grey. Mummy makes a clicking noise. "A damn foot!"

A foot? I can't take my eyes off it and get a funny feeling. "A rabbit's foot?" I ask.

The feet of the live rabbits moving away when I tried to catch one...

"Yeah. All the rotten fox left." She grabs it, brings the heel of her boot down on the trap's bow handle, the jaws open, and she sends it tumbling through the air.

She turns to us. "Now I want you kids to watch everything I do." She pulls on a chain attached to the trap till a rusty, iron pencil thing comes out of the ground. "This is the peg. You have to bang it into hard ground when you re-set the trap, to stop the rabbit from dragging it away on its leg." She puts the trap on the ground. "Always re-set it in a new place—

---

[1] A large bag, about two by three feet, made of heavy string.
[2] A short-handled digging tool with a narrow blade and a top like a hammer.

Figure 5.1: The countryside around the rabbiting place.

you don't have to move it far—in case the rabbit remembers where it was and avoids that spot."

She pushes at the ground with the peg in a few places, then looks at us. "The ground has to be hard enough, as I said." She uses the hammer end of the setter to bang it in, making the CLINK... clink... sound. "Now, pay close attention."

She means me, too.

"You have to dig a hole for the trap." The hole dug, she says, "This next part'll be hard for you kids—it takes strength." She again presses the heel of her boot down on the bow handle, opening the jaws. She looks at Claude and Amelia. "You might have to stand on the bow with both

Figure 5.2: A leg hold rabbit trap with anchor pin.

feet." Keeping her boot pressed down, she squats and uses a little stick to fasten a clip that she says keeps the jaws open and the square metal plate flat.

She slowly lifts her boot, and almost in a whisper, as if talking could set the trap off, she says, "See how I used that stick? The most important thing of all is to make sure you don't catch yourself. Always keep your fingers well away from the plate in case the jaws shut suddenly. Otherwise, you could lose a thumb or finger. Or your whole hand." Holding the open trap by its handle as if it's a frying pan, carefully settles it in the hole. "Now we're going to very gently cover it with dirt, and a rabbit has only to step on that to set it off." We all nod.

She's telling me how to set a trap, too. I give her all my attention.

"I want you to watch this next part carefully," she says.

Amelia says something to Claude, but I say, "I'm watching."

Mummy laughs. "That's a good girl, Leila, but you're a bit too young, yet." She looks at Claude and Amelia. "Pay attention, you two."

She's not talking to me at all!

"Hand me that sieve, Amelia." She fills it with dirt from the hole, holds it high, and sprinkles carefully till the trap's covered. "Once you've got a couple of inches of dirt on the plates, you can shake a bit faster. Oh yes, and make sure you cover the head of the peg, so the rabbit doesn't see it and get suspicious."

When the hole is full, she breaks a leafy twig from a nearby bush and gently sweeps the dirt.

"That's a trick my Dad taught me. When a rabbit comes along, it sees the smooth dirt and imagines another one's been rolling on the ground— they do that when they're playing. 'That looks like a nice place to play,' it thinks. Then, snap! It's caught."

But catching them when they're playing?

Mummy stands up and glances at the dirt covering the hidden trap. "There's another thing. You have to remember where you put every trap so you don't step in it. For instance, remember that this trap is just in front of the bush near this stone."

The sky is a lovely pink, and there's something like a red-hot coal in some clouds above the dark hills as we follow her down a slope.

She stops and sniffs the air. "Fox! Strong. That damn thing must've only just left. That'll be the mongrel that stole that rabbit! Can you smell it? Almost like that dreadful stuff they call garlic—you don't know it—only worse. Your Auntie Charlotte put some with meat she cooked once. Awful stuff."

A little farther on, she stops, holds up her hand, slowly turns her head with a finger over her lips and nods towards a spot ahead. "Fox," she whispers. A pretty orange animal with a long body and white-tipped tail is flowing like a wave over the ground. It pauses, looks at us, and then disappears in some logs and ferns.

"A person ought to always carry a rifle," says Mummy.

As we continue around the side of a hill, the pink fades, and the faces of the others become yellow in the sun. Again she stops, motioning for us to be quiet, then cups a hand behind one ear. A trembling, screech swells and fades, swells and fades.

Figure 5.3: Left to right: me, Amelia and Claude near the rabbiting place.

"That's a rabbit in a trap. The sound brings the foxes."

A little farther on, the sound stops, and ahead we see what looks like a brown stone sticking up.

"Keeping still, hoping we won't see it," Mummy mutters.

The "stone" has ears and large brown eyes. She reaches for the rabbit but it jerks away, the trap on its foot, till it's lying flat on the ground, trembling, the chain stretched out.

"The poor thing's trying to get away," Amelia says.

"It's not a *poor thing*. It's a damn pest." Mummy squats next to it. "Foot's nearly sawn off. Sometimes they escape—minus a foot, though."

Its ears are lying flat against its head, but she manages to grab them, then opens the trap and lifts the creature out. Next, her other hand goes round the neck, she transfers the one from the ears to the neck above the first, and twists in opposite directions. The rabbit's head flops over, eyes closed. And I'm crying.

She glances at me. "That's enough from you, Leila. It died in a second. Didn't feel a thing. They're pests and they have to be killed. That's what we're here for."

Her knife flashes around the rabbit's ankles. Soon what she's doing becomes interesting, and I stop crying. She whisks the knife through the glistening stuff between its skin and body, then pauses. "Damn things don't deserve sympathy. They're the worst kind of pest. This land used to be covered in grass. English toffs brought the bloody things to this country to feed the foxes they used for their stupid hunting. Another pest we have to thank them for."

As if she's undressing the rabbit, she pulls the skin comes away from its body, cuts it off from around the neck, and puts it in the large bag. As she hurls the body away, bits of black appear in the sky, descend and become crows, fighting over it as it hits the ground.

"Those crows must be really hungry," Amelia says.

Claude is staring up into the sky. "Look how many more there are up there."

But when I try to look, the sun makes my eyes close. "Where?"

Mummy's voice is gentle. "Squeeze your eyes nearly shut, like this."

I try.

"No, don't close them right up—leave them open a little bit."

Now I see more black shapes, and beyond these, specks swirling like tea leaves.

"Listen to them," says Amelia.

And I hear, far off, "Ahhhh... Ahhhh... Ahhhh..."

Most of the remaining traps have rabbits in them, but I shut my eyes so I don't see what Mummy does to them after she takes them out. As it gets warmer, the corners of my eyes begin to itch. Mummy looks up. "Chase those flies away from your eyes, Leila." She moves her hands in front of her face. "Wave your hands in front of your face like this."

When I do, my eyes stop itching and the flies go round and round my head, but they land again as soon as I stop waving. Mummy chases them away from her own face by letting one of her hands flop and hitting at them with the back of her wrist, or she makes her lips into a flat line, pushes the bottom one out and blows upwards, or makes a hole in one corner of her mouth and puffs at them out of that.

As I'm trying these things, she looks at me. "You don't need to blow them away like that—you can use your hands. Mine smell that much, I can't stand them near my face." Every now and then, she stands up and shakes her head and shoulders, sending the flies into a black cloud. "Mongrels! They always know when a person's hands are busy."

The flies keep coming back, and when the sun gets really hot, my head begins to hurt, and I cry and point to it. Mummy looks at Amelia. "The sun's burning through her hair. She indicates the white bag. "Find her hat in here, will you?"

Amelia puts my floppy white hat on my head, and it stops hurting. I can see better from its shade, too. But before long I get so hot I can hardly drag myself along. Mummy keeps telling me to hurry up, and then a low noise starts up. Up ahead, the others stop and look back, and I realize it's coming out of me.

"For heaven's sake, Amelia, take the kid's cardigan off! You can see I can't do anything because of these filthy hands. And give her some water."

The cardigan off, Amelia pours me a drink from the canvas water bag[3] "There you are," she says.

Mummy looks around. "She needs some shade. There might be enough under that jimmyburn bush for someone her size." She leads me to it. "Lay your cardigan on the ground, and sit on that," she says, then points to the bush. "Don't touch this—it stings. That's why it's called a jimmyburn." She looks at me. "Understand? You'll be alright here in the cool. We just have to go to the end of the ridge—we'll be back soon."

---

[3]In former times, a canvas bag was used to carry water in the bush.

The crows swirl up above, making their "Ahhhh... Ahhhh... Ahhhh" sounds. "No," I wail. "Don't go!"

Mummy sighs. "Whatever's the matter with you now?"

I wave my arm towards the sky. "Cwos."

"Crows? Oh, for heaven's sake! They're only interested in rabbits— and they have to be dead. See, this part of the trapline ends just down there?"

"No!" I cry, grabbing her trousers and holding on.

"Oh, for God's sake. Stay with her, Amelia."

Amelia frowns, but comes and stands next to where I'm sitting in the shade. My feet are hot and itchy, I try to take my boots off, and Amelia helps me.

But a few moments later, pain stabs my foot. I scream as it spreads into my leg and gets worse. Mummy comes running up the hill. "What's happened?" Her eyes are big.

"I dunno. She was just sitting there," Amelia says.

"You didn't see a snake or anything, did you?"

Amelia shakes her head. "No."

"Did you touch that jimmyburn?" she asks me.

Sobs see-sawing out of me, I manage, "N-n-nooo."

"Show me where it hurts."

I point.

"I can't touch her, Amelia. Lift her foot up so I can see underneath."

Mummy brings her face close and looks. "Turn it so I can see the other side." She peers, then flicks something off, picks up a stone, and bangs it on the ground. "A greenhead![4]

"A greenhead ant bit her on the foot," Amelia tells Claude, who's just arrived.

Mummy says to me, "Greenhead bites really pain. I've been bitten more than once. Nasty damn things. But it'll stop soon. And their bite isn't dangerous."

Claude looks into the distance and says, "If greenheads were as big as hens, the pain would kill you."

Slowly, the pain stops, and I can hear the "Ahhhhs" of the crows again. There's laughter in Mummy's voice as she stands up. "You'll live! I'd better get the rest of the rabbits out of the traps before they get stolen." She tells Amelia to stay, and takes Claude with her.

---

[4] An ant five to seven mm. long with a green head, which gives a very painful, but harmless, bite; endemic to Australia, its scientific name is Rhytidoponera metallica."

Figure 5.4: Left to right: my father beside Hungry and Cecil beside his horse, the animals laden with bags of rabbit skins.

Later, walking with the others again, I notice how, now, Mummy bends her knees and takes a deep breath each time she lifts the bag of skins.

It's really hot when we get back to the tents, and, after we've eaten, Mummy puts her skins on bows while we kids lie in the shade. Before we leave for the afternoon trap run, she gives Claude a bag with a lantern in it to carry as well as the setter.

When the sun sets, I have to put my cardigan back on, and soon Claude lights the lantern. On a hill, Mummy points to many lights moving over the countryside below. "The place is fairly crawling with them tonight," she says. "Rabbiters like us. More arrive every week."

Cecil's car is back, and down below is the black shape of Daddy in front of the fire. When we're closer, we see that he's holding a pan over the flames, and I hear crackling, and smell food. Seeing us, he sets the pan on a rock and stands up. "Gooday, you fullahs. Got some sausages in town." He kisses Mummy and tells her what's in some parcels, and hugs the rest of us. From one parcel, Mummy takes a loaf of bread and a block of something in white paper. "Butter!" she says "It's been so long! You must have got a good price for the skins."

"Well, yeah, I did. Thought it would be nice to have some for a change."

We usually put dripping on our damper, but now Mummy spreads slices of the fragrant bread Daddy's brought with butter and makes sausage sandwiches. As I bite through the sausage, tasty warm juice squirts into my mouth.

"Only got as much as I did after a fight, though." Daddy says. "That Armstrong bloke—useless bastard's never done a tap of real work in his life—tried to tell me the skins weren't much good."

"But you were so pleased with them."

"Best I've ever taken him. Told him so, too. Laughed in his face. He knew he was beat then—it was the laugh that did it. Amazing what the buggers'll try."

Chapter Six

STEPPING IN THE BILLYCAN

A few nights later, I finish eating while everyone else is still sitting around the fire, and the feet take me into the tent where all our things are. The full corn bags look like fat animals with ears, and soon I'm prickly with cold, and the feet take me outside again to where the fire blazes and crackles. When my front is nice and warm, I turn to warm my back, stepping to one side.

Pain! Screams rip out of me...

Big shadow Daddy yelling.... "What's happened?" Shadow Mummy, "What's she done?"

"Oh my God!" He grabs me under the arms, lifts me. "She's stepped in the billy of hot tea. Bring a blanket!"

Mummy runs off, brings one and wraps it around me, leaving the foot sticking out.

Daddy says, "I always sit it there... Why in God's name did she have to... in the dark! Wasn't watching..."

He carries me in the blanket, still screaming, sits on a log facing the fire, and starts rocking. "Shhhhh. Shhhhh. Don't cry. Oh, don't cry, my dear little girl." Then *he's* crying.

The pain is worse. "Hot! No!" I scream, arching my body and trying to pull away from the heat of the fire.

Mummy understands. "The heat from the fire's making the pain worse! Turn around so you're facing the other way."

Daddy gets up, walks to a log farther from the fire and sits back down with the dark before us. "It's alright, Pet. It's alright. Shhhhh." And he cries some more.

Mummy calls, "I'll melt some butter to put on it. Lucky there's some left."

"There, there, Pet. It'll be better soon—the butter'll stop the pain."
He calls to Mummy, "She's shivering. Get another blanket first."

She tucks it around me, and leaves again. When she comes back,
Daddy positions me with the foot sticking out over the ground. She lifts
a saucepan above it and begins to tilt it. "This'll help the pain."

Butter. Hot from the fire! "No! No! I shriek between sobs. "H-o-t!"

"Hot? No it isn't. I wouldn't put something hot on your poor foot.
It's only a little bit warm." She pauses. "Watch me." She dips her finger
in the liquid and holds it there. "See? It's not hot. Now, keep your foot
very still."

Even the touch of the butter hurts, and I scream louder, but manage
not to move. As she pours, the special butter spills on the ground like
water from one of Pod's drainpipes, till it's all gone. But, soon, the foot
begins to hurt less. And then the pain stops.

Mummy brings some white material and rips strips from it. "I have to
bandage your foot up, so germs can't get at it. And I need you to keep
really still. I know it'll hurt, but I'll be as gentle as I can possibly be."

She places the end of a strip on my leg above the burn, holding it in
place with her forefinger, and bandages downwards. She hardly presses
on my foot, but still it hurts, and I jump and cry harder.

She looks at me. "Please try very, very hard to keep still."

And, again, I manage to. The bandage makes my foot big and white.
Seeing her open a large safety pin, I scream again. She laughs. "I'm not
going to stick it into you—I have to pin the bandage on. Like this." She
shows me how she's going to do it.

After a while, my foot feels cozy all bandaged up, and I stop crying,
except for long, shuddering sobs that keep coming every little while. Then,
far away, I hear a trembling sound I've heard before that Daddy has told
me is the cry of a rabbit in a trap, my foot jerks, the pain comes back,
and I'm crying again. "It's best to keep still, Pet," murmurs Daddy. And
the pain soon stops again.

I never want to leave the smoky scent of his jacket. I look up to see his
face, but it's too dark. What I do see, far above us, are rabbiters' lights,
some brighter than others, but not moving. I pull my arm out from under
the blanket and point. "Look, Daddy. Wabbiters."

"What?" Daddy looks up and laughs. "They're not rabbiters' lights!
They're stars. They're pretty, aren't they." He looks at me. "You've never
seen them before, have you?" He says again, slowly and carefully, "Stars,"
and draws me a little closer, careful not to touch the foot. "They look

very small, but they're a long, long way away. Each one is bigger than all the land you can see from up on the hill." He pauses. "And look over there. That big round thing is the moon."

The next morning, I wake up crying; my foot is paining again, and even the tiniest movement makes it worse. Daddy, his face coated with white stuff, is looking in a mirror and scraping it off with a silver thing. When he's finished, he washes his face in a dish and calls Claude and Amelia. Cecil is going to drive him and Mummy and me to Scone, he says, and they have to stay with Joyce, Cecil's wife, till we get back.

Very slowly and carefully, Mummy dresses me in clean pyjamas. "We're taking you to the nice doctor," she says.

"No," I say, pulling the blankets up. "Want to stay here."

"You have to see him. He'll make your foot better. But you can stay in bed till we're ready to leave."

But it's not long before Daddy puts his hat on, and says, "Time to go, Pet."

He lifts me out of bed and carries me in a blanket up the track. He hands me to Cecil, who's standing next to his car, then sits on the back seat, folding his long legs in after him. "I'm ready for her now. Mind her foot." But it bumps against the doorway and makes me cry again. Then Mummy gets in in a flowered hat, and we set off.

Daddy carries me into a room where people are sitting on benches, coughing. Soon, a woman in a white dress and a white hat with wings tells us to come in, and he carries me into another room with strange but interesting smells, Mummy following. A man in a dark jacket with a silver and black thing around his neck shakes hands with my parents.

"Now be a good girl, and let the doctor look at your foot," Daddy says, and Mummy adds, "This is the doctor who's going to make your foot better. You have to let him look at it."

The doctor asks Daddy to lift me onto a bed thing. "No!" I say. But he does, anyway.

"Be a good girl, now," Daddy tells me again, more loudly.

"Keep as still as you can," says Mummy. "The doctor will try not to hurt you."

But I jump and cry out as he unpins the bandage. His hands stop and his big yellow eyes gaze into mine. "If you keep very, very still, it will hurt less," he says in a slow, strong voice. *"I know you can do it."*

It hurts as he unwinds the bandage, and I cry but do manage to keep still, like he told me to. The bandage gone, there is the foot, weird and white with big bubbles. His fingers flutter above it as he peers at it from above, below and the sides. "And what did Mum and Dad put on it when it happened?"

Daddy clears his throat. "Well, melted butter when she first did it last night."

The fingers stop. He stands and glares. "Butter! Are you mad, man? Butter! You put butter on a burn?" He shakes his head. "Don't you know that infection's the big danger with burns?"

Daddy looks down. "It was all we had."

The doctor says something quickly to the woman in the winged hat, nods to my parents and leaves.

"This is the nurse," Mummy says to me. She's going to bandage your foot."

She uses a piece of thin, flat wood to butter the foot with ointment. She's so gentle that it hardly hurts, but a terrible stink, worse than the fox, rises up. "This is Picric ointment," she says. "It smells like rotten fish, but it'll heal that burn like you won't believe."

"Thew!" says Mummy. "It does have a horrible smell."

The nurse puts a bunch of other flat pieces of wood, what's left of the ointment, and rolled up bandages in a paper bag and gives it to Mummy. "That ointment's wonderful stuff. I've seen it heal really bad burns beautifully." She smiles. "She'll be alright. Use the ointment to dress it twice a day. And of course, keep it very clean. Any worries, come back."

Just before we leave, the doctor reappears. "In future, never put butter on a burn," he says, shaking his head. "I know a lot of people do, but it's a very, very bad idea. If there's nothing else, plain cold water's best."

***

As we start for home, Mummy says in a high voice, "We were always told to put butter on burns."

Cecil nods. "So were we."

"That's what I was taught, too," Daddy says. "They always have to make a man feel bad."

The next day, I stay in the tent, and Mummy gives me a box of crayons and a book with outlines of animals and birds and flowers to fill in. Daddy props the tent flap open with a stone, so I can see him stretching his skins on bows, and I can still hear the CLINK... clink...

Every morning, and after tea[1] at night, Mummy gently unwinds the bandage. When I cry, she says, "I know it hurts. I know." And she butters my foot with the stinky ointment, and bandages it up again.

One evening, she says, "Look how well it's healing, Joe. The nurse was right—that Picric ointment *is* wonderful." And before long, my bare feet are floating over the hard dirt again.

***

One morning, Daddy, Mummy and I go up to where Cecil and Joyce are standing beside their car, the back seat full of their things. Daddy shakes hands with them both. "I'll get that tarp back to you as soon as I can, Mate," he says to Cecil. "It'll take us awhile to get all our stuff over to the house." Joyce hugs Mummy and me.

"We'll miss you all," says Cecil. "Shame the new boss wanted me to start right away."

We keep waving till the car has disappeared in a dust cloud. Then my parents hug each other and giggle. "Six months in bloody tents is more than enough," Daddy says.

Next to the house is the big water tank where Daddy used to get our water, and there's a verandah to run along, with a couple of big chairs on one end. Inside there's a fireplace and a table with little wooden chairs, a room for Claude and Amelia and me to sleep in, one for Mummy and Daddy, and an empty one.

That's where Uncle Bill, Daddy's brother, sleeps when he comes to stay, soon after we've moved in. He's tall with dark hair, dark clothes, and thick glasses, which he takes off when he first says hello, bringing his face close to mine, and his eyes slits, he tilts his head to one side and peers. He smells a bit like the doctor's office.

The next morning, he says, "Well, I better give meself me shot before breakfast." After he goes to his room, Mummy tells me that he has a sickness called diabetes and has to give himself a needle with medicine in it every morning.

The following day, I ask him if I can watch him give himself the medicine.

He looks puzzled. "Yes—I suppose so. If you're sure you want to."

First, he takes a glass tube with a needle at one end. "This is a syringe," he says. He points to a bottle, "This is insulin." He fills the syringe, then dabs his arm with strong-smelling stuff from a brown bottle.

---

[1] The evening meal in Australia in former times.

Figure 6.1: Left to right: Uncle Bill in his army hat, and my father near the tents at the rabbiting camp.

"Methylated spirits, or metho,[2]" he says. Do you know what germs are? They're so tiny you can't see them. But if I don't kill them, they'll get into my bloodstream and make me sick." He sticks the sharp needle in the place he dabbed—and doesn't yell out or anything.

After a few days, I start to like how he laughs—putting his head back and making a "Ssss... Ssss... Ssss..." sound through his teeth—and I follow him around, waiting for him to do it again.

One morning, I'm running along the verandah when a board breaks, and the same foot that got burned crashes through. I dangle there, caught near the top of my leg, screaming. Mummy lifts me out. On my thigh is a wide stripe of pink and red lines, and it really hurts.

"We'll get Uncle Bill to take a look at that," Mummy says. "He's a

---

[2]Methylated spirits or rubbing alcohol, which is a disinfectant when used at a concentration of seventy percent.

kind of doctor."

He takes his glasses off and peers at the stripe, then straightens up. "It's just a simple abrasion. All it needs is some disinfectant."

After Mummy has put Solyptol on it, I ask Uncle Bill if he's a doctor. "No, Pet. Not really."

"You may not be a doctor, Bill, but you know an awful lot about medicine," says Mummy. She looks at me. "He was in the Medical Corps in the army during the war." She turns to Uncle Bill. "Do you ever wish you'd become a doctor?"

He considers. "Well, yes. But I couldn't have worked as a doctor, being a diabetic. The stress of a job like that would've been too much for me. Even if I could somehow have got into university and paid the fees."

"Can I be a doctor when I grow up?" I ask.

He stares down at me. "You? No, you can't."

"Why not?"

"Because you're a girl."

I don't understand, but Uncle Bill is striding towards Daddy, who's at the other end of the verandah.

"I went to a woman doctor once," I hear him say. "All I had was a sore toe, and she examined me *all over*." They both laugh loudly.

Chapter Seven

DANDELION BABY

We haven't been in the house long when Mummy tells us that she and us kids are moving to a town called Gundy a few miles away, but that Daddy will be staying at the rabbiting place for a while longer and will come to see us on weekends.

The Gundy house is grey and splintery like the fence around the horse-yard at Pod's, and it's at the edge of the little town. Behind it are low, dry hills with a scattering of trees. The front path is made of bricks in a pretty pattern, with, on both sides, a row of big, golden bottles sitting at an angle, their necks stuck in the ground. I like their colour and the way their shape repeats, and say they're pretty, but Mummy makes a face. "Ugh I don't like *beer bottles* in the garden!"

She soon pulls them out, and loads them into bags. And, with everyone except me carrying one, we set off for what she calls the "dump," where you throw things you don't want.

It's a hill of rubbish surrounded by clumps of fleshy, bluish plants twice as tall as Mummy, she calls "cactuses." Slipping on cans and bottles and other stuff, we climb halfway up before they let the bottles out of the bags. I watch them clink and rattle down the hill till they find a place to stop. Then we explore the rest of the hill, looking for things. Claude finds a book with a black leather cover by someone called Tennyson; Mummy says she's read his poetry in school and that the book is very old. We also find a small sewing machine that she says "will come in handy." Claude carries the book and the sewing machine home, but as we're walking up the brick pathway, the machine falls and breaks in two.

"Oh no!" cries Mummy. "That's the trouble with *cast iron*—It breaks if you drop it."

The next day, while Claude and Amelia are in school, she and I go to the shop in town to buy some things, and on the way home, we notice a house, not far from ours, with what Mummy calls a "latticed-in[1]" verandah, and stop to talk to a little girl in the garden. Her name is Nora, and she's four, the same age as me. Then the front door opens and an old couple come out. Mummy tells them we've just moved to Gundy and points to our house. The old woman says I can come and play with Nora any time, and Mummy tells her that Nora can come to our place to play with me, too.

When Amelia and Claude get home from school, Mummy tells them that we met "the Thorn girl."

"Nora's mummy and daddy are old," I say.

Mummy clears her throat. "They're not her mummy and daddy," she says. "They're her grandparents. Nora's mother had to go to the city to work." And she adds something to Claude in a low voice.

"Does Nora know who her father is?" Claude asks, but Mummy frowns and shushes him.

Nora comes to play with me a couple of times, and then Mummy takes me to her place to play. The old couple are out, but Nora lets me in anyway. We draw for a while, but have to share one stubby pencil.

"Let's play doctor," I say, though I've never played a game called this. "You can be the doctor." Making it up as I go, I take off all my clothes, get a chair, climb onto the kitchen table and lie down. *What to do next?* Nora is standing on a chair, looking at me expectantly, the pencil in her fist. "Put the pencil there," I say, pointing to a place above where I wee.

A loud voice. "What sort of game do you two think you're playing?" It's Claude. "Get down off there, Leila. Right now—and get home!" Feeling bad, I put my dress back on and follow him.

I don't know if he tells Mummy, but she doesn't seem upset with me and says nothing about it.

One afternoon not long after this, Mummy and I get back from a walk to town to find Claude and Amelia in the house. Laughing, Claude tells us that Nora was in the kitchen when they got home from school. He climbs up on the table and shows us how he roared at her, frightening her so badly that she ran away. Mummy and Amelia laugh, too.

"I think she might be a bit light-fingered," says Mummy. "I've noticed a few little things missing after she's been here."

A few times after this, I knock on Nora's door and ask the old couple if she can come and play, but they always say she can't, so I stop asking.

---

[1] Criss-crossed slats of wood form one of its walls.

***

Daddy is coming to see us, and Mummy and I watch for him through the window. Finally, he rides up on Hungry, waves and jumps down. A moment later, the door bangs open, and his hat nearly hits the top of the doorway as he hurries in. He grabs Mummy, and they kiss for a long time.

When they separate, he leans down. "And how are you poppin' up, young lady?" he asks, as always. "Want a pony ride?"

I nod, his hands come to my sides, and he lifts me and carries me to the big chair, where he sits and bounces me on one leg till I giggle. But after Mummy comes and sits on an arm of the chair and snuggles against him, he puts me on the floor and she slides onto his lap. I try to hang onto his trousers, while they kiss and kiss. Then she says, "Just a minute," gets up, takes the piece of wood we call my car, and puts it halfway down the room. "Why don't you go and play with your nice car?" she asks in her bird voice.

I'm pushing it around when they go into the bedroom and start jumping about on the big bed. Every now and then, Mummy squeals like one of Pod's horses when another one bites it. Then I hear her say, "Don't. She'll see." Through the door, I glimpse a flash of pale flesh.

"She's too busy playing to be interested in what we're doing," I hear Daddy say.

Wanting only to disappear, I suddenly feel huge. I'd go outside, but that would make them notice me more. So I stay as still as I can, except for pushing the "car" a little bit with one hand.

We all eat together that night, and Daddy talks to Claude and Amelia about their new school. The next thing, I wake in his arms as he's carrying me to bed.

When I get to the kitchen the next morning, he's not there. Mummy sighs. "Oh he left hours ago—off to catch more rabbits. I know you miss him, but don't worry—once we're on our own place back on the mountain, he'll be home all the time."

***

Mummy and I walk on the hills near the town, along narrow tracks that twist and turn and cross over one another. "I know it's hard to imagine," she says. "but these tracks were made by meat ants[2]" She points to dark

---

[2] A member of the genus Iridomyrmex (iridomyrmex purpureus) endemic to Australia, with a dark bluish body and red head and 6-7 mm. in length.

ants down on the path, about as long as my little finger is wide. "They eat dead things and keep the countryside clean," she adds. "And they don't have a nasty bite like greenheads." We come to their nest—a pile of little stones Mummy says they've collected, almost as tall as I am. We watch them coming and going through their front door holes for a while before we continue to the top of the hill.

She gazes at the countryside below. "This is a dry damn place," she says. "I can't wait to get back on the mountain where there's plenty of rain."

We walk home alongside the gravel road. It's hot, and she shows me the heat shimmering above the cream grass. A bit later she stops, sits on a stone, and points to some yellow daisies with black centres at the road's edge. "Those are what your father calls 'black-eyed Susans,'" she says. "They must have just come out—the rest look as if someone's sifted flour on them. See?" I think of the squeaks of Mummy's flour sifter as her hand turns the little wooden handle when she's making a damper. "Dust from the road is choking them to death."

Then I notice white powder on my new black boots with the beetle buttons Mummy's mother sent me. "It's getting on me," I say. "Come on!" And I try to pull her.

"Dust won't hurt you."

I pull harder. "Mummy! Come on!" But I can't move her. And then I see how fat and tired-looking she's become, and stop pulling.

Her voice scrapes out, "We've come a long way, and I need to rest." She stares into the distance for a moment and then looks into my eyes. "Listen. There's something I have to tell you." Her voice is heavy. "You're a big girl now—four. But you're on your own all day with Claude and Amelia in school. She pauses. So I'm going to the hospital soon to get you a little brother or sister to play with—a new baby."

A playmate. Like Nora. Rivulets of sadness trickle through me.

***

When Mummy goes to the hospital, Claude and Amelia and I stay with Cecil's mother, an old lady with white hair who lives next door and wears slippers.

A few days later, my parents come home in a truck driven by a man I don't know. Mummy gets out, a white bundle in her arms, leans down and shows me, in the middle of it, a pale, round face.

I dance ahead of her, "Look," I say, pointing to the yellow flowers that have bloomed out of the spaces between the bricks in the path while she's been away.

She sighs. "Dandelions—weeds."

I look at the bundle. "Can I play with it?"

"Not it—him. Can I *play with him*. His name's Laurence." She pauses. "He's too tiny yet."

As usual, Daddy is gone when I get up the next morning. And, the baby asleep in his pram in the house, Mummy gets me to help her pull the dandelions out. She shows me how to take hold of the plants just above the ground, below where the leaves fan out, and pull. The first plant breaks, and I show her. She laughs. "Mine broke, too. Damn things do, half the time. The roots stay in the ground and grow again—that's why they're so hard to get rid of."

White stuff that looks like milk oozes from the broken ends of the leaves onto my fingers, and I lick them, but it tastes horrible, and I pull a face. She grabs my hands. "How do you know that stuff isn't poisonous? *You don't, do you?*" She pauses. "For all you know, just licking it could kill you. You must *never* do that again. You only taste things when you *know for sure* they aren't poisonous. Understand?"

I look down.

"Don't worry—dandelions won't hurt you," she says more gently. "And, by the way, that taste is what we call "bitter.""

We lay the dandelions that do come out with their roots on the edge of the brick path. "Sun'll soon shrivel them up," she says.

Then she shushes me, a hand cupped behind one ear. The baby is squeaking, and she hurries up the steps and inside, me following. His face is crinkled and red, and loud cries come from a hole at its centre. Talking to him in her bird voice, she lifts him up, lays him on the table and changes his nappy. He's as thin and pale as a dandelion root, and after she's fed him, white stuff oozes from his mouth. Once he's asleep again, she puts him back in his pram, and then we eat something, and have a little sleep.

His squawking wakes us, and she goes through the same thing again, then settles him in the pram.

"Can I play with him, now?" I ask. But again she says he's too little.

When we check on the dandelions the next day, the flowers and leaves are all frizzled up and the roots are curled over one another.

Later, she bumps the baby's pram down the steps, and sits it in the garden.

When Amelia gets home, Mummy tells her she's going to take a photo of me holding the baby, and she wants her to stay close by to keep an eye on me. She puts the baby in the blue and white and red hat with the pompoms that came in the mail from her mother, and brings the box camera and a kitchen chair outside. "Sit on the chair, and then I'll give him to you," she tells me.

When she's taken the photo, she'll let me play with him! I quickly climb onto the chair.

"He can break, you know—you have to be very, very careful with him," she says as she settles him on my lap. She puts my arms around him, and shows me how to hold my hands together. Shading the camera with one hand, she steps back, looking down at it and moving this way and that.

I shift on my bottom to get more comfortable, the camera clacks onto the pathway, and she jumps to us, arms outstretched. "You *have* to keep still!" She tells Amelia to stand closer.

I wish she'd hurry up and take the picture so I can play with him. As soon as she's taken it, I ask, "Can I play with him now?"

But she lifts him off my knee and puts him back in his pram. "Not just yet. I told you, he's a bit too little yet."

He's not for me to play with at all. I wish she'd never got him! I look at him lying in the pram with the sun shining on him, and wonder if he'll shrivel up like the dandelions.

Figure 7.1: Me, four, holding baby Laurence.

Chapter Eight

THE HOUSE BY THE RIVER

The baby has been with us only a little while when Mummy says, "Your father has had enough of rabbiting and is going to be cutting down trees near Stewarts Brook, so we're moving there so he can come to see us easily."

A fellow in an old car drives us to our new house on the bank of the brook, and it's as old and splintery as the last one.

The day after we get there, Mummy puts on some leather gloves and starts cleaning up the backyard. She digs out high, dead grass, scraggly bushes, blackberry vines and small trees she doesn't know the name of, with thin, red stems and a bunch of leaves fanning out at the top. She finds a lot of old bottles and rusty tins with nasty spiders in them, and shows us one with red on it she's squashed. "This is a redback spider[1] Red for danger. Its bite could kill you or make you very sick, so be careful. That's why I wear gloves."

The next day, she heaves the bits of the strange trees, which smell a bit like foxes, over the fence and onto the river bank. Bored, I go inside to where Amelia and Claude are, but the next thing she's calling us. A long thin black thing dangles from her hand. "This is a snake," she says. "I killed it with the hoe. You can be sure it has plenty of friends and relatives slithering around, so be careful. A snakebite can kill you, but you usually have to step on one to get bitten, so always look very carefully where you're about to walk when you're outside."

She digs up the ground where the strange trees were for a garden, but a week or two later, their red shoots are poking out of the earth all over it. She digs them out, then rakes the dirt to make sure she hasn't missed

---

[1] A highly venomous Australian spider (Latrodectus hasseltii) found throughout the country.

any. "If that damn plant isn't a noxious weed,[2] it bloody well ought to be," she says. She puts all the pieces in a bucket, together with the bits she threw on the river bank, and, once the fire is well alight that night, throws them in a few at a time.

We've been in the house a few weeks when a neighbour with a telephone brings a message from Daddy to say he's coming to see us that afternoon. Mummy asks me to take a note to Claude and Amelia at their school on the other side of the river, telling them to come home early. She says to cross on the swinging bridge she's pointed out. Pleased, I run off with the note in my pocket.

My legs can hardly reach up to each next step as I climb up to the bridge, and when I begin to cross, a board is missing in a couple of places. Then I come to a really wide gap, catch a glimpse of the river sliding far below, and feel woozy. Keeping my eyes on the bridge, I hold onto its side till I feel better. Then I try stretching a leg across, but my foot can't even touch the other side. I think of stepping around one edge of the hole, but there's hardly enough space for even my little feet, and not much to hang onto, either. I decide to climb down and cross the river where the cars do.

The water gets deeper and faster and colder as I wade in. When it's up to my waist, it's pushing me so hard my feet are lifting off the bottom, and I realize I could get washed away. It takes all my strength to pull myself back out of the water. I walk home shivering in my wet dress, and feeling bad that I couldn't do what she asked me to.

Mummy is feeding the baby when I get back. "The river was too strong," I mumble.

She stares at me. "The river? Why didn't you cross on the bridge like I told you to?"

Explaining about the gaps is difficult, but then a sad look comes onto her face. "Listen to me," she says. "You must *never* try to cross the river by yourself again. *Never*. You could have drowned!"

When Claude and Amelia get home, they're surprised to find Daddy there. Mummy says, "You kids cross the swinging bridge every day, don't you? Leila says she couldn't get across because of big gaps."

Claude nods. "There are spaces, but we just jump over them."

"This is how you do it," says Amelia. She walks backwards, then runs forward, and leaps. "See? It's easy."

***

---

[2]In Australia, a plant declared so under an act of parliament because it is considered to have the potential to harm; land occupants have an obligation to control such plants.

One day, we kids go picking blackberries from the bushes that are ev- erywhere, and when we get home, Mummy tells me that a woman called Violet Rose has invited her and me and the baby and the baby to morning tea at her place up the river the next day. "She seems nice," Mummy says, "but I wish I didn't have to go—I've got that much to do."

Before we leave the next morning, we wash in the tin tub and put on clean clothes, and, with the baby in his good hat in the pram, we set off. On the way, she points to a lot of birds and tells me their names—magpies, crows, currawongs, galahs, and a red-breasted robin. "I love birds," she says. "Just imagine—there are people in this world who keep them in cages! That's one thing I *can't* stand."

We stop at a gate in a high wooden fence partly covered by a vine with purple flowers. "Morning glories," Mummy says. Inside, there's a garden in front of a big house with lattice on the front like that on Norah's house, and I feel sad for a moment. But an old woman almost as tall as Daddy, but much bigger round, is coming down the path, smiling. She shakes Mummy's hand, tells me what lovely curly hair I have, and waves to the baby.

We walk through a garden, looking at roses, white daisies, and many other flowers, and she and Mummy talk about how much manure and water and shade and sun each one likes. Mummy shows me tiny white aphids with legs like hairs in a pink flower she calls a gladioli, and I find them in all the gladioli flowers, but it's really hard to see them in the white ones. Every now and then, I hear strange squawks and screeches. Then we look at apple, plum, and peach trees, and a pomegranate bush with large red fruit, which I like best.

The sounds become very loud as we climb the steps to the verandah. A thin, bent-over old man stands next to two big cages full of birds, and we can hardly hear Mrs. Rose as she introduces her husband, Jim.

"Hello, Flossy," he says to me, and, to the baby, "Hello, little man."

I wait for Mummy to say something about the caged birds, but she keeps smiling and doesn't mention them.

"Shall we have some tea and scones?" Mrs. Rose asks. "Jim's busy with his aviaries, so he won't be joining us." She looks down at me. "Oh, I'm sorry—aviary is a big word—it means a place where birds are kept."

She takes us to the latticed-in verandah, and everything is set out on a white cloth with pink flowers, which Mummy touches, saying she loves "fancy-work." The scones are like little dampers, but instead of the enamel mugs and plates we use—some with glittery black patches—Mrs. Rose has white cups and plates with roses or violets on them.

"The same flowers as your name," Mummy says.

While Mrs. Rose is getting the tea from the kitchen, I say, screwing up my face, "Mummy, the birds are in cages!"

"Yes, they are."

I stare at her. "But that's awful!"

"Shhh," she says, then whispers, "You're right. But it would be rude to say so to Mr. or Mrs. Rose. Understand? You mustn't say anything."

"But—"

"Not one word! Now behave yourself." She picks up one of the little dampers and says loudly, "Let me butter you a scone. Would you like honey on it?"

Mrs. Rose comes back with a big teapot with roses on it. "I see you're trying our honey. Jim's an apiarist, too."

Mummy looks at me. "He keeps bees," she explains.

"I like to use the correct word so they'll learn," says Mrs. Rose. "I hope you don't mind."

"Not at all. I do the same thing," Mummy says. She nods towards the teapot. "That teapot is beautiful, Violet. I've never seen roses that look so real on china."

I point to its edges. "That's real gold," Mummy says, adding to Mrs. Rose, "My husband and I panned for gold for a living one time—at Kangaroo Creek up on the mountain."

"My goodness! Did you now? I know they found some up there in the old days. There was quite a bit of gold mining around here, too, as I'm sure you know." She pauses. "But what I want to ask you is, how are you managing in that dreadful old house?"

"It *is* a funny old place, but it's alright for now. I can't wait to get back on the mountain, on our own place. But I've been making a garden to grow vegetables in," she says, telling of her battles with the strange trees, but Mrs. Rose doesn't know what they're called, either. Just then, the baby wakes, and Mummy gives him a bottle while Mrs. Rose says how sweet he is.

I don't want to go when Mummy says it's time. Mrs. Rose puts eggs, butter and a jar of honey in a wooden box, and then adds, from the vegetable garden, dark red tomatoes—she gives me one to try and it tastes really nice—green beans, corn, carrots, squash, and lettuces. Mummy keeps telling her she's giving us too much, but she keeps saying, "No, no. You're helping us out—we have far too much for our own use."

Before we leave, she hugs us both as if she's known us a long time, and I have a lovely warm feeling as, with the box of vegetables in the pram and the baby in Mummy's arms, we set off. But before we get to the front gate, Mrs. Rose calls from the top of the verandah steps, waving a parcel. "I forgot to give you this." She rushes down to us and shoves the parcel into the pram.

Looking puzzled, Mummy tears aside enough of the newspaper it's wrapped in to see the rose-patterned teapot. She stares at Mrs. Rose. "Violet! You can't give me this!"

Mrs. Rose smiles and shrugs. "You admired it, and now it's yours."

"But I didn't mean... You mustn't think... I didn't want you to *give* it to me."

"I know you didn't, but I want to. I have far too many things like it." And she looks really happy.

In the end Mummy puts the teapot back in the pram and, as we walk home, she keeps smiling and shaking her head.

***

On the way to the Roses' one day, a beautiful orange, green and black bird with long tail feathers flies up from the riverbank. Mummy doesn't know what it's called, but we find a small tunnel, its floor covered with shining insect wings, which she says must be its home.

When I tell Mrs. Rose about the bird, she says, "That'd be a rainbow bird. Don't tell Jim or he'll shoot it."

But Mr. Rose loves birds, and I don't believe her, so I hurry to where he is and tell him about the bird. "A rainbow bird!" he says. "I shoot every one I see. They eat bees. I've seen one sit next to a hive and pick off every bee that flew out."

***

One sunny day I'm by myself in the Roses' garden when I notice a line of small black ants crossing the cement path. A hammer happens to be lying on the ground nearby, and I pick it up and bash the next one that crawls onto the path, the next, and the next. Soon, all my attention is on watching for them—I don't want to miss one.

A shadow falls across me. "What do you think you're doing?" Claude snaps. "You should be ashamed of yourself! Stop right now! Those ants have as much right to live as you do."

I understand his meaning instantly and know he's absolutely right. I lay the hammer down. And although I feel badly about killing the ants, now, inside me is a good feeling because I've learned something important.

***

The days are hot, Claude and Amelia don't have school, and most days we go to the water hole near our house. They swim to the middle where it's deep, but I can't swim, so I stay in the shallow part, hanging onto the willow fronds and kicking my feet. One day, I copy how they're moving their arms and kicking their legs, and find myself moving through the water. "I'm swimming!" I yell. "I'm swimming!"

"You can't swim," Claude calls. "You've got your toe on the bottom!"

"Yeah. You can't swim," says Amelia. "You haven't learned."

"I can," I say. "Look, I'll swim out to where it's deeper so you can see." I do, and then they believe me.

Very happy, I swim and swim, and when the sun goes down, we get out of the water and lie on the coarse grey sand, still warm from the sun, the popping and clacking of frogs loud in our ears. Around dark, our mother calls us, and we walk up to the house. I have a lovely heavy, sleepy feeling.

When I tell Mummy I can swim, she says, "Oh yeah? That's good."

Figure 8.1: Me, four, Amelia, eight, holding baby Laurence, and Claude, eleven at Stewarts Brook.

Chapter Nine

THE BATTLE OF THE GIANTS

Amelia is very excited when she discovers a piece of gold as big as a matchhead by the river. Daddy finds his gold pan—a big metal dish—and says he'll teach us how to wash for gold. He puts sand and dirt from the place where she found the gold into it, fills it with water, swirls the water and dirt round and round many times, then tilts the dish, and as the water runs out, scrapes the topmost gravel and dirt off with the back of his hand. Then, over and over, he fills the dish with water and does the same thing, until all that's left is a bit of black sand, either scattered with gold specks or not. He washes many dishes of dirt, but none of the nuggets he finds is as big as the one Amelia found.

Daddy is very tall—six-feet-four—but when he meets the Roses' son, Trevor, he's even taller—six-foot-six. The two of them talk about gold, and places in the hills and mountains round about where there might be a rich reef. They decide to go prospecting, and early one morning, Daddy gathers up picks and prospecting dishes and puts them into bags. Mummy says, "Why can't you stay home? You're hardly ever here as it is."

"When I find the mother lode," he says, "We'll never have to work again."

Then Trevor arrives and the two of them disappear down the road, the full bags bumping against their backs. "Where's Daddy going?" I ask Mummy. She points to a hill as big and dark as a blackberry bush, and with torn-off bits of cloud caught on it, and says in a scratchy voice. "Up that damn hill." She pauses. "Why on earth he's always got to be tramping off on another wild goose chase, I'll never know."

***

Trevor asks my parents if we'd all like to come to a dance at a place called Woolooma, which isn't far away, in a couple of weeks. The night of the dance, he drives us to a big square building with a crowd of men standing around the front door. Like all the other women, children and girls, we kids sit with our mother on a seat that runs around the walls, while Daddy and Trevor stay outside with the other men.

On a platform at the end of the big room opposite the door, people play music, and when my eyes start to close, Mummy takes me to a room behind where they are, puts a coat on the floor, and has me lie on it, then covers me with a blanket. I like the music, but soon fall asleep.

Loud voices wake me. The music has stopped, and, sitting up, I see through the doorway Daddy and another man in the middle of the dance floor, hopping around one another with their fists up. Around them are other men shouting, and a bit farther back, Trevor and Mummy, frowning. Suddenly, there's a strange "thwack" sound I've never heard before as Daddy punches the other man, who thumps onto the floor and lies there, bellowing. People hurry to him, kneel down and ask him if he's alright, while Mummy goes to Daddy, takes his arm and leads him off the dance floor, Trevor following.

The next thing, she's picking me up and carrying me out to the car; Claude and Amelia are already inside. As soon as we set off, she says to Daddy, "Why did you have to get yourself into such a state that you ended up in a fight?"

Trevor cuts in, "That's quite an uppercut you got there, Joe!"

When we get back to our place, Daddy asks Trevor if he'd like a beer, and though Mummy says he's had enough, he goes to the well and turns an iron handle, which creaks as up comes a clinking wet bag. He opens one of the bottles from the bag, and he and Trevor sit on a log drinking frothy yellow liquid from enamel mugs, and talking about the money that can be made from boxing.

"I don't want you boxing, Joe, Mummy says. "It's too damn dangerous."

A week or so later, Daddy and Trevor go to Newcastle, a city a long way away, for a few days.

They arrive back late one afternoon, and as soon as Daddy gets out of the car, he grabs me and throws me into the air. Then, his hands over mine make me clap as he sings in a thick voice, "Clap hands, Clap hands till Daddy comes home."

When Mummy comes out, he puts me down and says to her, "There's a bloke that wants to put on a fight between me and Trevor."

"Oh, you're very happy, aren't you?" she snaps. "I can smell the happiness on your breath! Fancy coming home in that state! Boxing is too damn dangerous!" She goes back inside and slams the door.

Daddy gets some beer from the well, and as they drink, they talk about something called "the exhibition match," and "getting in shape."

I ask him for a drink. "It's beer," he says. "Would you like some?" I nod, and he pours a bit into an empty mug.

I like the taste, but Mummy rushes out, grabs the mug, and throws the beer onto the grass. "For God's sake," she yells. "What do you think you're doing, giving the kid beer? Can't you have a bit of sense?" To me she says, "It's past your bedtime," and takes me inside.

The next day, Daddy talks to Mummy more about the match that's being arranged between him and Trevor. "It won't pose any danger at all," he tells her. "I'll tell you why." I don't hear the rest of what he says, but after this, she stops saying boxing is dangerous.

Now he talks about being "in training," and he and Trevor cut pieces of rope off a roll, make a knot at each end, and use these for skipping. They also fill big cans with cement, nail one at each end of two long sticks, and call them "dumb-bells." Every day when he's home, Daddy puts on shorts, runs out of the house and comes back later puffing, his face shining. Then he skips for a long time, lifts the dumb-bells over and over, and gets down on the floor and does what he calls sit-ups. He eats raw eggs, as well as fruit juices and raw vegetables, all from the Roses.

Mummy, Daddy, Trevor and Claude talk and talk about the upcoming match, which is to be in Newcastle. The men need boxing shorts, and Mummy somehow finds out where to buy old silk parachutes and sends away for one. It arrives in a big parcel in the mail, and she dyes the silk blue for Daddy's shorts, but leaves it white for Trevor's.

When the shorts are finished, the men say something is missing—boxers always have an emblem on their shorts, for luck. Trevor says he'll get his mother to sew something on his, and then they talk about what emblem Daddy should have. Someone suggests a kangaroo and someone else a bird, and they all like the second idea better. "But what kind of bird?" they ask. Someone says an eagle, but Daddy cuts in, "Not an eagle! God knows how many imperialists have eagles on their flags and things."

Mummy wonders whether a flower would work. But the men laugh so hard she stomps off to the kitchen.

One day, when she and I are alone in the house, she says she's thought of an emblem she's pretty sure will work. When Trevor comes over that evening, she brings out Daddy's blue shorts. "What do you think of this?" she asks, lifting them up by the elastic, and there, pinned to them is a red hammer and sickle she's cut from the cover of the "Soviet Union," a magazine that comes in the mail and has pictures of smiling people working in fields on its cover. Mummy has explained that the sickle is a tool for cutting grass, but that on the magazine, it represents "the peasants" who now rule Russia.

I think the red looks pretty on the blue, but although the others like the idea at first, they start frowning and shifting in their seats. Then Daddy says, "Course a bloke with that on his shorts might end up in gaol.[1]"

In the end, they all decide it would be wiser to have something else, and eventually choose a crossed pick and shovel, a symbol the gold miners used in the old days.

A few days before the fight, Daddy and Trevor set off for Newcastle in Trevor's car. We don't own a wireless,[2] but Mrs. Rose does, and she invites us to her place for tea on the big night.

There seem to be even more flowers in Mrs. Rose's garden now, and I notice sweet peas, honeysuckle, hollyhocks taller than I am, and sunflowers as big as plates she tells me follow the sun as it moves across the sky. The air is full of butterflies, perfumes and the winding sounds of crickets. When we sit down at the table, she brings us plates loaded with vegetables from her garden and pieces of golden meat. As we start eating, Mummy says how tasty the chicken is.

"It does taste like chicken, doesn't it? It's the butter it's cooked in."

Mummy looks at her. "Oh?"

"It's rabbit."

Mummy is silent for a moment, then, with a kind of stiff look on her face, says she'd never have known and goes on eating it.

When they find the right station on the wireless, a man with a nasal voice is talking about "The Battle of the Giants," and mentions how tall Trevor and Daddy are. When the fight begins, he sounds excited, but it's not long before he's snarling things like, "Are these blokes fight'n' or danc'n'?"

The fight ends when Trevor is knocked down and doesn't get up before the count of ten—which Mummy explains means that Daddy won. The

---

[1] Jail.
[2] A radio.

man sounds even more disgusted, and says things like, "If that was boxing, I reckon I'm packin' the whole thing in."

Mrs. Rose turns the wireless off, and she and Mummy have funny looks on their faces. Something was wrong with the fight, but I don't understand what.

When Daddy and Trevor get back the next night, they wind the clinking bag of beer up again, and this time we all sit around the well and Mummy drinks a mug, too. Before long Daddy is laughing. "Trevor was down on the floor groaning and holding his belly. And then I see him wink at me, and they counted him out." He takes a mouthful of beer. "After the fight was over, this big bloke from Queensland comes up to me. 'I was going to fight you,' he says, 'but I reckon I'm heading back to Brisbane after I seen what you done to that big bugger.' "

After Trevor has gone home, Mummy tells Daddy about the food at Mrs. Rose's. "Imagine—I had to eat *rabbit!*" She shudders.

"Well, I don't think I could've eaten it—even to be polite. The very thought makes me sick. I still have nightmares about that awful rabbiting business and the stink on me hands."

Figure 9.1: Cecil Rossington and Joe in his boxing days.

Chapter Ten

GOODBYE TO THE RIVER

I'm five when Daddy buys a truck, and Mummy tells me we're going back to the mountain to live on our own place—the one her parents used to own. The day before we're to leave, Amelia and Claude stay home from school to help with the packing. Mummy sings songs like, "Come back to Erin," and "Home Sweet Home" in her lovely voice.

They pack all morning and after we've eaten the midday meal of corned beef and damper, Daddy and Mummy gulp tea between bursts of talk about what they "have to do" or "mustn't forget," as they scribble notes on the backs of old envelopes.

Mummy butters a slice of bread. "Thank God for Violet."

Daddy looks around at us. "From now on, we'll have all the butter we can eat."

"And you'll have plenty of boiled eggs," says Mummy, knowing how much I like them. To Daddy she says, "We have to talk to those people about getting the chooks."

"Yeah, and we've got to see that bloke about the sheep, too. God, it'll be good to have our own meat. No more rotten bully beef!" He pulls a face.

But I like the scent and taste of the red meat. "But bully beef's nice, Daddy."

He pulls another face and says, "Errr," then looks at Mummy. "The first thing next Spring'll be to get a vegetable garden going."

"And don't forget my flower garden."

"Well, I'll let you look after that. We can't eat flowers."

"Can't eat flowers!" She gets up, gathers the mugs, and bangs them into the washing-up[1] dish.

---

[1]In the Australian bush in former times, "washing-up" referred to the washing of dishes,

Claude and Amelia say they're glad they won't have to go to Stewarts Brook School any more.

"Yes, thank God for that," Mummy agrees. "Correspondence school will be better." She looks at Claude and Amelia. "You kids will remember getting your lessons in the mail when we were at Pod's. I'll be what they call your "Supervisor" again from now on. There's no school near enough for you and Amelia to go to—the closest is at Ellerston, fourteen miles from where we'll be."

Daddy sounds pleased. "Yes, your mother'll be your teacher from now on." He scrapes his chair back and stands up. "She'll do a good job, too." He plants a kiss on her forehead. "She always wanted to be a teacher. You kids don't know how lucky you are. I didn't do any schooling after I was eight. Well, only a bit here and there, anyway."

"Yeah, I remember, Dad," Claude says. "Your father took you out to work on the roads. Did you like school?"

"Well, I did and I didn't. The other kids give me a terrible time because of me red hair. "Ginger," they called me—among other things. A mob of them would follow me round, singing out, "Why did the donkey buck?" And then they'd laugh, and one of them would yell, "Because he had ginger on his back." And they'd laugh and laugh." He stares outside. "So, no, I wasn't real sorry to leave. And starting work made me feel like a man." He pauses again. "I wasn't learning an awful lot in that school, anyway.

"Me brothers, your Uncles Bill and Sid, helped me with me reading. You haven't met Sid yet. We'd read Wild Wests[2] of a night, and if I didn't know a word, I'd ask them. And being with Dad, I learned a lot about the old gold mining days... there was always some old fullah calling in and telling stories. How they had to fight for their rights and that."

He pauses. "As I said, I did get back to school for a while now and then. One time when I went back, the teacher had just taught the other kids long division—I'd never learned it. Anyhow, he gave everyone a test on it, and, somehow I managed to figure out how to get the right answers. But when he asked me how I'd got them, I couldn't explain, so he said I'd cheated."

He stands up and looks at the pile of bags and boxes. "Anyway, I've got to get this stuff loaded." He gets Claude and Amelia to help him, and they all start carrying things outside and putting them onto the back of

---

and the "washing-up dish" was the dish in which they were washed.

[2]Cowboy adventure stories.

our truck or in the boot of Trevor's car, which he's left at our place for us to load.

Mummy and I get ready to visit Mrs. Rose, and as we're leaving, Daddy says, "Say goodbye to Violet for me."

Today, Mummy and Mrs. Rose drink their tea in silence. Afterwards, Mrs. Rose gives us a small box with a parcel in it. "Rat traps. You always need extras." As we go through the kitchen, she begins to fill other boxes with eggs and jars of jam, honey and butter, then goes to the cellar and comes back with carrots, turnips and potatoes and piles these in. When she brings a large bag of apples, Mummy says, "Now you really are giving us too much, Violet." But not till she goes close to her, looks into her face, and says, "Violet, it's too much," does Mrs. Rose stop and stare at her, and then at the overflowing boxes. "Oh, dear! You're quite right, Gwen. You must have an awful lot of things to take. I wasn't thinking."

Mummy nods and says softly, "Yes, we do. I think I'd better just take what's in the boxes already." And together they lift them into the stroller.

They hug goodbye and as they separate, Mrs. Rose turns away, her back making odd movements. Mummy stands behind her, her hands fluttering, as if she doesn't know whether to touch her or not.

After some deep breaths, Mrs. Rose blows her nose and faces us again, her eyes watery. "I'm sorry, Gwen. I've become so fond of you, and you'll be a long way away. I can't remember the last time there was another woman living near us."

Mummy's eyes are wet-looking, too. She clears her throat. "Oh, Violet! It's not goodbye really, you know! We'll still come to see you. And you'll have to come and stay with us."

"Well... I know you mean what you say. But I remember what it was like for me and Jim when we first bought this place. You'll have that much to do. I'm sorry to say it, but I don't envy you. Now, at my time of life, loneliness is the problem."

"Whatever happens, we'll have to go to town to get things, and we'll make a detour to see you. And you *will* come and see us, too, won't you?"

Mrs. Rose suddenly gives a big smile. "Yes! You're quite right. There's no reason to be gloomy. No reason at all. I'll bring you the things you can't grow up there. Tomatoes and lettuces... melons. And cucumbers..."

But Mummy is frowning. "It's not as hard to grow things up there as people think. A lot of vegetables grow a damn sight better there than they do down here—or just as well. Dad even grew tomatoes one year—*and* lettuces."

Mrs. Rose looks surprised. "Is that so? I'm sorry, Gwen. It's just that I know you're up pretty high, and there's snow in the winter, and people always say how cold it is."

"Yes, it is high—over four thousand feet," Mummy says. After a moment's silence, she lowers her eyes, "Well... It *was* that really hot year that he grew the tomatoes." She pauses. "But it just shows that you can grow all kinds of vegetables there if you persevere—and pick a nice warm spot, of course. Where you plant things makes all the difference." She stares into the distance. "You should taste the parsnips that grow up there—it's the frost that does it. The ones from warm places are the most insipid things! And Dad used to grow huge carrots. Dark red. You should have tasted their juice—talk about sweet!" She pauses, then smiles. "Anyway, it's *you* we'll want to see. You don't always have to be giving us things, you know."

"But I love giving you things."

"I know you do. And... I spose a few things would be nice—till we get the garden going, anyway. Moving up there in mid winter isn't the greatest idea, but we couldn't wait any longer—we've been away so long. And it gives us time to get settled before we have to plant the potatoes in the spring—they'll be our main crop." They're silent for a few moments, and then Mummy says, "Come on, Leila, it's time we left."

Mrs. Rose squats down and looks into my eyes. "I'm going to miss you." She puts her arms around me and holds me close.

She's mussing up Laurence's hair and saying goodbye to him when Mr. Rose comes and says, "Goodbye, Flossy. Bye-bye, little man. Bye, Gwen." Then he disappears back into the great ball of noise from his birds.

I skip down the path through the straggly flowers the frosts have left, Laurence's stroller squeaking along behind me. Mummy unlatches the front gate, and I run through, but her voice stops me. "Don't just run off without waving to Mrs. Rose." I turn around, and there is her solid figure. As I wave, my legs want to run back for another hug, but Mummy says, "Now we can go." Wanting to cry, I run as fast as I can.

***

The next morning, Daddy stands beside Mummy, who's holding Hungry's halter and Dolly's bridle, as we wait outside for Trevor, who's walking to our place. All loaded up, Hungry looks as if he has a little house on his back. Mummy, Claude, Amelia and I are going up in Trevor's car, which has a rope across the boot. Trevor arrives, folds his long body into the driver's seat, and sits waiting for us.

Daddy hugs and kisses me. "Bye-bye, Pet." He squats to kiss Laurence, who's holding onto Mummy's trousers. "Ta-ta, young fullah." He strides over to Amelia and kisses her, then goes to Claude and stands in front of him. "See you soon, mate."

Mummy's words, "He'll be home all the time..." echo in my ears. "Isn't Daddy coming?" I ask. But she's looking at him as he comes towards her with a big grin on his face and doesn't hear. "Well, me girl, we finally made it," he says, "No more bloody rabbiting and..." The last of his words are muffled by her hair as he hugs her close.

Now my voice is a squeak. "Isn't Daddy coming?"

But again nobody hears. Daddy takes the bridle from Mummy, throws the reins over Dolly's head, fits his boot into the stirrup and heaves himself up, then takes Hungry's halter. With his boots dangling below Dolly's sides, he turns her, slaps her with his knees, and the little house thing sways above Hungry's rump as they move off.

Mummy is staring at the house we're leaving, and I hear her say, "Horrible old place."

"Now the snakes can move back in," says Claude.

"And the mice," adds Amelia.

"They never left," Mummy's voice rasps out.

A loud wail bursts out of me.

They all stare at me. I point to Daddy and the horses, now small and far away. Suddenly, Mummy's head goes back in a laugh. She looks at me kindly. "Oh, for heaven's sake! He has to take the horses up, silly. How else would we get them up there? He'll be there later tonight. Then he'll come back with Trevor and get the truck." Her arm warm around my shoulders, she grins at the others. "Stop your crying. You're a big girl, now. Five, remember?"

***

In the car, Trevor's knees stick up on either side of the steering wheel, and his hair is near the ceiling. With Amelia in the seat next to him, and Mummy, Laurence, Claude and me squeezed into the back, the car moves off.

Chapter Eleven

TO THE TOPS

As we speed along the dirt road, it gets warm and Mummy opens the windows. Then she's busy with Laurence and I lean out, enjoying the wind pressing on my face. Small trees up ahead get bigger and bigger, whip past, and then shrink and disappear behind other trees or hills or the big brown cloud boiling up behind us and smudging across the fields. Down near the road, gravel and stones fly up and crack against the mudguards.

Mummy tugs at my dress. "Sit down on the seat. You might fall out."

A little while later, she points to a tree up ahead covered in big pink flowers. Even Mrs. Rose doesn't have a tree that pretty. Trevor stops the car.

"Isn't it beautiful!" everyone keeps saying. Trevor usually speaks slowly, but now his words rush out. "They're a terrible nuisance to the wheat farmers out west, you know. I was working out there a few years ago. Miles of them lined up on the telephone wires. Ground underneath looked like someone'd gone along with a broom full of whitewash."

Mummy sighs. "The tree looks like it's in bloom."

"What is it, Mummy?" I ask.

Amelia turns to me. "They're not real flowers, you know." She glances at Mummy. "They're pink galahs,[1] aren't they, Mum?"

All of a sudden, the "flowers" start moving, then lift into the air and become a flock of pink and grey birds, voices scratching the sky as they whoosh over the car, leaving behind an ordinary dead tree. It's as if I've just seen magic, and inside me is a warm, airy feeling.

Soon the road has a yellow dirt bank alongside of it, and we're winding around the sides of hills. "The Yellow Cutting," Mummy says. "See the

---

[1] Eolophus roseicapilla, one of the most common and widespread cockatoos, found in open country in almost all parts of Australia; also known as "pink and greys."

river down there?"

It's like a shiny worm in a green field. After the cutting ends, Mummy points out a shop and pub, and says, "That's Moonan Flat," as we drive past.

A little while later, the road crosses a river. "Dicky Dan's Crossing," Mummy says. The water looks deep, and I grip the seat in front. Slippy-gluggy sounds—from the tires sliding on stones, Mummy says—come from underneath as we cross. Leaning out of the window again, I see that the water nearly covers the tyres, and Amelia has her head out of the front window, too.

"Stop leaning out of the windows, you two," Mummy orders.

Amelia props her shoes on the dashboard. "The water'll come in if it gets any deeper."

"Get those shoes off that wood this instant!" Mummy snaps.

The shoes thump back onto the floor. Mummy picks up a crumpled ball of paper, leans forward and wipes at the dashboard. "I'm sorry, Trevor."

"Don't worry about it, Gwen. It only looks like wood. Marvelous what they can do these days—probably made of emu feathers or something."

After we've climbed up out of the river, he says, "But I've been wanting to ask you—the place you're moving to used to be your father's—is that right?"

"Yeah. He selected it way back in 1923. Seven hundred acres. Most of the properties up there are twelve-eighties—twelve hundred and eighty acres. But the soil on our place is very rich. All bush, when he got it—still is, except for the valley where the house is. All he managed to clear. It was back-breaking work getting that place to the point where he could plant crops and run stock. He had to use draft horses, and, luckily the coal miners down in the valley were on strike, so he paid some of them to give him a hand. They ringbarked[2] the big trees, and dragged the saplings, old logs and leaves into heaps and burned them."

"What's ringbarked?" Amelia asks.

"It means that they remove a strip of bark off the trunk of a tree all the way round, which cuts the vessels carrying the nutrients and water up from the soil, so the tree dies. Once the leaves have withered and fallen off, the sun can shine onto the ground, and grass and crops will grow." She pauses, and says to Trevor, "As soon as he could, he got a vegetable garden started and planted an orchard.

---

[2]See my mother's explanation of the term, which follows the word. In the old days, this was the easiest way of allowing the sun to reach the ground so that grass and crops could grow. A tree so treated, is said to have been "ringbarked."

"The place needed fencing, too, and they had to build a house, so he had to keep working for other people till he'd earned enough money for those things. Joe helped build the house, which was finished in 1936, the year we were married.

"Dad loved that place—Mum was the only reason he left—she came from Sydney and always wanted to get back to a damn city. Anyway, a year or so after the house was built, my brother won five hundred pounds in the lottery—a lot of money—so he and my parents bought a farm at Grose Vale, near Sydney. That's when we decided to buy the place."

After a silence, she says, "Sometimes I can't believe it's taken us so long to save enough. We always wanted our own place on the mountain, and to run Hereford cattle. But we had to have enough to pay the mortgage, buy machinery and stock, and to tide us over till we could get some potatoes growing."

"Spuds, eh?" says Trevor. "Well, they're something everyone needs." He's quiet for a while and then asks, "It'd get pretty cold up there of a winter, wouldn't it?"

"Not half as cold as people think. We usually get a fall or two of snow—but it *is* four thousand five hundred feet above sea level, so you'd expect that. The highest place up there is Carey's Peak, which is over five thousand feet."

After we drive around some more hills, we cross a creek, and Mummy points to a chimney among some bushes, and says to us kids, "That's all that's left of the house your father's family used to live in—this place is called Dry Creek. There's a beautiful rose bush, there. 'Cloth of Gold,' it's called. I must get a cutting." She points to one of two small buildings with ridged silver roofs not far away. "The school your father went to for a while. And that's the schoolmaster's house next to it. Both empty for many years now."

As we go through a little creek, she says, "Eleven more miles to go."

We stop at a gate. When Mummy tells Claude and Amelia that one of them has to open it, they start arguing with one another. Trevor stretches, yawns and rubs his chin, and Laurence starts wailing.

"For heaven's sake, you two!" Mummy says loudly. "There are eleven more miles to go, and ten more gates. Take turns. You open this one, Claude."

"With all those gates, it must take quite a while to get to Scone from your place," Trevor says.

"It's pretty good now. In the early days with buggies, it used to take a day or two. But Joe was talking to someone from up here and he said it's four hours by car now. Sometimes rivers flood, though, and if there's rain the roads can get slippery—or boggy."

The hills crowd in closer and closer, and then we're going around the side of a mountain and Mummy points out sheep so far below us in a valley that they look like the aphids in Mrs. Rose's garden—but without the hair-like legs.

As we continue to climb, I lean out of the window again and look for more sheep down in the valley next to us. But suddenly, I feel the movement of the car in my belly, and the next thing, I hiccup and out of my mouth yellow stuff pours down the car door. Mummy yanks me inside, and holds a towel under my chin.

"I'm really sorry," she keeps saying, as she wipes my face and dress.

But Trevor says, "Don't worry about it, Gwen," and pulls the car off the road as soon as he can.

My throat is burning as Mummy takes me to a stone and tells me to sit on it. She gives me some water from the waterbag, and the burning stops. "Don't worry—you'll be better soon," she says. "You're just carsick. That's what happens when you lean out of the window!"

She takes the water bag back to the car and washes the sick onto the road. "Kids!" she says to Trevor. "She would keep leaning out." Then everyone has a drink, and Mummy says, "Water from water bags always tastes so good. It's the canvas, but I like it."

I'd rather water without the funny taste. I wish they'd be quiet. I feel like being sick again, and it's so bright I close my eyes.

But before long, the sick feeling has gone enough for me to stand up and walk around, and soon it disappears altogether.

When we start off again, Mummy puts me in the middle and makes me hold the towel on my lap, saying, "Just in case."

After we've climbed some more, we come to a flat place, and Mummy asks Trevor to stop. We all walk to an edge and gaze into and across a huge blue valley. Then Trevor, who's wandered away a bit, calls, "Come and look at what I've found! There's a fullah here that looks like he's wearing a football jersey." Clinging to the stalk of a tussock[3] is an insect as big as Mummy's thumb with a red and blue striped body and bluish wings.

---

[3] A plant of tussock grass or bunch grass, which is in the Poaceae family; each plant appears to be separate from the others, unlike grass as we usually think of it. A tussock can be several feet tall.

Figure 11.1: Overlooking the valley from the Black Cutting. Joe on the left, Gwen, Laurence and Claude. The road edge is bottom left.

Mummy smiles. "I haven't seen one of those for years," she says. "That's a katydid[4]—they're relatives of grasshoppers. People call that particular one a "mountain devil." She stares into the distance. "When I was a kid, there was an old fellow up on the tops who knew a lot about insects. He had a big white umbrella. He'd hold it open under a bush, and shake it to collect all the insects and things, and then he'd examine them. And he showed me one of these. He reckoned there were all kinds of creatures up here nobody knew about."

As we continue, the road goes around the mountainside. "This is the Black Cutting," says Mummy, and she tells me to keep my eyes on the bank. But the valley and the blue hills on the other side are so pretty that I do look at them quickly a couple of times.

"Black boys," Claude and Amelia shout, pointing to strange trees near

---

[4]An insect in the same family as grasshoppers but with longer antennae, and sometimes very brightly coloured.

Figure 11.2: A Xanthorrhoea plant near the Black Cutting.

the road with black trunks and long, brown sticks coming out of grassy tops.

Mummy says, "Those are grass trees—Xanthorrhoea."

"Mr. Wilson told us about them," Amelia says. "and he said they're called "black boys" because black men stand on one leg like that. See? The trunk's his leg, and there are his spears sticking up."

"That old Wilson's an idiot. The trunk looks nothing like a leg—it's too thick. And the spears, as you call them, are the dead flower stalks."

"But it does look like someone wearing a grass skirt," Amelia insists.

"Mummy, what's a black boy?" I ask.

"That's what some people call men with black skin," says Mummy. "You've never seen one—they don't live around here."

After the cutting, the road levels out, with bushes and trees on either side that almost meet above us. Then the bush thins and there is pale grass and many tussocks.

Mummy keeps pointing out birds. "Mountain Lories!" she sings, as two red, blue and green ones fly out of a low tree, screeching. And a little farther on, we see green and orange birds. "More parrots—Rosellas," she says.

"You know all their names," says Trevor.

"I love birds, and Dad taught me a lot about the wildlife up here."

We go down a steep hill and cross a creek. "The third Hunter," Mummy says. "The big Hunter River down in the valley starts up here as three little creeks—the first, second and third Hunters. One of them is on our land. That's why the place where our property is, is called Hunter's Springs."

Beside the road at the top of the hill are big white-trunked trees, and just after this, in a valley below us, is the orange house with its silver roof, with the huge dead trees around it. Mummy's voice drifts down to me. "There it is."

Part II

BACK ON THE MOUNTAIN

Chapter Twelve

OUR OWN PLACE

Taking a turn-off, we go down the hill, and stop at a gate. Mummy points to a drum on a forked stick on one side. "Our letter box," she says.

As we drive towards the house, the windows blink, and the tops of the dead trees nearby disappear into the sky so I can see only their big trunks. Laurence is asleep on Mummy's lap, and when we stop, nobody seems to want to get out of the car.

Mummy's voice is scratchy. "It looks the same." She points to the other end of the valley, where there's a big white house half hidden by dark green trees with pointy tops, in front of a hill dotted with sheep. "Our nearest neighbours, though I don't expect we'll be seeing much of them. They think they're too good for the likes of us."

The hills that form the valley's other sides are covered in bush, and on the valley's floor are many cream tussocks. Mummy points to rows of twiggy purplish trees behind the house. "Dad's orchard," she says. "The garden seems to have pretty well gone, but we'll soon get it going again."

Trevor is the first to get out, followed by Mummy with Laurence bundled up in her arms, and soon we're all standing near the car looking round. Trevor shivers and puts on a sweater, and a cold wind blows right through my dress, making me long to get back in the car where the warmth of the place we've come from still lingers.

Trevor glances at the nearest hill, where the bush looks as if it's boiling. The roar of the wind steals most of his words, but I hear him say, "Quite a gale."

"It *is* mid-winter," I hear from Mummy, "... just as cold down below..."

She leads us through a small wooden gate to the house, and we cross a verandah to a door, which she unlocks with a big silver key. The room we walk into is large with chairs and a couch covered in material patterned with leaves and flowers, arranged around a fireplace. "Mum's furniture," Mummy says.

It looks as if her mother and father still live there, and might appear at any moment, but she says, "Oh no! They've been down at Grose Vale for years now."

She lays Laurence on the couch and piles cushions around him, and then taps, with the toe of a shoe, the shiny green floor covering, patterned with circles of orange, black triangles and lines. "This linoleum's good, Trevor. A lot easier to clean than those damn boards."

Noticing that I'm shivering, she gets Trevor and Claude to bring in the ports,[1] finds my sweater and helps me into it.

She frowns at the brownish walls. "It's so dark in here! Mum *would* have them painted in that colour. 'Stone,' it's called. All the fashion then. I'll repaint them as soon as I can."

Trevor touches a wall. "What are these walls made of?"

"Tar paper. All they could afford. The outside's tin, as you probably noticed."

We all follow her into the kitchen, where there's a wooden table with chairs around it, all alike. She keeps pointing to things and talking about them, and everyone gets in front of me, and although I say, "I can't see," or "What?" they don't seem to hear. Then Trevor lifts me up, and I can see everything. But he soon says, "You're heavier than a bag of spuds!" and puts me down again.

Then I want to wee and Mummy tells Amelia to take me to the lavatory. At the back of the house, a stone pathway leads to a tall, narrow, tin building with a ridged silver roof. The door opens with a soft ripping sound, and thin, ragged white stuff waves from its edges, and those of the doorway. "Spiderwebs," Amelia says, then points to black spiders running across the board floor and disappearing into cracks.

We've always had lavatories with holes in wooden platforms, and this one doesn't smell, but the platform is so high I only just manage to get up onto it. And as I'm weeing, I notice other spiders watching me from their tents high up in the corners. I finish quickly, jump down, and run back to the house, Amelia following.

Mummy is standing next to the doorway of a little room at the end of the verandah. "This was the room Mum ran the telephone exchange from," she says. "It's big enough for a single bed." She moves into the kitchen and stands up tall next to a doorway. "And this is our bathroom,"

[1] Formerly used for suitcases in Australia.

she says in a high voice, sweeping her arm towards it. While everyone else is giggling, I manage to slip in first.

"Our bath!" she announces, as the others crowd in behind me and press me against a long, bluish tin bath, so deep it comes up to my chest. On the tin, is a pattern like frost on a window. I rub my hand on the inside, and it feels greasy. "Errrh!" I say. "It's awful!"

Mummy glares down at me and snaps, "There's nothing wrong with it!" Then her eyes widen. "Your face is *filthy!*" There's a tearing sound as she pulls a cloth off the edge of the bath, and she scrubs my cheeks with it.

It's rough and smelly. "Ugh!" I say.

She smiles up at Trevor. "They never like having their faces washed."

"It stinks!"

Mummy swings round. "Don't be cheeky!"

They go into another small room. "The storeroom,[2]" she says.

They're all in front of me again, so I wander back into the room with the pretty chairs. On the table is a bottle of red ink, paper and a pen, and I put these on the linoleum, lie next to them, open the ink and start scribbling with the pen.

Mummy's voice comes from the little room. "It'll be so good to have a storeroom... Oh, there's Mum's meat safe, Trevor... Looks in good shape..." She pauses. "Good—she's left a few bottles of jam... Smells alright."

"How long has that jam been here?" Trevor asks.

"Doesn't matter. Jam'll keep forever if it's cooked properly." There's a clink of glass. "See these big jars? By next winter I'll have them full of preserves. You can bottle everything, you know—not just fruit. Meat. And vegetables... Dad built this bin. Solid wood." There's a creak. "Nothing much left in it."

"Must be six feet long. It'd hold enough to see you through a siege."

"Could, just about. Now I can buy things in large bags. Let's see... We'll need one of flour. And one of sugar."

They come into the room where I am, walk by me and into the hallway.

"Nice collection of books in this bookcase, Trevor." Mummy sighs. "What on earth? Oh no! Damn rats. Mum's books. Rotten things will eat anything. Looks like I'll be needing those traps your mother gave us. She thinks of everything."

---

[2]Pantry.

They go into the room next to the one I'm in and I hear Mummy say, "You and Leila can sleep in here, Amelia. And Claude, you can have what used to be the telephone room off the back verandah for now. You can sleep on the front verandah in summer, if you like."

On the couch near me, Laurence starts crying, and Mummy hurries to him. The others wait while she changes his nappy. Then she picks him up and says something about taking a look at the orchard and shed, and they all go outside, their voices becoming fainter till I can't hear them any more.

Something scratches on the tin outside of the house, and a cold breeze blows on my legs. Then I glimpse a big grey spider sliding across the floor towards me and jump, knocking over the ink. I quickly set the bottle upright again, and then see that the "spider" is a gob of dust. A small red pool is on the linoleum. The floor is so pretty, and Mummy likes it so much! I crumple the paper I was using and try to wipe up the ink, but the red stain just gets bigger. *First the sick down the car door, and now this!*

Not knowing what else to do, I roll onto my back. Outside, I see mist drifting through the broken limbs of a dead tree, and the cold linoleum prickles my skin through my sweater. *I wish I'd gone with the others.*

I hear wood being chopped and jump up to look out the window, but it's too high. I try to open the door but can't reach the knob. Then I hear them coming back and lie over the stain, which is dry now, to cover it up. I concentrate on my scribbling as they come in with buckets of wood chips and armfuls of wood for the fire. Mummy drops her load next to the fireplace and walks over to me. "What happened here?"

Twisting round, I see some of the red poking out from under me. "It spilt."

"Oh dear. Well." And, smiling, she lights the lamps.

Soon Trevor has a big fire going and I stand in front of it, watching Mummy light the stove in the kitchen and start cooking.

Tiny tapping sounds start above us and grow louder.

Trevor grins. "Makes quite a racket."

Mummy looks up to the ceiling and sighs. "I've missed the sound of rain on the iron roof."

After the rain has stopped, when it's nearly dark, we hear clinking outside, and I follow Mummy to the window. She lifts me up. "See? There's your father now. Told you he'd come." I can just make out his tall shape topped with his broad-brimmed hat alongside the horses. He comes in, his coat dripping, hugs Mummy and us girls, and says hello to Claude and Trevor.

The next morning, I wake to sunshine, and go to the window. My breath comes out in a cloud, and everything on the ground is white, even the logs and sticks. Amelia gets up and stands alongside of me. "Look how heavy the frost is up here!"

Shivering, I dress quickly and hurry to the kitchen ahead of her. Only Mummy is there. "Where's Daddy?"

She points to a breadboard on the table with half a loaf of bread, crumbs and a knife, its blade striped with butter. "That's where he made sandwiches before he and Trevor left. He had to go back down to get the truck, remember?"

"But you said he'd be home all the time."

She pauses. "Do you want some toast and Vegemite[3]? Mum left some here."

---

[3]The brand name of a very popular vegetable extract Australians spread on bread and butter.

Chapter Thirteen

EXPLORATIONS

Ever since we've come to live here, Mummy has been saying she'll have to prune "those poor orchard trees." And one day she brings a stepladder from the shed and carries it, together with big scissor things she calls "secateurs," into the orchard and gets started. Late that afternoon, she brings an armful of long, thin sticks onto the front verandah, and lays them on the floor near the front door. "These canes are from the top of the pear trees—they'll make *lovely little switches*," she says with a strange smile. "You kids had better behave yourselves from now on."

I don't know what she means, so I ask.

"They're for hitting kids who misbehave."

I still don't understand. *Maybe she's just playing with me.*

***

Most of the ground where she's making the flower garden is covered with a mat of the reddish plants she calls "sorrel," with little leaves that squeak when you walk over them with shoes on. She says that in some parts of the world people make sorrel soup, but she doesn't fancy it. She gets me to bite into a leaf and it's really sour.

One day she starts digging up the plants. She jabs the prongs of her gardening fork through the "mat," stands on its shoulders to make the prongs go down deep, and levers up a square of earth. Then she digs into this with the fork and her fingers, frees the plants from the soil, and lays them in the sun so they'll die.

***

Claude and Amelia ask if I want to play hide-and-seek, and Mummy says she'll play, too. She's never played with us before, but now she runs around laughing like we do, and we have lots of fun.

But a few days later, when I ask her to play with me, she says, "I have far too much to do to play silly games. And *you* could do something useful, too." She gives me a bucket, takes me to the wood heap, and shows me how to gather up wood chips and small sticks to start the fire.

***

Claude, Amelia and I go exploring. As we're passing through the orchard, we see, on its web, a light-brown spider with yellow on it, and call Mummy.

She smiles. "Oh, that's a Saint Andrew's Cross—a garden spider. It won't hurt you—most garden spiders are harmless." She pauses. "But always be suspicious if you see red on a spider. The redbacks I showed you at Stewarts Brook—that live in old tins and things, remember—are around here, too.

She pauses. "And another thing. If you happen to see holes in the ground, don't go poking your fingers in them. My Dad suspected they were the homes of nasty spiders. I've seen black legs poking out of them, but I've never actually seen one of them." She stares into the distance for a moment, kind of shakes herself, and then says, "Anyway, I haven't got time to stand around here yapping all day."

Amelia and I are following Claude around the side of the hill above the house when he stops suddenly and holds up his hand. "Look." He slowly moves his hand forward, as if he's pushing at the air, draws it back and pushes again, then looks around. "That's the strongest spider's thread I've ever seen." He tells Amelia to feel it, too, adding, "Be careful not to break it, though." She steps forward and her hand moves like his did.

"I walked right into it and it didn't break." He nods to tell me to have a go, and Amelia shows me where the thread is. But as I reach out, Claude yells, "Be careful!"

My hand jerks back, but then I reach out again till I feel the thread on my palm, and push it gently. Looking up, I see a spider move on a web as big as a tea towel high on a sapling next to me. It's large, and black with red and black legs.

Claude's voice vibrates against the skin at the back of my neck. *"Red for danger."* Reaching past me, now he bounces his hand on the thread. The web sways wildly, and the spider rushes back and forth. "Watch it dance," he laughs, making it move faster and faster. Suddenly, the web billows out, and we all jump back as it and the spider drift down. *He broke it after telling us not to!*

As we walk on, the thought of the spider makes me prickle, but I also think of its work making the web and feel sorry for it.

We climb up the hill, and walk into the bush, our shoes crackling over dead leaves and streamers of pink bark hanging from trunks. In the air is a sharp, fresh scent like Solyptol, which Amelia says is "eucalyptus," from the leaves of the trees all around with the same name—though everyone calls them "gums.[1]" A brown animal as big as a large dog but low to the ground runs away, and Amelia says it's a wombat. A bit farther on, we notice a hole in the ground, which she and Claude say is its burrow.

As we emerge from the bush, the end of our valley opposite to where the neighbour's house is below us, and beyond this is more bush. Hopping along the flat are three grey kangaroos Claude calls "wallabies," which he says are smaller than other kangaroos. And, on the floor of the valley next to the hill opposite us, is a broad sweep of what looks like orange grass.

"To the swamp!" Claude shouts, and he and Amelia race down the hill, jumping tussocks and small logs, while I follow more slowly. The swamp is the orange grass, and when we reach it, we hear frogs croaking, though they're not as loud as the ones at Stewarts Brook. Then our feet start sinking into mud.

"It's probably quicksand!" Claude shouts, hurrying back to solid ground with us following.

Amelia looks frightened. "It isn't, is it?"

"Could be." He looks at me. "You know what quicksand is?"

I shake my head.

"It sucks you down so quick you can't get out. And no one can pull you out, either. Mr. Wilson told us about a man who rode into some, and it swallowed him and his horse—only his hat was left on the surface. That's how they found out what had happened to him."

I keep away from the orange grass and make sure my feet aren't sinking as we head for the bush at the end of the valley.

"Look—bulrushes!" Claude and Amelia shout, pointing to tall, coarse grass with long, soft-looking brown stuff on stalks at the edge of the swamp.

"Just like in the pictures we saw at school," Amelia says. She looks at me. "Moses was found in the bulrushes."

"Moses?"

---

[1] There are more than seven hundred species of eucalyptus, most native to Australia.

Figure 13.1: Three giant trees which were ringbarked long ago, close to the house on our property at Hunter's Springs.

"He's in the bible. He was found in a basket when he was a baby," she explains. "Mum says it's just a story, though."

Every time I see more bulrushes, I look for a baby, anyway, but don't find any.

At one place, Claude points to oily-looking orange stuff floating on the water. "That could mean there's oil here. We could be millionaires, like the Americans. They're always finding oil, Mr. Wilson said."

After the swamp ends, on the banks of the creek that runs into it, is a magical forest. The trees are small and most of their limbs have long green beards of moss. Some of the branches are so light we can lift them with one finger, and Claude and Amelia say they're dead, and have dried out over a long time. Most of the lower trunks are covered with layers of what look like scalloped, overlapping leaves cut from pale green paper. In the soft green grass are small pink or green flowers like elves' hats, which Amelia and Claude call "orchids." We become quiet as we look carefully at everything, and all I can hear is the creek tinkling. I know fairies aren't real, but if they were, this is where they'd be.

Eventually, we decide to walk to the opposite end of the valley where the white house is. On the way, Claude finds a patch of what he calls "sphagnum moss," which he says we could sell because people pack plants in it. He rips a chunk up and underneath, racing away, are brown beetles, red, white or yellow spiders with bodies as small as pinheads, and bigger, nasty-looking black ones.

As we continue, Amelia and Claude start talking about Jane, one of the other kids at Stewarts Brook school. They joke about sending her a perfume bottle with wee in it. Pretending to be her, Amelia dabs some behind her ears, then notices its smell, makes a horrible face, starts coughing and pretends to throw the bottle away. They laugh and laugh.

They talk about how, when they first went to Stewarts Brook School, the teacher and other kids asked them what religion they were, and when they said they weren't any, the teacher asked, "But what religion were you christened in?" They didn't know, and asked Mummy. She told them we don't believe in God, and they hadn't been christened. But the other kids—especially Jane—were mean to them when they told them. Claude and Amelia wish they'd just said "Church of England," and left it at that, and they say that's what they'll tell people if they're ever asked again.

I ask them what "christened" means, and they say that the minister of a church puts a little bit of water on a baby's head, and then it has the religion of that church.

As we walk, grey and white birds Claude calls plovers cry out or strut a few feet in front of us. And then we discover some bushes with long, sharp thorns.

"You could use these for sewing," Amelia says.

"And give injections!" Claude tries to grab her arm, and then mine, but we jump away.

Not much farther on, at the edge of the swamp, water as wide as our swimming hole at Stewarts Brook shines like a mirror.

"Yippee!" Claude yells, and we all run to it. He rolls up his trousers, and we wade in. He pulls a straw from a tussock on the bank. "Look," he says, "It's hollow," and he sucks water through it.

Amelia peers into the water. "There's an awful lot of mud down there."

When I try to look, all I see is sky and clouds, so they show me how to bend down closer. When I'm so close that my face feels cold from the water, I see a brown cloud swirling up around my legs.

"If we stand really, really still, it'll settle," Claude says, so we try this, and, after a while, the water above my feet, which are buried in mud, is clear. I'm like a plant. Then I start shivering. "It's c-c-cold."

"What do you expect?" Claude snaps. "It's winter. The water'll warm up in the summer."

Amelia pulls a face. "But it'd be horrible swimming with all that mud."

"It'll all get washed away in the next flood," he says loudly. "The mud collects here in the winter. Summer rains'll wash it away."

I try to wade back out, but my feet are like chunks of wood. I start to cry.

Claude twists up his face. "You're such a baby. We shouldn't have brought you." But a moment later he sighs, takes my hand and helps me onto the bank, where I sit, still crying and wobbling, my teeth clattering against one another. He pulls some dry grass from a tussock, squats in front of me and starts rubbing my feet with it. It hurts, and I pull away.

He throws me a kind look. "*You* rub them yourself, then. It'll make them feel better. What you've got is *pins and needles*. It's the feeling you get when cold feet start warming up. You'll feel better soon." And after I do what he says, they do feel better, and we continue our walk.

Chapter Fourteen

THE WHITE HOUSE

We're close to the fence between our place and the property where the white house is when a pair of small brown-speckled birds with kind of round bodies run in front of us and disappear in the grass. Claude and Amelia say they're quails, and they talk about someone called Annie Oakley who used to shoot them in the eye.

Then we see a boy and girl about the same age as Claude and Amelia on the other side of the fence, everyone says, "Hello," and, after a silence, Claude asks, "Does your mother teach you school?"

The boy's chin lifts. "Mother? Oh, heavens, no! Right now we're on holiday, but normally we're at boarding school." He pauses. "I'm Timothy, by the way, and I'm at Kings." He looks at the girl. "And this is Rosemary—she's at PLC."

"PLC?" Claude asks.

The girl smiles. "Pymble Ladies' College."

Claude asks where their schools are.

The boy looks surprised. "Oh! In Sydney. Where do you two go to school, anyway?"

"Well," Amelia pauses. "we lived at Stewarts Brook before we came up here, and went to school there, but now Mum's going to teach us with correspondence. She reckons it's better. We haven't started yet, though. She has to write to the school in Sydney to get them to send the lessons. For Claude and me, that is." She points to me. "She hasn't started yet." She pauses. "We haven't been up here very long."

The boy looks at Claude. "Why don't you go to boarding school?"

Claude frowns. "I dunno. Mum reckons correspondence school's good."

Timothy nods towards our property. "Is that your father's place, now?"

"Yeah."

"What's its name[1]?"

Claude frowns. "It hasn't got a name."

"No name? How very odd. Oh well. You two do have names, I suppose?"

"I'm Claude, and she's Amelia." He glances at me. "She's Leila."

A little smile keeps coming to Rosemary's face, but she doesn't say anything.

Timothy points to our muddy feet. "Why do you not wear shoes?"

We all stare at our feet, and then I notice that the strange children are wearing shoes, and white socks with the tops folded.

Claude says, "Going barefoot is better for running and stuff."

Then a high voice, like the one Mummy used when she was showing Trevor our new bath, calls, "Timothy! Rosemary! It's time for your cocoa." I glimpse a stout woman partly hidden by shrubs in the garden of the white house.

"There's Mother," says Timothy. "Sorry—we have to dash." And they both turn and hurry towards the house.

As we walk slowly back up the flat to our house, Amelia says, "It's a pity they had to go in."

Claude doesn't seem to hear her. "Boarding school... I wonder what that'd be like."

"I didn't think there were any kids up here. Remember Mum said there weren't?"

When they tell our mother about the kids, all she says is "Oh?"

The next day, we're with her in the garden, when we notice Timothy and Rosemary out in their yard. "Look, Mum, there are those kids," Claude says. He turns to Amelia, "Let's run down and talk to them. Can we, Mum?"

I run out of the garden with them, and she calls after us, "Don't be surprised if they won't talk to you."

After we've said hello, Claude asks if they want to come exploring our place.

Timothy looks at Rosemary. "W-w-well, I don't quite know..."

Rosemary looks at Claude, and is about to say something when the same voice as before calls, "Timothy. Rosemary. Come inside now, please."

---

[1]Usually in Australia, large properties have names, whereas small ones do not, so those associated with a property without a name may be seen as lower class by class-conscious people.

Timothy gives a short laugh. "Mother calling. Guess we can't." They walk away slowly, as if they don't want to go, talking in low voices.

That night as we're having tea, Claude and Amelia talk about the kids.

"Told you, Joe, didn't I?" says Mummy.

"Yeah." Daddy looks at Claude and Amelia. "You fullahs don't want to waste your time on those kids. They think they're better than you."

Claude tries to explain. "But they *wanted* to talk to us—it was just that their mother called them in."

"Yeah, they did want to talk to us," Amelia echoes.

Daddy booms, "But their *parents* didn't want them to. That's why their mother called them in."

"They're damn *toffs*—that's what *they* are," Mummy says. "They know the Whites—or are related to them or something. They're people who own a huge property down near Scone and hobnob with the Royal family when they come out here." She's silent for a little while and then shakes her head. Her next words come out in little pops. "What utter nonsense—as if anyone's blood is better than anyone else's!"

Daddy cuts in, "The truth is, they never wanted anyone to have this land. See, they used to run their sheep here, and if your grandfather hadn't bought this place, they could have kept using it for free. They've got a big property of their own, but that's not enough—they want our miserable seven hundred acres as well. God-given right! People like that don't think the likes of me should even own land. Ought to be working for some useless buggers like them."

Mummy nods. "There are a lot of people like that in the world." She looks at Daddy. "Remember that bank manager when you went to get the loan for this place?"

He sighs. "Yeah. He was ready to write a man off, without even hearing me out. Looked at me like I was some kind of bug that had crawled in." He screws up his mouth and speaks in an odd voice. "'And how would you be planning to repay the loan?' he asks. 'I'll pay it back alright,' I says. I reached into me pocket and pulled out a big wad of notes, and when I told him what I'd made rabbiting, he nearly fell off his chair." He shakes his head and laughs. "Well, he couldn't refuse me then." He stares into the distance for a moment. "'The bank doesn't usually loan money for land to men such as yourself,' he says. And as I was leaving, he calls after me, 'Mind you don't keep us waiting for those payments.' Had to get one last dig in."

He folds his arms and adds, kindly, "No, you don't want to let people like that worry you. I've had to deal with them all me life. Bastards who wouldn't give you a crust if you were starving."

Mummy looks at him. "*My* life, Joe—*my* life."

"Me life—my life. It's all the same."

After a silence, Amelia says, "But it wasn't the kids. They *did* want to talk to us."

"Yeah, they did. You could see they did." Claude sounds sad. "They're the only other kids up here. There probably aren't any others till Moonan."

"Well, you might be right that they wanted to. But you saw what happened—their parents, or one of them, stopped them." Daddy takes a breath. "*I tell you, you can't let people like that worry you.* Put the whole thing right out of your minds."

Whenever my parents are out of earshot, Claude and Amelia tell each other again that Timothy and Rosemary wanted to talk to them. But the next time we're down near their place and they're outside their house, they don't even look in our direction.

Knowing that there are people who think there's something so wrong with us that they won't even let their kids talk to us gives me a slithery feeling inside. It was so much nicer at Stewarts Brook with the Roses. Now, whenever I walk near the white house, I look down at my dirty bare feet and think of the white socks and shoes Timothy and Rosemary wear. Their place has a name—Hunter's Springs—and ours doesn't, and near their house are big green trees, whereas ours is surrounded by dead ones.

One day as Mummy and I are walking along the road past their house, she points to the trees there and says, "Those trees are," she twists up the next word, "*European.*" She pauses. "See? They have needles instead of leaves. And cones." She leans down and picks up a shiny brown thing at the edge of the road, and shows it to me. "This is a cone—where the seeds are."

"Can I keep it?" I ask.

She says I can, but she won't let me climb through the fence to get others. "We'd better be getting home," she says. "It must be late."

As we turn around, I glimpse the plump woman, again almost hidden by bushes. *Maybe if Mummy talked to her, she'd get to be a friend like Mrs. Rose.*

As we walk home, the cone in my hand, I think how scraggly gum trees are—you can always see bits of the sky through them—whereas the

European trees are thick and blot out everything. Under them on a hot day, you'd be so cool, and if it was raining, you'd never get wet.

A few weeks later, I'm with Daddy, who's getting the bag of mail from the mailbox, when a man sitting up very straight in his saddle comes riding up the road. "Gooday, Hunter," Daddy says.

The man pulls his horse to a stop, nods and clears his throat. "Bit of a cold spell we're having," he says. The horse shakes its bridle.

Daddy shifts on his feet. "Quite a bit of rain the other day."

With another nod, the man taps the horse's neck with a stick thing, and the horse moves off.

Daddy watches him disappear over the hill. "Can hardly bring himself to speak to a man. That's the father of those kids you fullahs have been trying to get to know. Uses a riding crop, instead of a switch like we do," he says.

***

Two days a week, a truck leaves a big canvas bag containing our mail in the mailbox, and whoever brings it to the house empties it onto the kitchen table. One day, out tumbles a fat yellow envelope with Claude and Amelia's school lessons in it, and early the next Monday, they sit at the kitchen table, Mummy reading aloud what she says are the "Instructions for the Supervisor" and "Instructions for the Pupil." Once they get started, she goes outside and works in the garden, coming back every so often to check on them and answer any questions.

I tell Mummy I want to start school, too, but she says I can't till I'm six, and that because my birthday is in March and the school year begins in January, I'll be nearly seven before I can. It feels like a long time to wait.

Often when Claude and Amelia have finished their lessons for the day, they go exploring, but they don't ask me to go with them any more. And if I ask to go, they say, "You're too little," or, "You can't walk fast enough."

Chapter Fifteen

BROKEN STITCHES

One morning, the ceiling seems shiny when Amelia and I wake up, and through the window, almost everything is white. Mummy says it's snowing and shows us things like white feathers twirling down from the sky. "Snowflakes."

When the flakes stop falling, she takes us outside. Even what was ugly or dirty has been made new by the white covering. She shows us how to make snowballs and snowmen and we have lots of fun, but then it starts raining, and we have to go inside, and soon every bit of snow is gone.

Every morning after this, we look for the shine on the ceiling, and sometimes we think it's there when it isn't.

But, gradually, the days get sunnier and warmer and Daddy begins digging up a paddock for potatoes, not far from the magical forest. One day Mummy packs the meat and bread and jam and cake for the midday meal in a box, and we go over to where he's working. I watch him swinging the mattock[1] high into the air and bringing it down with such force that a deep huh sound comes out of him.

Seeing us, he comes over puffing and wiping his shiny face with a big handkerchief. He grins, and then drinks a couple of pints of water from the water bag hanging on a gum sapling. After we've eaten, we all stretch out on the ground in the sun for a while.

After he's dug up a small patch of ground with the mattock, he breaks up the clods with a potato fork, which has a long handle like a hoe but prongs like a garden fork, separates out the weeds, and throws these into heaps.

---

[1] A digging implement with a long handle, and, at right angles to this, a heavy, narrow blade.

Figure 15.1: Snow at Hunter's Springs.

When he gets home that night, he keeps stretching and rubbing his back, and he looks really tired. "That digging's a backbreaking job," he says.

***

I mostly wander through the forest of tussocks in the orchard. They were as pale as Mummy's hair when we first came, and as tall as me, but now they're green, and I'm six and can see over them. Mummy is usually busy with Laurence, or gardening, or cooking, or riding out into the back paddock to check up on something.

Late one washday afternoon, Mummy is outside taking clean clothes off the line when I come into the house to find Claude and Amelia listening to the wireless we have now. When they see me, Claude switches it off, and I ask him what they were listening to.

He screws up his face. "It was about mad people. Like you. You're just a Dill." He starts chanting, Dill-Dill-Dill," and Amelia joins in. Then they sing, "The greencart's coming... the greencart's coming to take you away." Claude grabs a towel from a pile of clean laundry on the couch, throws it over my head, and pulls it tight. I try to get away but Amelia helps him hold me. They twist it till it burns my skin and presses on my eyes. Everything's black, and I can hardly breathe. Really frightened, I struggle but can't get away. I scream, but only a little sound comes out, and then I'm sobbing, but you can't hear that, either.

Footsteps on the verandah. The towel falls to the floor just before Mummy bursts through the door, arms stretched around a load of laundry. Claude and Amelia are sitting, pretending to read, and I'm sobbing.

She drops the laundry on the couch, and then picks up the towel. "What's this doing on the floor?" No one answers, and she folds it and sets it aside. She frowns in my direction. "What's the matter with you this time? I've never seen a kid that cried as much as you do."

***

After that day, whenever I'm pulling a dress over my head, if it gets stuck and everything's black, I have to fight my way out of it, and the stitches rip.

When Mummy finds the dress, she stamps her foot. "Why are you so damn careless? How many times do I have to tell you to *take your things off carefully?*" She sighs. "You have to learn to think of *others*. As if a person doesn't have enough to do!"

I try to explain. "When it gets tight—it's all *black.*"

"Black won't hurt you!" she says as she stomps down the hallway to the sewing machine to mend the dress.

One day, she picks up one of my dresses, looks at the torn stitching, and says, "Another one! I've had enough of this!" She goes out the front door, comes back, grabs me and hits my legs with one of her "lovely little switches." I lie on the floor, crying, my legs criss-crossed with stinging red marks.

***

A few days later, I squat beside Mummy, who is at the sewing machine in the hallway; it's hot outside, but a nice breeze blows through the open front door. She's cutting oblongs from the edges of a thin old towel with a hole in the middle, and sewing several of them together, the silver foot racing around the edges and criss-crossing at the wad's centre.

"What are you making?"

"Nothing you need to know about," she replies in an odd voice. "Yet."

Just then, a small black insect flies past my ear and into the keyhole at the centre of the long front drawer of the machine, and a thin whining starts up.

She stops treadling, and nods towards the keyhole. "You're wondering what that sound is. It's a hornet[2]—that's the noise they make when they're building their mud nests. Why they always insist on making them in that keyhole, I'll never know." Just then, one flies out of the hole, and goes through the open doorway. "Off to get more mud!" She scrapes back her chair and stands up. "Come and I'll show you."

In the garden, at the muddy edge of a little lake of water under the tap on the water tank, two black insects move back and forth. "They're gathering mud on their legs. But you'd need a magnifying glass to see it," she says.

And no matter how hard I peer, I can't see any.

Back at the sewing machine, the whining sound continues. "They make the dearest little clay pots," Mummy says. "And you'll never guess what they put in them." She pauses. "Spiders. Tiny spiders. After they catch them, they inject them with something to anaesthetize them—put them to sleep. And, in every pot, they lay an egg—imagine how tiny their eggs must be. Specks. They seal each spider into a clay chamber with the egg, and when the babies hatch, they have nice fresh food."

"Can I see the pots?"

"No. The trouble is, I can't show them to you without destroying the nest."

After a while I ask, "But won't the spiders bite the babies?"

"No. I told you, they're anaesthetized. Deeply asleep. They can't bite anything."

"But why don't they wake up?"

"They can't," she snaps. "Listen, I've got better things to do with my time than arguing with you. Find something useful to do. Tell you what—

---

[2]No true hornets exist in Australia. The one she refers to would be a spider wasp, and member of the Pompilidae family.

you can get some chips from the woodheap for the fire. The bucket's on the back verandah."

The days are warm or hot, but usually in the late afternoons what Mummy calls "the coastal mists" come over the hill and fill our valley, making the nights cold, so we need a fire.

When I don't move, she says, "Get going now, if you don't want me to give you the switch again."

The wood heap where the wood is chopped is a pile of grey mush scattered with big, new chips, and I get an idea. I almost fill the bucket with the mush, then put a couple of layers of new chips on top. I put the full bucket near the fireplace, and in no time I'm squatting by the little lake again.

Mummy appears. "Did you get the chips?"

"Yeah."

"Show me."

I do, and she nods, frowning, and goes to the kitchen to start tea.

I'm inside when Daddy comes home from his day's work, and starts making a fire. "Who brought the chips?" he asks.

"Leila—after I threatened her with the switch," Mummy says.

"He looks at me with shining eyes. "What a good girl!."

I feel myself smiling. It's as if magic has happened, though, deep down, something niggles. I wander out to the front verandah, and hear Daddy say, "Well, I'll be damned! She's put a layer of good chips on top of a bucket of old muck!"

I hear Mummy's footsteps as she goes to look. "Oh for heaven's sake. What'll that kid get up to next?"

He calls me, and I go to him slowly. He points to the bucket of grey stuff. "What have you got to say for yourself? And I told you what a good girl you were!" But there's the hint of a smile on his face.

Mummy glares at me. "If you don't mend your ways, you're going to end up in serious trouble one of these days!"

I wait there, full of fear. But Mummy shivers. "Hurry up and light the fire, Joe. It's freezing in here."

"Well, that's what I've been trying to do," he snaps. He hurries out to the verandah, but, over the sound of pumping as he fills a jam tin with kerosene to get the fire started, I hear him muttering and giggling.

***

Figure 15.2: Joe milking a cow.

A few days afterwards, Mummy calls, "Leila, come and look." She's in front of the sewing machine, and points to a small pile of what looks like dirt on the machine's table. "I decided to clean the hornet's nest out of the keyhole after all. These are the pots." Now I see what look like tiny cups made of dried mud with curled-up spiders in them, as well as pots that are still sealed up, and lots of broken ones. "The spiders aren't dead— they're anesthetized, like I told you. Watch this." She takes a paper clip, straightens one part, tips a spider from a cup, and carefully moves the wire over, and just above, its body, making the curled-up legs straighten out. But as soon as the wire has passed, they curl up again. "If the spider was dead instead of alive, the legs wouldn't curl back up—they'd probably break off," she says.

"Can I see one of the eggs?" I ask.

"Remember that they're too tiny to see." She shakes herself. "We have to get rid of this rubbish now, so I can get tea going." She sweeps clay and spiders onto a piece of paper, and throws them into the garden.

***

I'm up near the cow yard one morning, when I hear a deep, rhythmic sound I've never heard before. Daddy is sitting on a wooden block next to a cow. He stops what he's doing and looks up at me. "I'm milking. See, this is the udder where the milk is, and these are her tits. Watch how I do it." His big hands squeeze one white tit and then the other, the streams of milk making loud sounds as they go through what look like soap suds, and deep into the bucket between his knees. Then he stops and pats the cow on a flat place next to her tail, just the right size for his hand. "This is Nancy. Do you like her coat? It's called "brindle.'"

She's kind of striped in red and brown, and pretty. After I've watched him milk for a while, he says, "She can be your cow if you learn to milk her." He gets up and has me sit on the block. My legs have to stretch out a long way for the bucket to fit between them. Squatting behind me with his hands over mine, he shows me how to squeeze the tits. The first stream hits his ear, but he laughs and wipes the milk off with his handkerchief. But before long, every time I squeeze, milk lands in the bucket.

As we're walking back to the house, he says, "Now that Nancy's yours, it'll be your job to bring her and her calf in each afternoon, to lock the calf up for the night." He explains that otherwise, the calf would drink all the milk. He looks at me. "Don't worry—there's plenty for everyone."

Chapter Sixteen

DANGERS SMALL AND LARGE

Late one afternoon, Mummy takes Laurence and me for a walk. "Before we start off," she says, "I want to remind you two of a couple of things I've told you before. Whenever you're walking anywhere, look carefully at the place where you're about to put each foot. And, wherever you are, inside the house or out, watch for *movement where none should be.* It pays to be really careful, because most creatures—even snakes—won't hurt you unless you hurt them first."

We set off up the road, and at the top of the hill, she searches the ground underneath the huge white gum trees there, collects tiny lumps of white stuff that look like icing sugar and holds them out in her palm. "Manna," she says, smiling as she puts a piece into her mouth. "I'm not sure if it's some kind of sap, or it's made by insects, but it comes from these white eucalypts, and it's nice and sweet. Try some." It tastes like icing sugar, and we eat all we can find.

A little farther on, she shows us a pile of ants on the ground. "This is a Pet ants' nest," she says. "They look a bit like those awful greenheads, but you'll notice the heads of these ones are reddish instead of green, and they don't bite. That's why we call them Pet ants." She holds her finger among them and lets them crawl on her hand. "See?"

Farther on, we stop for a rest, and I flop down on a tussock, but pain jabs my ankle. I jump up and stand there, almost crying. Mummy comes and looks at the place that's hurting, and then searches the ground where I was sitting. She points to a black ant as long as her thumb is wide, with pincers. "You've been bitten by a bull ant," she says. "You must have brushed against it and hurt it. It was only trying to protect itself.

The bite hurts, but it's not dangerous—and it isn't *nearly* as painful as a greenhead's. It'll stop hurting soon."

After it's stopped hurting, she frowns at me. "You *must* get into the habit of looking very carefully *before you sit down*, as well as before you step."

The hills around the valley are yellow with blooming wattle trees, or "acacias," as Mummy calls them. She shows us the tiny balls of fluff that are their flowers. A little while later, we find a bush covered with white flowers; but when I bring my face close to sniff their perfume, bees rush out and make me jump.

***

When it's warm enough, I always go barefoot. One day, I'm walking on the flat in front of the house with Mummy and Laurence, when, again, pain jabs into my foot. She sits me down and shows me, stuck in my foot, what looks like a curved hair topped with a tiny yellowish gob. "That's a bee's sting," she says, "and the yellow bit is torn from its body." She points to a bee trying to crawl across some white clover flowers. "It'll die, now, so I might as well put it out of its misery," she says, squashing it with her shoe. I'm not sad. She flicks the sting out with a fingernail, and then says, "Always avoid walking barefoot on white clover flowers. Bees love them." My foot is swollen and red where the sting was, and it hurts.

I hop home hanging onto her. There, she makes sure that all the sting is gone. My foot is swollen, and she says she's heard that the blue you rinse white clothes in is good for bee stings, and puts some on it. Now I have a weird blue foot! The next day, the swelling has gone and my foot hardly hurts.

Bees aren't the only things that sting. One hot night as I'm undressing for bed, I notice a flying insect with transparent wings and a thin red body hitting the hot globe of the lamp over and over. But, suddenly, it veers off and stings me on my tummy. I cry out, and call Mummy.

"An insect stung her," Amelia says.

"Did you hit it?" she asks me. "By accident, I mean?"

"No. It just stung me."

Amelia nods. "Yeah, Mummy—it did."

Just then, it lands near the lamp. "Oh, that's a red hornet[1] Damn thing!" Mummy bashes it with her slipper, then shows me the long sting

---

[1] A wasp.

on its squashed body. "Sometimes they *do* just sting for no reason." To me she says, "It'll only hurt for a while."

"Maybe it hurt itself on the hot globe," Amelia says.

"Maybe," Mummy agrees.

***

One Sunday when I'm in the house by myself, a man with a strong voice talks on the wireless about God, who is kind of like a person a long way away in the sky or somewhere, who's really, really strong. He also has magic, and can stop accidents and save people. The man is explaining how you can ask for God's help by praying—a special kind of talking—when Mummy comes in. "Why are you listening to that rubbish?" She switches it off.

"What's God?" I ask.

She sighs. "Some people think there's someone called God up in the sky who controls everything, but there's no such person. They talk about him in a book called the bible. He's supposed to be able to save you and do all kinds of things. But he doesn't exist. That's religion."

But I think God is interesting. And the next day, Daddy is late getting home from Scone, where he's gone to sell the truck and buy a lorry, and I ask Him to make sure he's alright, and he comes in grinning a little while later.

The next day, we all go to see the lorry, which is dark green. Daddy shakes a yellow cloth out of a packet. "Chamois leather," he says. "Feel how soft it is. Only thing to clean windscreens with, the bloke that sold me the lorry reckons." The material feels soft and strong at the same time. He soaks it in metho and uses it on the windscreen. Then he points to the back of the lorry and says he'll be able to bring the tractor home on there when he buys it, and adds that it'll hold a lot of bags of potatoes, too.

"Can I get up there?" I ask, and he lifts me up. It's a big space with a board floor, a low wooden wall, and boards behind the cab.

After he lifts me down, he says, "Why don't we all go for a spin?"

He shows Claude and Amelia how to climb onto the back by using a tire as a step, and gives them bags to sit on. Then he bows and holds the door open for Mummy, who has Laurence in her arms. I sit near the door. Before he starts the engine, he shows her how to press on the brake to stop the lorry if it starts rolling when it's parked and she's in it but he isn't. As we drive along the road, I hear Claude and Amelia singing, and through the back window I see them standing behind the cab.

The first time we go to town in the lorry, it's raining a lot, and Claude and Amelia would have to ride on the back, so they stay home. We need to leave very early, and, after Daddy wakes me, I shiver into my dress, my breath coming out like steam from a kettle. In the loungeroom, he is in front of a huge, crackling fire, toasting bread with the long-handled wire toaster he made. When a slice is done, he lays it on his big palm, and spreads it with chunks of the butter Mummy makes. At breakfast, the partly-melted chunks of butter on the toast look like boulders stranded on a riverbank, and when I bite into a slice, butter dribbles down my chin.

The stars are still in the sky when we leave. Mummy, with Laurence on her lap, sits next to Daddy, and I sit on the outside and will have to open all the gates. The valley next to the Black Cutting is filled by a huge pink cloud, and I feel as if I could walk across it. After the cutting, the road gets very steep, and the engine grinds out a noise like the one I used to make to show Mummy I was really trying when she sat me on the potty and told me to do my jobby.[2] The grinding gets louder and louder, till my face is buzzing.

"The lorry wants to race down the mountain, and doesn't like being held back," Mummy says.

Daddy glances at me. "Don't worry—the gear's holding her. And if it slips out of gear, I can stop it with the brake. See?" As we come to a stop, there's a sound like dried peas being poured into the saucepan before Mummy cooks them. "Hear the wheels slipping on the gravel?"

None of the other valleys beside the road on the way to town is as big as the one next to the Black Cutting, and the rest of the cuttings are wider, but the part of the road I like best runs between two hills.

In town, my parents keep stopping to talk to people. After everyone has said hello, the men fold their arms and say something about the weather. And there are long silences in which I, and any other kids my size who are there, kick at things or twirl. Every now and then, one of the men says something about crops, sheep, horses or cattle, or the prices of things, and the women smile.

We go to a place called the Vogue Cafe, where we sit at a table, Mummy reads a list of the food they have, and tells the man there what to bring. Later, we drive to a shop where my parents buy things like flour, sugar,

---

[2] A word formerly used by children to describe faeces; to "do one's jobby" meant to have a bowel movement.

Figure 16.1: Scone as it was in the 1950s.

tinned food, vegetables and fruit, load them onto the lorry, and cover them with a tarp.

It's dark and rain is pouring down when we leave for home, and every time we come to a river crossing, Daddy stops the lorry, peers at the water in the headlights, and says, "It's *full* but not up,[3]" before we cross.

"The next river we'll come to is Dicky Dan's Crossing," he says. And he tells us how, when he was about my age and his family lived at Dry Creek at the bottom of the mountain—and all they had was a horse and buggy[4]—his sister Charlotte got so sick that Grandfather had to take her to the doctor in Scone, and Daddy went, too. He says that she had something called "appendicitis," which Mummy explains means that a bit of your insides has gone bad and a doctor has to cut it out or you'll die. Leaving her in the hospital, they started for home. It was dark and

---

[3]My father used the word "up" to mean that a river was in flood.
[4]A horse-drawn carriage.

raining when they got to Dicky Dan's, he says, and Grandfather stopped the horses, handed Daddy a lantern, and told him to go down the hill close enough to the river to see if it was "up." He hadn't gone far when, with a roar, a wall of water as high as a house burst into the valley below where he stood. If they'd been crossing, they'd have drowned, and if the river had been flooded on their way to Scone, Charlotte would have died.

As we roll down to the crossing, the lorry's lights show fast-moving clear water. "It's a bit high," Daddy says, "but we'll make it across."

The water swirls around us, and all I can think of is that wall of water. I silently ask God to let us get to the other side, and, after what seems like a long time, we do.

Not long after we start on the Black Cutting, Daddy yells, "Hang on!" He's spinning the steering wheel fast one way and then the other, his elbows jabbing out, and Mummy's leaning against me. *We're heading for the edge! Stop! Stop!* thumps in my head. *Please, God, please don't let us go over!* On the edge of my seat, I stiffen my legs as if I have my own brakes and push down.

We stop just in time. Daddy sits staring ahead for a moment. "Rain's made her greasy." Then he starts inching the lorry back to the centre of the road.

I ask why he didn't use the brakes.

"Can't use them when it's slippery. Have to steer into the slide."

I can hardly get the words out. "How can we stop, then?"

He's too busy spinning the wheel again to answer—we're sliding towards the dirt bank of the mountainside.

Please, please God, don't let us hit it! Again, we stop just in time.

Back and forth like this we go, me praying to God and pushing my feet hard against the floor. By the time the cutting ends, my legs are aching and my head hurts from the words jabbing into my forehead.

Just then, headlights come towards us and grow larger till a lorry roars past, a long load of logs swinging back and forth behind it.

"Timber jinker,[5]" says Daddy. "Bringing logs from the *other end*." He means from farther out on the mountain. "If we'd met it on the cutting, it would've put us over. Them blokes can't stop—no brakes." He glances at me. "We normally drive along the middle of the road, but we're supposed to be on the left, so coming up the mountain, we have to go to the edge if another vehicle comes towards us."

"Stop it, Joe!" Mummy snaps.

---

[5] A lorry with a long trailer used for carrying logs.

He laughs. "Well, it's true. There's nowhere to pull over."

We cross the last creek, and as we start up the hill before home, Daddy says he hopes we don't get bogged. Again I ask God for help, and though we slip a bit, and the engine grinds, we keep going.

Inside the house, Mum and Amelia start cooking, while Daddy lights the fire. As he and I are warming ourselves in front of it, he looks at me. "We were lucky with that jinker," he says in a low voice. "Dangerous buggers. No brakes." His face looks serious, but I notice the corners of his mouth twitching in an odd way.

Chapter Seventeen

BOGGED

We go with Dad in the lorry over to the potato paddock to help harvest our first crop of potatoes. Just before we get there, the engine grinds as we go through a swampy part, but we don't get stuck.

The potato plants were dark green when I last saw them, but now they're dry and grey, and sprawl over the ground like big dead spiders. Daddy and Claude dig them up, and the rest of us fish the potatoes out of the dirt and throw them into piles—the large, solid, smooth ones to sell, any half rotten ones for the pigs, and the small or knobby, "second-growth" ones, as Daddy calls them—explaining that they must have stopped growing because of a dry spell and then started again after rain—for seed, or for us to eat.

There are a lot of things going on around me. Dragonflies sit crackling their wings, plovers cry as they swoop over, or strut across the grass nearby, and kookaburras land, pull big worms from the dirt and swallow them, then fly up to a high branch and laugh. In the ploughed ground, I find small frogs among bunches of sticky-looking eggs, and other tiny eggs shaped like hen's eggs that Mummy says belong to lizards. Sometimes I find large, fat, white witchetty grubs[1] in a piece of rotten wood. The Aborigines eat these, and we tried them once, fried in butter; they tasted like nuts, but nobody liked the thought of eating them, so we never had them again. I also see thin, dark brown grub things called millipedes, that are a few inches long with many legs and a peculiar smell. Mummy told me that these look like tiny trains, which she showed me a picture of, and told me about. Millipedes are harmless, and she taught me how to tell them from centipedes that also have a lot of legs, but can make you

---

[1] The name given in Australia to the large, white, wood-eating larvae of several moths, and eaten by the indigenous people.

very sick, or even kill you; they are bigger, broader, paler and flatter, and without a smell.

"You're supposed to be working, not playing." Mummy has come up behind me, but there's a smile in her voice.

I start picking up potatoes again and throwing them onto the piles, but then I see a strange-looking stone. It's oblong, black, and twice as big as my hand, with one edge thin. I hold it up. "Daddy?"

He glances over and keeps working. "Found a stone, have you?" But I just know this one is special, and take it over to him. He glances and then stares at it, takes it from me and turns it over. "That's an Aboriginal axe," he says, his voice rising. "Leila's found an Aboriginal axe," he calls to Mummy.

She comes over. "Oh, for heaven's sake. There were Aborigines up here before white people came. Black people who knew all about the land."

"Up here?" I ask.

"Oh yes; they were all over Australia when the British came," Daddy says. "But they probably only came up here in summer. They didn't wear clothes or have warm houses, see."

Mummy stares into the distance. "No, they'd just make a bit of a lean-to to sleep in, and light a fire nearby to keep warm. When we came to live on the station, there was an aboriginal ceremonial ground not far from the house. You could still make out the circles where they danced, although the grass had grown over some parts. You can't see any of it now—they ploughed that place up."

Daddy says, "When I was a young fullah working on Curricabark station down near Gloucester, there were fifty or sixty piles of stones at the foot of this plateau, near the track they walked up to get here. The old hands reckoned that every time an Aborigine set off up that track, he left a stone to tell the others where he'd gone." He pauses.

"And do you know, I went to school at Ellerston—that's fourteen miles away down the mountain—for a while, and the kids were always finding aboriginal axes and bringing them in. The teacher used to throw them down the toilet." He hands the stone axe back to me. "Put that in the glove box, Pet, so we can take it home with us."

Half-way through the afternoon, Daddy starts putting the potatoes into bags, sewing up the tops with what he calls a packing needle,[2] which is very big, and string, and heaving the bags onto the back of the lorry. Then,

---

[2] A thick needle about six inches long with a large eye; threaded with string, it is used to sew the tops of bags such as cornbags together.

everyone except him leaves—Mummy to get tea, Amelia and Claude to do some school work, and I, to bring Nancy in to lock up her calf. Mummy tells me that Daddy will cover the bags of potatoes on the back of the lorry with a tarp and walk home.

The next day, by the time we leave the potato paddock, all the potatoes have been dug up and thrown into piles, and the rest of us leave Daddy to finish bagging them and drive the loaded lorry home. But he isn't back by dark, and we wait and wait for him, tea in the oven. At last the lights of the lorry appear and we hear his boots crossing the verandah, heavy and slow. He holds onto the edge of the table as he sits down, and winces a couple of times before he speaks.

"Lorry got bogged," he says. "I bagged up every last potato—even the ones for the pigs. Loaded every damn bag on the back and set off." He looks down and sighs. "Bloody thing got bogged in that swampy bit. All the extra weight. Tried every trick I knew to get it out—packed the wheel tracks with stones and branches. It wouldn't budge—the wheels just kept digging in deeper and deeper. In the finish, I had to unload the whole bloody lot. Whole bloody lot! Course once the lorry was empty, it got through, no trouble." He sighs again. "Then I had to lug all the bags over to where the lorry was and load them again. It bloody near killed me." He's almost crying, and Mummy puts her hand on his shoulder.

His back is so bad the next morning that he decides to rest that day and take them to town the following one. In the afternoon, Amelia and Claude are outside somewhere, and Mummy is in the kitchen making tea when Daddy comes in. "After what happened last night, I've been thinking. I really need more help on this place." Claude's thirteen, now, and maybe he could leave school to help me."

Mummy frowns. "He can't leave till he's fifteen."

"Well, I think if we explained our situation... There must be some way he can." He pauses. "You left at twelve."

"You weren't supposed to leave till you were fourteen at that time. But Dad wrote and told them about Mum being away, and they gave me special permission."

"Well, if we explain that I can't carry on without his help, I don't see how they can refuse us. After all, his life's going to be on the land; I don't know what else he could learn at school that'd be of much use to him."

Mummy's voice sounds sad, "He's too young to leave."

Daddy sighs. "Well, I don't know what else to do. We'll never get this place the way we want it without more help, and we can't afford to pay anyone. If he can't leave, I don't know how we'll survive."

"Well, I suppose I could write and ask."

Later, when we're all sitting around the fire, Daddy says to Claude, "Well, son, you're almost a man, now."

Claude grins.

"I need to talk to you about giving me more of a hand here. You've had a fair bit of schooling, and one day this place will be yours, and you'll need to know how to run it. Now, as I see it, you aren't going to learn much about that at school." He takes a breath. "The thing is, unless I get more help, we could lose this place. We can't afford to pay anyone full-time. And if we do lose it, well, it won't be ours to leave to you. So your mother and I want to write to the school to see if you can leave. I don't think they'd be able to refuse us, under the circumstances."

Claude looks serious, but then he grins, and nods. "Yeah. Well, OK, then."

Chapter Eighteen

NASTY GAMES

When my parents are taking the load of potatoes to town, nobody can ride on the back of the lorry, and Mummy says I can't go. "Amelia has to see the dentist," she says, and explains, "Laurence will be on my lap, and you're too big for her to nurse[1] all the way. We'd be crammed in like sardines." Even after what she's said, I continue to try to persuade her that I *can* fit in every now and then, and after a few times, she disappears, rushes back into the kitchen with one of her switches, grabs me and beats my legs.

The next day, I watch everyone else except Claude heading for the lorry where, the engine running, Daddy sits far up in the cab staring straight ahead, his hands on the steering wheel. Mummy looks at me. "Come on—you're a big girl, now," she says. "You don't have to look like that just because I'm leaving you for a few hours. Claude'll look after you."

She helps Laurence up into the cab, she and Amelia climb up, and the vehicle with its load of lumpy bags moves slowly up the hill. I want to run after it, and once it disappears over the top, I hold my breath and listen till I can't hear the engine any more. The great dead trees tower over me, the bush up on the hill swirls, and I feel very small and alone.

Claude comes out of the shed and I follow him around. But, suddenly, he stops and turns. "Why are you following me like some damn poddy calf[2]?"

I stop. He kicks at the grass, then picks up stones and spins them at the fowls; one hits a hen and makes her squawk and jump into the air before she runs away. He walks to a sapling, and starts turning over its leaves.

---

[1] In Australia, to "nurse" someone commonly means to have him or her sit on ones lap.
[2] An orphaned calf fed with bottled milk, and which often have a large belly.

I move slowly to where he is. "Spitfires,[3]" he says, showing me, on the underside of a leaf, a row of bristly little black grubs side-by-side, yellow stuff oozing from their raised-up heads. He points. "Vomiting. That's why they're called spitfires." He rips the leaf from the sapling and drops it on the ground. I stare at it, and then him. A shadow passes across his eyes. "Pests," he says. "Destroying the tree." He pauses. "Anyway, the leaf'll keep them alive. For a while."

I walk over to the woodpile, and sit on one of the logs at its edge, and Claude sits across from me. He picks up a stick from the ground, and scratches among the yellow surface chips as if he's angry with them, then jabs at the grey muck underneath. He points the stick at the clothesline, where there are some toweling things like the ones I saw Mummy sewing. *Nothing you need to know about. Yet.*

"You know what those are?"

I don't answer.

"They're what Mum uses for her monthlies. You'll have them, too, when you're a woman." He jabs at the grey muck again.

Monthlies? What's he talking about?

"Approximately one cup of blood drips out of a woman every month," he says slowly, staring into my eyes. Then an ugly look comes over his face, and he nods at the line again. "That's what they're for."

"What—what—?"

"She pins them on to soak it up. The blood." The toweling things writhe in the breeze. "The blood starts to drip when you're old enough to have a baby." He scans my face. "You don't believe me do you? It's the truth."

I somehow know it is, but I hate the ugly way he's talking.

One of his boots kicks up gobs of the grey muck under the chips, some landing on my bare feet. "Do you know what you're made out of?"

"Made out of?"

"Yeah."

"No."

"You're made out of horrible slimy grey stuff." watching me, he screws up his face. "Like this grey muck. Dad squirted slimy grey stuff into Mum to make *you.*"

I look down at my muddy bare feet; and notice the smell of a pile of fresh cow manure nearby. But I say, in a good, strong voice, "Well, then, you're made out of it, too."

---

[3]The larvae of the sawfly wasp that does not sting.

He stares at me, and then his face gets twisty. "Nah. Not me." He gives a laugh. "He put some new chips in when he made me." He jumps up. "I'm going for a ride."

Horrible feelings inside me, and nasty images flashing, I notice him putting a bridle on Dolly up near the shed. Wanting not to see him any more, I look over at the trees on the hill.

A drumming on the ground. Dolly, Claude on her back, his legs kicking her belly to make her go. Coming at *me*! I scrunch up.

She stops suddenly, just before me, sending chips flying onto my bare legs and feet. He turns her and jogs away, hiccuping laughs coming out of him.

Frozen. Can't move. Again and again, he comes at me on the horse. Splinters of light. Chips hitting.

Then, Dolly's legs are standing in front of me. His voice from high up. "Ah, don't be so silly." He slides onto the ground and stands there, shifting from boot to boot. "She wanted to run over you, but *I* stopped her." After a silence, he says, "I wouldn't hurt you." He says it again when I don't speak.

He leads Dolly back up the the shed and I'm relieved to see him taking her bridle off. He walks back past me, through the gate and into the house. *I hope he stays in there.*

But soon he's back, standing in front of me. "You can have these if you don't tell Mum and Dad." In his palm are two silver threepence's. "They're yours." He pauses. "*If* you don't tell."

They're like fairy money. *But why does he think I'd tell them?*

He reaches into his pocket, and, the next thing there are three threepences in his hand. "I'll take you up the creek for a walk, too."

My eyes are on the coins. *I wouldn't have told, anyway, but he doesn't know that.* I reach for them, but he closes his fist over them.

I should have known.

"You've got to promise first. Promise you won't tell." I nod.

"Promise."

"I promise."

A while later, we set off for the swamp. Feeling better, and the coins in the pocket of my dress, I follow him along its edge.

He stops. "Shhhh. Listen."

A rustling, then everything starts to move. The wind. But he's peering into the grass. "Don't you hear it?" he asks.

"No."

"Rustling."

"It's the wind."

"No. The other sound. Slithering. Like a snake. Hear it now?"

I don't.

He curls two fingers of one hand, and jabs them at me. "Snakes have fangs like that. When people get bit, the poison makes them swell up and go black before they die." His eyes dart to the grass near my feet. "There's one! Run!" He bounds away, me following.

We don't stop till we reach the little creek where it runs into the swamp. We're standing there, when he yells, "Snake!" He grabs me, lifts me onto a stump, and quickly climbs up himself.

I'm only a bit frightened, thinking it's probably another trick. But he points down, and there, winding through the water of the stream is a black snake, flashing red from its belly. *He protected me after all.*

***

The others get home in the late afternoon, and after tea, when we're all sitting by the fire, Mummy smiles at me. "Well, it wasn't so bad being left at home with your big brother, now was it?"

Claude is watching me, and I grin a bit and nod. I wouldn't know how to describe what happened, anyway.

***

One day Mummy takes me to Scone to get my munization—which means that I get a needle to stop me from getting sick. The doctor with the yellow eyes tells me to hold out my arm. "Now you'll feel a little prick, but I want you to keep very, very still. Now, don't look." There's a prick, and I do watch him pull the needle out.

The next day, for the first time ever, Mummy tells me to take Laurence for a walk. His hand in mine feels really nice as we go down the flat towards the swamp. At last I can play with him. As we're passing the needle bushes Claude and Amelia found when we went exploring, I get an idea. "I'll show you something," I say, tearing a thorn off the bush. "Now, hold out your arm." He does.

"I'm going to give you your Munization so you won't get sick. Now keep still and don't look."

But every time I try to push the thorn in, he cries out, "No. Don't! No!" and jerks his arm away. He's bucking about so much I have to hold his arm really tight. "Come on, now," I say firmly. "I told you, you've got to get your *Munization*." By now he's crying. "Keep still," I order again, in a loud voice. He gets away and runs for home, sobbing.

"You're just a baby!" I yell after him. "Baby! Can't even play a game."

He disappears into the house before me. As soon as I'm inside, Mummy steps in front of me, glaring. "What have you done to him? What's this about needles?"

I don't answer.

"He told me you stuck something in his arm. Did you?"

"No, I didn't," I say. *It wouldn't go in.*

"Laurence? Come here." She turns his thin arm to show me two red marks. "Did you make these?"

After a while, I mumble about the *Munization*.

"What a horrible damn game! How can you be so cruel to your little brother?" She shoves her face close to mine and says through clenched teeth. "You're a nasty piece of work. If I ever hear of you doing anything like this to him again, I'll take the horsewhip to you."

I start to cry.

"I don't know what you're crying about. He's the one who got hurt."

I'll never play with him again.

Chapter Nineteen

RESCUED FROM THE TUSSOCKS

Spring almost here, Mummy again starts digging up the sorrel, but, like
when she was trying to get rid of the strange trees at Stewarts Brook, bits
always hide in the ground and grow again.

"Another bloody noxious weed," she says, her face purple as she searches
through the dirt, flinging every bit she can find onto a heap.

Not far away, Laurence plays with his red lorry, and asks many questions. She waits longer and longer to answer each one, and her answers
get shorter and shorter. Then suddenly, she stands up, her hands, red
with dirt and trailing bits of sorrel, on her hips. "Can't you give a person
a moment's peace?" she yells. "I'm trying to get rid of this rotten bloody
sorrel—that's enough for anyone to cope with."

The orchard is full of tussocks, and I spend most of my days wandering
among them. That's where I am a little later when Mummy and Laurence
pass. They're walking slowly, and she's back to answering in her pretty
voice, and when he wants to look at something, she waits as if she has all
the time in the world.

"I see the green dragon." Amelia is standing not far away. "You're
jealous. *Full of green poison.*"

Somehow I know what jealousy is. I'm surprised at how well green
describes it. I keep looking straight ahead as if I haven't heard her, though
she's at the edge of where I'm looking, watching me. When she finally
goes away, I walk through the tussocks, and they brush my arms and face,
as if they like me.

In the mornings, if breakfast isn't ready when I get to the kitchen, I
walk among the tussocks until Mummy yells from the back step, "Leila!

Figure 19.1: Tussocks near one of the dams that were built later.

Get back in here for breakfast right now!"

Later in the day a cold breeze often comes up, and I squat; it's warmer low down. Often, a little, shiny brown lizard pokes it's head out, and looks at me, a tiny bump ticking in its throat. If I stay still, it glides all the way out, pausing to look back at me every now and then. The moment I move, it disappears. I see small, black ants, too, following one another, and carrying grass seeds or an insect leg.

On warm days, I stay in the tussocks until the afternoon mists come, wetting my dress so I can see through the material. When I get too cold I go inside and stand in front of the stove, where the fire burns all day.

As I'm walking in the orchard one day, I see a lizard as long as my foot with rough, grey skin. Suddenly, it opens its mouth wide to show bright orange inside, and jumps a few inches towards me, making me jump, too. When I look again, I can't find it. I tell Mummy about it later, and she says she's never seen one like this.

When I get the feeling of wanting to wee, I wait till it really hurts before I go, and, sometimes, little bits of water fall into my panties. When I take them off, if they smell bad, I hide them under the mattress.

One washday, Mummy calls me; she's beside the copper[1] where she boils the whites. She nods at a pile of washing. "How come you wet your panties?" she snaps. "I found the ones you hid under your mattress."

I don't know what to say.

"You mustn't wait so long before you go to the lavatory."

Soon afterwards, something worse happens. I wake to find the bed cold and wet, and when I turn back the covers, a nasty smell rises up. I don't understand, and go to breakfast. Later, Mummy calls me into the bedroom, and points to my sheets. "You wet your bed."

Then I remember dreaming that I was weeing, but don't know how to tell her this.

She stamps her foot and yells, "First your panties, and now this. Did you go for a wee before you went to bed?"

"Yeah."

"Then you must have drunk too much last night. From now on, you're not allowed to drink *anything* after we eat."

So now I can't drink the strong, milky tea I like so much in the evenings. But still, every few mornings, she calls me into the bedroom, her face dark. "You drank after tea, didn't you?" I didn't, and say so, but she

---

[1] A large receptacle made of copper and arranged so that a fire can be built under it; before electricity and washing machines, a copper was used for boiling white linens.

doesn't believe me. I stand there, my eyes on the floor. I'm asleep when it happens, so I can't stop it, but I feel as horrible and dirty as the wet sheets.

"This is damn disgusting!" she yells, screwing up her nose.

***

Daddy says there are too many rabbits on our place, and decides to put out what he calls bates—bits of carrot with poison on them. A few days later, I see him up in front of the shed and go there. He doesn't notice me, and I pick up a rusty billycan from near him and have fun twirling with it in my hand.

Suddenly, he jumps up and grabs the arm holding the billycan. "What do you think you're doing?" he yells. "Give me that!" He picks up a bit of rusty barbed wire from the ground, and taps me on the legs with it. It doesn't hurt, but he's never hit me before, and I sob.

"That can is what I used to mix up the strychnine I put on the carrots," he says.

Mummy appears, and asks what happened, and he tells her I was playing with the billycan he mixed the poison in.

"How did *that* happen?"

He looks down. "She just picked it up."

"How come it was where she could get at it?"

"It doesn't matter. She has to learn not to touch things she knows nothing about."

That night, there's something on the wireless about kids being bad, and Daddy says, "The parents let them get away with too much. Time and again, I've seen a father discipline a kid, and the wife get mad at him. That won't teach a kid a damn thing. Parents have to back each other up when it comes to punishment."

Mummy nods. "A kid treated like that wouldn't know what to think." She pauses. "Most parents are too damn lenient. Kids have to learn the difference between right and wrong."

"Another thing they do is, they give a kid a slap and then cuddle it and say they're sorry. That's sending a double message."

***

Daddy looks up from reading a letter that's just come in the mail. "Well, now that summer's here, Bill's leaving Queensland and coming to stay with us for a while."

Claude says, "I remember him. He stayed with us when we were rabbiting."

"Yeah, he did. He can't stand the cold, so he spends the winters in Queensland. And, in spring, when it gets too warm up there, he comes back down here. He mostly stays in Newcastle with Grandma and Grandfather, but I expect we'll be seeing more of him now we have our own place."

I remember watching him giving himself a needle.

Mummy says to us all, "You'll like Uncle Bill—he's really nice."

Daddy rubs his chin. "He isn't a well man, and I want you all to help him as much as you can. He's as good as blind because of the diabetes. And he can't eat as many sweet things as we do. He has a special diet."

A week or so later, Daddy goes to town, and when he gets back, a tall man wearing a dark jacket and glasses gets out of the lorry.

Mummy makes tea, and as we're drinking it, Uncle Bill says, "I've been staying at the Palace in Brisbane."

We kids all stare at him. "The *palace?*" I ask.

He laughs. "It's not a palace like that. I mean the People's Palace. It's a hostel run by the Salvation army. The rooms are small, but it's clean."

Uncle Bill comes to the dinner table in white trousers and shirt. "Time to get into me summer whites," he says. "In the tropics, people wear white in summer. It reflects the heat."

Mummy appears with a steaming enamel jug, and pauses next to him, smiling. "Try some of this lovely pea water, Bill."

He shifts in his seat, frowns, and drawls, "*Pee* water, eh Gwen? *Pee* water. Hmmmm. I don't think so. No. No thank you. Not today." And a bit of a giggle escapes from him.

Mummy—who tells us "pee" is a rude word, and to say "wee"—looks surprised. "It's the water the peas were boiled in—I always drink it, and it's delicious. Good for you, too."

"Well, y-e-s, I'm sure it... could be." The corners of his mouth twitch. "But I don't think I'll have any, just the same." He glances at Claude and Daddy, and they all roar with laughter, Amelia and I joining in.

Mummy's face goes red. "Oh I don't know what on earth's the matter with you all!" She stamps off, and sets the jug back on the hob of the stove.

By the time she puts the plates of food in front of us and sits down, everything's quiet again except for a few giggles. The Tilley lamp[2] is on

---

[2]The brand name of a lamp that runs on kerosene pumped up with air to make it gaseous,

Figure 19.2: Uncle Bill.

the table—it was in the house when we came, runs on kerosene, and has to be pumped up—and around it are many insects. Then, a moth with dark wings as wide as my hand burrrrs in through the open window, and lands on the edge of the saucer where the milk jug sits, red eyes sparkling.

Everybody gazes at it, Mummy smiling, and she and Amelia say how beautiful it is. Then, something like a wound up feeler appears from the lower part of its head, straightens out and dips into a drop of milk.

"Look at it's tongue," Mummy says. "It's like a watch spring."

"The poor thing's thirsty!" Amelia carefully pours a tiny pool of milk next to it, and we all watch it drink from this.

The moth stays there till we've eaten our pudding, then turns and burrs back out the window and disappears.

***

Uncle Bill sleeps in the little room off the back verandah, and noticing his door open the next morning, I look in. "I was just about to give meself me insulin," he says. "Are you OK seeing me do that?" I nod. He rubs his arm with metho, and sticks the needle in. And, like before at the rabbiting place, he doesn't cry out or anything. I ask if it hurt.

"You get used to it." He pauses. "Listen, Pet. I'd feel better if you didn't watch me give meself me injection. It makes me nervous." He hesitates. "If you don't mind. Could you do that for me?"

I nod.

After breakfast, he says, "I was wondering if you could show me round a bit."

As we walk, I tell him about watching the lizards, and he says. "You want to keep a good lookout for snakes, too, Pet. Nasty customers."

After that, he gets me to walk with him every day; he seems to like being with me, and never gets cranky. Although I haven't wet my pants or the bed for a while, every now and then I imagine Mummy telling him about the wetting and get a horrible feeling. I still check the sheets every morning, but everything stays nice and dry, and, as more and more days pass and he's still nice to me, I stop worrying that she'll tell him. And after a while, I know the bed wetting has stopped.

***

---

and has a mantle which glows and gives off a very bright light.

One night, Mummy gets out her paints and a board to paint on, and I stand next to her chair and watch her squeeze paint from the tubes onto a plate and add a little pool of linseed oil, and I breathe in its lovely scent. Next, she uses her pallet knife to squash dark blue into the white to make sky blue, then studies the black and white photograph next to her, dips a small, stiff brush into the blue she's just made, and makes a wavy line the shape of the hill in the photograph. She uses a bigger brush to sweep pale blue upwards from this till the space above the line is full. Mixing white and green, she uses a different brush to paint the hill. Then, with a brush like a teardrop, she makes a series of black Y's on the green, and, using a small stiff brush, dabs dark green around them till she has a forest.

I need to hear her voice. "Why do you paint trees like that?"

"Like what?"

I demonstrate the dabbing.

"Why?" She frowns. "Because that's the way you paint trees, that's all."

"But couldn't you do them other ways?"

She swings around. "No!"

"Why?"

"Stop asking stupid questions," she snaps. Then she sighs, and asks in a pained voice, "Can't you ever give a person a moment's peace?" She finds some paper and a pencil, and gives these to me, saying, "Why don't *you* try to draw something?"

I draw a tree, and she teaches me how to make crows in the sky. When the drawing is finished, I show it to her and she says it's good. *Maybe I'll be an artist when I grow up.*

***

One morning, as Uncle Bill and I are walking around the hillside above the house, he runs into a spider's web and is afraid the spider is in his hair, and I look but it isn't. I tell him about the brown tarantulas nearly as big as saucers that live in the house and have been in every house we've lived in. He knows about them. "They catch flies," he says. "They're our mates, and they're not poisonous, you know. "

When we get back to the house, he says I've been telling him about the tarantulas, but Mummy says, "Oh yes, the Huntsman spiders."

Then, in case he doesn't know, I tell him what Mummy told me—that they won't bite you unless you hurt them first, and also that, even if you do happen to get a bite, it won't make you sick unless the spider hasn't cleaned its teeth.

She and Uncle Bill laugh, and he says, "It's a good idea for you to clean your teeth, too—I'm sure she's told you that as well."

"The only time you have to kill a tarantula is if it gets in your bed," I add.

"Yes, they don't make good bedmates, that's for sure."

A few mornings later, Uncle Bill and I are the only ones at the breakfast table. Laurence is playing on the floor, and Mummy is making toast on the stove and stacking the pieces on a plate on the hob next to it.

I notice Uncle Bill feeling beside his plate. "Leila—can you see my knife, Pet?"

"Find Uncle Bill's knife for him," Mummy says over her shoulder. I lean across the table, and hand it to him.

"And pass me the butter too, Pet, if you don't mind."

I push it towards him till it touches his hand. "There it is, Uncle Bill."

"Ah." He jabs at it with the knife till he gets a gob on the blade, then holds it upright in his fist, waiting.

Mummy sets several pieces of toast on a plate on the table next to him. "There you are, Bill."

"Good. Can't wait too long to eat after me injection." He takes a slice.

My chin on my hands, I stare till he separates into two. Vaguely, I see him jabbing at his toast with the knife with the butter on it, but mostly missing, and then, the toast shaking in his hand as he lifts it. But, suddenly, I see "movement where none should be"! I focus. A tarantula! Shifting back and forth to keep its balance on his toast as it wobbles towards the cave of his mouth!

I yell, "Uncle Bill! Spider! On your toast!"

Laurence lets out a wail.

Mummy looks round and yells, "Throw it on the floor, Bill!"

He flings the toast across the room, then jumps up, knocking his chair over, and furiously brushes at his clothes. "Where'd it go? Where'd it go? Is it on me?"

By now, the spider is racing up the wall near where the toast landed.

"It's gone, Bill. It's OK," Mummy says, picking up Laurence, who's crying loudly.

'It's gone?" Bill looks from her to me. "I had a spider on me toast? How in Gawd's name did it get there? Where'd it go?"

Mummy touches his shoulder. "One *was* on your toast, Bill. But it's gone. It's over there," she points, "on the wall. They—they live in the space between the stove and the hob next to it. It must've crawled onto the toast when I wasn't looking."

"On the wall? Where?"

Mummy leads him there, and shows him where to look.

He takes off his glasses and peers. "Well, I'll be damned."

I pick up his chair, and now he sits on it again. "Nasty Customer! Good thing you saw it, Leila. Bloke like that could've put a diabetic like me in hospital for a month. If it didn't kill me!"

"They only make you sick if they haven't cleaned their teeth," I remind him.

He laughs, then says seriously, "Not when you're a Diabetic. Infection's the problem with bites like that. They'll make anyone sick, but they can *kill* a Diabetic."

Mummy flushes and looks down. "I'm sorry, Bill. The trouble is, they're nearly the same colour as the toast. That's why I didn't see it. The crack next to the stove makes a nice, warm home for them, I spose." She clears her throat. "But now, you still haven't had your toast. Let me make you another piece."

"Thanks, Gwen. But I think I'll have one without a spider this time. Just for variety."

Too soon, Uncle Bill's visit is over and Daddy takes him back to town to catch the train to Newcastle.

Chapter Twenty

AUNTIE COMES TO VISIT

One mail day Daddy hands Mummy a letter. "Charlotte wants to come and stay."

Mummy reads, and then says, "She doesn't say she *wants* to come—she says she *is* coming."

"Well, *wants to, is*—it amounts to the same thing, doesn't it?"

She kind of growls. "There's a lot of difference! What if it isn't convenient for us to have her? It would have been nice if she'd given us the option."

"Convenient? Why wouldn't it be?"

Mummy sighs. "I've got that much to do, and I won't be able to get a damn thing done with someone staying."

"Who's Charlotte?" I ask.

"Your father's sister. You've never met her." She turns to Daddy, "And where will she sleep?"

"Can't we put an extra bed in the girls' room?"

"The girls' room? You know what she's like!"

"Well, we'll find somewhere, anyway. We can't put her off. She's had us stay with her enough times. You stayed there when the kids were born."

"Well, Claude and Amelia. That was a long time ago."

After a pause, Mummy gets up and flings the letter at the table, missing; Daddy picks it up from the floor.

But soon they're planning for her visit. Mummy says we're to call our visitor Auntie or Auntie Charlotte, and Daddy tells us that she has something called asthma—which gives her trouble with her breathing if there's a lot of dust, say, or she gets upset, and sometimes she has to go to hospital because of it. The day before she's to arrive, Daddy and Claude

131

carry a spare single bed down from the shed and put it in the room Amelia and I share, and Mummy makes it up.

Amelia and I do a lot of housework and cooking now, and, while Daddy goes to town to meet Auntie's train we help Mummy get the house ready. She bakes cakes and biscuits and pies while we clean, tidy, wipe, dust and polish. We let the fire in the loungeroom go out, remove the ash from the fireplace, and arrange paper and chips and wood in there to light later. We let the stove go cold, and paint it with some silver paint stuff that Mummy's mother used—we found a tin of it in the house. The fire burning in the stove again, a hot paint smell fills the kitchen. We scrub the verandah floorboards, mop the red dirt off the linoleum inside, and wax and polish it. We pick flowers from the garden and put a vase in several rooms. Then we go outside and rake up the cow and horse manure, throw these on the garden, and sweep the paths.

By late afternoon, the scents of floor wax, hot paint, flowers, cakes, pies, and a leg of mutton roasting in the oven fill the house. When it's time to change, Amelia says she wants to wear the black crepe dress Mummy's cousin Jenny gave her because it shrank so much when she washed it. It fits her perfectly, but Mummy says, "It's *black*. And you're only ten!"

Amelia keeps saying she wants to wear it, though, and in the end, Mummy says she can, but adds, "You can't wear it to town, though, so don't get the idea that you can."

At last, Amelia and I are at the window watching the lorry roll down the hill. We start to go outside, but Mummy keeps doing things. "Aren't you coming, Mum?" Amelia asks.

"I spose a person should," she says, her voice scratchy, and she follows us.

The excited dogs are jumping up at a thin woman with black hair, who's laughing and calling in a soft voice, "Shoo, you wretches! Shoo!"

Mummy steps forward and bellows, "Peggy! Jock! Cut it out!"

The dogs shrink down, and I feel like doing the same. The smile disappears from the woman's face and she stares at Mummy for a moment before she opens her arms. "Gwen. How *are* you?"

They embrace briefly, and Mummy gives a short laugh. "Damn things must jump up on anyone new."

"This is your Auntie Charlotte," Daddy says.

Smiling, she looks at each of us. "Call me Charlotte," she says. Her hairline comes to a peak at the centre of her forehead. "It's so long since I've seen you all," she says. Looking at Amelia, she puts her head on one side, smiling. "My goodness. You're such a young lady now. And so elegant in your black."

Mummy clears her throat. "I said she could wear that dress, but only around here."

Auntie shakes Claude's hand. "And you, Valiant. What a handsome young man you've become!"

Then, she leans down and looks into my eyes. "And you're Leila. You were just a baby the last time I saw you, and now you're a quite a big girl, with your gorgeous head of curls." She touches them with the tips of her fingers, as if they're flowers, and a lovely light seems to shine on me. She hugs me, her soft cheek brushing mine, and I get a whiff of scent.

Laurence is standing to one side, one arm shading his eyes from the afternoon sun and the other holding the handle of a red cart Daddy made him not long ago. Auntie squats next to him. "Hello, young man," she says. "I'm Charlotte, and you must be Laurence." She touches his cart. "And what's this?"

"Daddy made it for me."

"Did he now?" She examines it. "Why, it's wonderful. You must be able to carry all sorts of things in it." And she nods as he lists them.

In the loungeroom, for the first time ever, we have tea in cups with saucers. As always, Daddy and Claude beat the sugar in with their spoons and gulp it down, but the rest of us stir quietly and sip. Every now and then, Auntie Charlotte makes a joke, her words coming out with little puffs of air till she's laughing; and sometimes she doubles over, and kind of screeches. Mummy smiles as if she's enjoying talking to her, and Daddy starts telling funny stories from when he was young. It's as if magic has made everything and everyone nicer.

That night, we have an embroidered tablecloth, and for dessert, instead of the usual stewed apples or slimy, grey rhubarb, there's an apple pie and Auntie says how nice it is.

"Talking of apples," Daddy says, "Bill and I were camped way out at the back of a property one time—we had a contract ringbarking and grubbing.[1] Anyway, someone give us a great big bag of apples. There was no way we could've eaten them all before they rotted, so we chopped them up, skins and cores and all, and boiled them with some water in a kerosene tin on the campfire. We hung the tin on the limb of a tree so nothing could get at it, and every night when we got back from work, we'd be dying of thirst—we were working like bullocks to get our contract

---

[1] Digging out the stumps and roots of trees that have been cut down previously.

finished—and we'd drink mugfuls of it. God it was good. There'd always be bits of apple and skin and cores left in the mug we'd suck the juice out of."

"One night, I see Bill sucking on something that looked kind of strange." He laughs so hard we have to wait till he can continue. "I didn't say anything, but I got the lamp and lifted it up." He laughs again, even longer, then wipes his eyes with his handkerchief, and looks at Auntie. "You know how bad Bill's eyes are. Well, he was sucking on a bloody great—a bloody great—"

Auntie has a smile fixed on her face as he again roars with laughter, while Mummy shifts uncomfortably on her seat.

He takes a breath, and, very calmly begins, "He was sucking on a— a bloody great—" Then, out of him explodes, "tarantula!" followed by another roar of laughter.

We all join in, though the thought of sucking the spider is horrible.

When everyone is quiet again, he explains, "It'd drowned in the juice. Thought he was sucking an apple core."

Mummy shoots him a look, but he isn't finished.

"You should've seen him when I told him. He threw the thing down the gully, and took off spitting and gagging. "The next day, we took the bucket down and had a look. Well, drowned in there was every kind of beetle and spider and ant and bug you could imagine."

Everyone is quiet for a time, except for cackles that keep escaping from Daddy.

"That's not a very nice story to tell at the dinner table," Mummy says quietly.

"Eh? Oh. Well." Folding his arms over his chest, he looks down but continues to smile.

Auntie says, "Poor old Bill. He always did have such terrible eyesight." She turns to Mummy. "Tell me, Gwen, can you grow gladioli in this climate? They're all the rage in Newcastle."

"*This climate?*" her voice is sharp.

"Perhaps I should have said, *at this altitude*. It's what, five thousand feet here?"

"Four-thousand, five hundred." Mummy takes a breath. "I'm told that gladioli grow very well here; I'm planning to plant some when I can." And she tells Auntie all the things she's learned about growing them.

"You always wanted a garden, Gwen—and you're so knowledgeable!"

After we've eaten, I follow Auntie to our room and watch her unpack.

"Why's your hair like that?" I ask.

"Like what?" She looks puzzled. "Show me what you mean." She stands beside me in front of the mirror, and, with my finger, I show her how her hair comes down in a peak at the centre of her forehead. "Oh!" She touches its point. "This is called a *widow's peak*. You have one, too." She holds my hair back with her hand, and it's true.

"What's a widow?"

"A woman whose husband has died."

"Did your husband die?"

"No, Pet, I'm divorced." She explains that this is what it's called when a couple decide they don't want to be married to each other any longer, and their marriage is "dissolved."

"Will I be a widow?"

Auntie laughs. "Of course not. I don't know why they call it that." She pauses, and looks serious. "But, about what I just told you. Please don't tell anyone else I'm divorced. The church doesn't allow it, you know. I always tell people I'm a widow. It's more respectable." She giggles. "The widow's peak helps."

"The church?"

"Well, I was brought up in the Catholic Church. We all would have been Catholic if Mum had had her way. But the boys were mostly working and camping with Dad, and he wasn't for the church at all. He was a Socialist. Course, I never go to church now, either. But not just Catholics don't like divorce. People gossip, religious or not. So just don't tell anyone. OK, Pet?"

I nod.

She lifts something fluffy and bright pink out of her suitcase. It's a sweater. "It's called angora—it comes from a special kind of rabbit. Would you like to feel it?"

I do, and it's the softest thing I've ever touched. I lift my hand up till I can just feel the hairs stroking my palm; they're really long, and so fine I can hardly see them.

"I keep it in the freezer at home—the cold stops it from shedding.

Auntie is shaking out a grey dress when Amelia comes in. "Finished the washing-up[2]?" she asks her. "Sorry I didn't help. I can't believe how weary I am. The journey, I suppose. I promise faithfully to do my share once I've settled in." She fits the dress onto a hanger, then looks at us

---

[2]In the Australian bush in former times, "washing-up" referred to the washing of dishes, and the "washing-up dish" was the dish in which they were washed.

both. "By the way," she says, then pauses. "Since I'll be sharing a room with you girls, I—I'd better warn you." She pauses again. "I have only one breast." She gestures vaguely towards her right side. "This one's a falsie."

She picks up a blouse and fits it over the dress. "I had a lump and they thought it might be cancer." She hangs dress and blouse in the wardrobe and turns around. "Right away, I said to the doctor, 'I'd like you to remove my breast.' His mouth fell open, and I had a job convincing him, but in the end he agreed that it was the safest thing. I didn't want it to spread if it was cancer, you see."

I think of a cow we saw in a field when we were going to town once. It had a big, black sore on its neck Daddy said was cancer, adding that it must be in pain, and ought to be shot. "That's the sort of beast they put into that bully beef you kids like so much," he told us.

"Was it?" asks Amelia. "Cancer?"

"No. I was lucky. It turned out to be benign."

"Benign?" I ask.

"Benign means something that doesn't hurt you. But I'd lost my breast by then."

I decide that, when I get breasts, I'll do the same thing if I get a lump. But I want to see the place where they took it off. "What does it look like?" I ask.

Auntie stares at me. "Look like?"

"The place where they cut it off."

"Leila!" Amelia's eyes jab at me.

But Auntie says, her voice a little wavy, "It's well—it's just a scar, Pet."

"Can I see it?" I persist.

Auntie's face goes kind of lumpy, and she doesn't look at me as she takes the last of her things out of her suitcase and puts them away.

I've gone too far.

Amelia has come over. "Leila!" she hisses. "What an awful thing to ask." Then, she says aloud, "That was really rude. You ought to be ashamed."

I watch the movements of Auntie's back. Into my mind flashes the image of Mummy pointing to my stinking sheets, and I feel terrible.

Later, when Amelia and I go to wee before bed she says, "You know Auntie has problems with her breathing if she gets upset. You could've given her an attack—and asthma can kill people!"

I don't look in Auntie's direction after we're back in our room, but quickly undress and get into bed. I wish so hard I hadn't asked! *And yet, I still want to see that scar.*

Chapter Twenty-one

A FEW WORDS

Auntie starts saying things like, "Look at all the work your poor mother has to do—you girls should help her more," and, "You should be nicer to your mother—she's got a lot on her plate."

One morning, just after I've finished sweeping the loungeroom, she points under a chair. "See that lump of dust there? I've been watching it for three days."

I sweep it out with the broom. *Even Mummy wouldn't get upset like that over a bit of dust!*

Although Mummy hadn't wanted Auntie to come, she seemed to enjoy her visit at first. And if Amelia or I did something she didn't like, instead of yelling, she'd tell us in a whisper when Auntie was around, or in a normal voice if she wasn't. But as time went on, her whispering became louder, till she was saying angry things in a normal voice, even when Auntie was in the bedroom. I hoped she couldn't hear what was being said from there till one day I was in the bedroom when Mummy got cranky with Laurence in the kitchen, and although she was talking and not yelling, I could hear every word. Knowing that Auntie could hear made me feel horrible. Things worsened till Mummy was yelling in front of Auntie, but hitting me only when she wasn't in the house. But now she's yelling most of the time, and, hitting me in front of Auntie.

But what's really interesting is that her constant yelling feels normal to me, and I've realized that this is how things were long before Auntie's visit.

Mummy always gets crankier than ever on washdays, and one morning, the fire burning under the copper, which is full of bubbling water, tells me it's that day again. She appears with her arms around a load of dirty sheets, and lets them fall in to boil. She's shown me the white "bloom"

137

on new plums, and the sheets have a red "bloom" from dirt.

She has to wash everything by hand, and it takes a whole day. She's shown me all the things she has to do. First, she fills many buckets with water from the corrugated iron tank and pours these in the copper. When the sheets have boiled long enough, she lifts them out with a stick and puts them in a tin tub, wringing them by hand when they're cool enough. Then she rinses them twice in clean water, and once in water with "blue" in it, wringing them each time. After hanging the whites on the line, she washes the other clothes in the sudsy water they were boiled in, the cleanest first, rubbing soap on any dirty places, and scrubbing the material between her knuckles. Claude's and Daddy's trousers, heavy with dirt, are washed last, and when she empties the copper, she has to scrape the mud out. Late in the afternoon, Mummy brings in armfuls of fresh-smelling whites, trousers stiff as iron and towels like graters, and dumps these on the couch—and she still has to sort and fold everything.

Today, while she does all this, like always, Amelia and I keep the stove alight, and make morning and afternoon tea—Claude and Daddy and any others working with them generally come back to the house for these. And we also make the midday and evening meals.

Late in the afternoon, Mummy comes into the kitchen where Amelia and I are peeling apples to cook for pudding, and she asks, "Have you girls put the meat on yet?"

"I was going to, but— " Amelia begins.

"Don't waste time talking. It has to be put on *immediately!*"

"But I thought— " I start.

"You thought!" She bangs through the pots and pans in the cupboard. "You don't think—that's your trouble." She takes a pot out the door, and I hear her go into the "meat house"—the little building at the back where the meat is kept. She comes back with a slab of corned beef in the pot, covers it with water and puts it on the stove.

"When I was your age, I did what had be done, *when* it had to be done, and I did it properly. Nobody ever had to tell *me* to do anything."

She lifts the lids of the pots on the stove with vegetables in them, dipping a finger in the water of each and licking it. A lid in hand, she turns and glares at us. "There's no salt in this."

"Not yet," Amelia says.

"If you leave it till the last minute, you'll forget. You have to put it in as soon as you've added the water." She grabs the coarse salt jar from the shelf above the stove, shakes some into her palm, and throws it in. Next, she scans the table, picks up a curl of apple peel from the pile next to us, and waves it in front of our faces. "Look at the thickness of that peel! Is that how I taught you two to peel apples?"

We stare back at her.

Her voice breaks. "There are hardly any left as it is." She peers at some pumpkin peelings among the ones from the apples. "More damn waste! That's the way your father peels pumpkins!"

She pauses. "And where are the potatoes? You haven't even started doing them, and it's after five. The men'll be home for their tea and they won't be cooked!" She goes into the storeroom, and looks in the potato bag. "Only a couple left." She stamps back out. "Leila! Get up to the shed and bring some back! Now! That's an order."

We stand frozen.

"Haven't you anything to say for yourselves?" She pauses. "Oh what's the use of even trying!" With a sob, she starts for the loungeroom, then stops, turns and looks hard at me. "Are you deaf? Go and get those potatoes. *Immediately!*"

"I was just going to finish doing the apples first."

"Can't you tell the bloody time?" She grabs the strap from its nail by the stove, doubles it and lifts it as if she's going to hit me. "Get up to that shed this instant or I'll thrash you to within an inch of your life!"

I drop the apple I'm peeling, leaving the knife under its skin, grab a bucket, and hurry outside. Once she can't hear me, I stamp and mutter, "Bloody-bloody-bloody!"

The shed door is open, and inside, Laurence squats in front of the bag of potatoes, guiding his toy truck filled with little stones along the dirt floor. *Making that stupid buzzing noise. He doesn't have any jobs to do—just plays all the time. It's not fair!*

"Why don't *you* ever have anything to do? Oh you're just a ba-by! All you do is play with your stupid toys. Well, you can just bloody well help me get these bloody potatoes!"

The truck stops, and he stares up at me.

"Come on!" I yell. Do something for a change!"

He doesn't move.

"I can't even get at the bloody potatoes with you there. Get this thing out of my way!" I give his truck a kick, and it lands a few feet away, spilling its load. He still doesn't move. I pull him to his feet, and he starts sobbing and hitting me. "Stop that!" I shout, hopping out of range.

Still sobbing, he goes to where the truck is, sets it back on its wheels, and starts gathering up the stones. My anger gone, and feeling a bit sorry for him, I start putting the potatoes into the bucket. I look up to see Mummy striding towards me, the strap twisting in her hand.

"What've you done to him?" she yells, grabbing me and yanking me to the middle of the dirt floor. She swings the strap out, thrashing my legs, and yelling, "Rotten-useless-little-mongrel!" Screams rip out of me. I hop in pain as she hits, and try to pull away.

She pauses, her fingernails digging into my arm, staring at me with gritted teeth. Then she hits and hits and hits again. When at last she stops and drops my arm, I fall onto the dirt floor sobbing, the root of my arm paining. She bangs potatoes into the bucket, takes Laurence by the hand, starts out the door and then turns. "You've been a trouble to me since the day you were born," she throws back before she leaves.

I sob and sob, curled up on the dirt. *I hate you I hate you I hate you.*

After a long time, the crying thins. Stops. I sit up. Everything is quiet. Then, my body sucks in a big breath, and a weird wail shudders out of me. The same thing happens every few minutes, and I can't stop it by holding my breath. On my right thigh is a painful, red swelling. I get to my feet. It's almost dark, and between me and the house is the yard scattered with cow pats, chook manure and bones. I hate the thought of anyone seeing me, but I have to get to the house.

When I think the noises have really stopped, I start off, shaking, and my teeth clicking. The grass is cold on my bare feet. Another jagged noise, so loud that anyone in the house could have heard it. I stiffen my legs to try stop them wobbling.

I open the gate near the back of the house slowly, but it squeaks. Knowing my mother will be in the kitchen off the back verandah, I turn left, creep along the side of the house, climb the front steps, tip-toe across the verandah, and open the glass front door without a sound. *Nobody in the hallway.* I creep to the door of the bedroom where I sleep. *Auntie might be in there.* A galloping in my chest. *If she is, she'll have heard. Please, God, let the room be empty.* I listen. Nothing *Good—she's still on her afternoon walk.*

Slowly, my hand pushes the door. A wire hanger on a hook on its back clangs. At the edge of my vision, a dark shape on the bed. I don't look at it. Wait. It doesn't move. *Maybe it's her eiderdown[1] bunched up. Or she's asleep and didn't hear.* Then one of the horrible noises rips out.

---

[1] A bedcover, traditionally stuffed with down, and similar to a North American duvet.

Auntie's gentle voice says, "Come over here, Pet."

I risk a glance. She's sitting up in her bed, the eiderdown over her legs and feet. Beside her, an open book. *Good. She was reading and didn't hear... But maybe she did. "Rotten-useless-little-mongrel... a trouble to me since the day you were born."*

Another glance. She's looking at me, one arm held out in a curve, inviting me. An image flashes, of the hurt look on her face when I asked to see her scar.

"Come over here, Pet," she says again.

I take a couple of steps. *An image of her hitting me.* But the curve of her arm... her face, soft and kind...

"I'm not going to hurt you, dear."

Somehow, I know it's true, and go to her. Her arm comes round me, warming my back. She draws me close. And I'm crying again. A different crying. When she releases me, she looks into my face. "I know what happened. I was watching through the window. I heard everything. I thought your mother had gone mad."

Her brown eyes have flecks of gold, and I see tears.

What?

"It's not you who has the problem—it's her. I've seen what's going on. *She picks on you.*" She hugs me again. "If she ever tries to do anything like that to you again, I want you to promise me you'll run to your father."

Daddy's sweet face as he rescues me... him getting angry with Mummy. But then I remember his and Mummy's rule that parents must support one another when punishing children. He probably wouldn't help me if I did go to him. But I can't explain this to Auntie—she might think I was bad for not trusting her brother.

She shakes me gently. "Promise?"

I nod. "Yes." And for a moment, the idea that he'd protect me becomes real again.

Auntie draws me closer to her and says, "I love you."

Nobody has ever said these words to me before, but, somehow, I understand the beautiful thing she's said. And I nestle in the warmth of her arms.

When Daddy calls us to tea from the hallway, the thought of sitting at the dinner table, especially with Mummy, is horrible.

Auntie says, "Would you like me to bring you something to eat in here?"

"Mummy wouldn't let you."

"Don't worry—I'll handle her."

I hear her saying, in a strong voice, that I'm not up to coming to the table for tea, and adding that she'll make me a boiled egg. Before long she's back with it and some toast. She helps me get ready for bed, and I climb in and eat sitting there, while Auntie goes to the kitchen for her tea.

She's soon back, with Amelia. They talk in low voices. Then I have to wee, and Amelia gets a flashlight and takes me out through the front door and around.

The next day, I can't look at Mummy, and she talks to me only if she has to. But after a couple of days she's shouting at me as usual. When she does, I repeat Auntie's words in my head. *Your mother picks on you. I love you. It's not you who has the problem...* And Mummy's voice becomes like someone talking on a wireless in the next room. And now, after Mummy has said or done mean things to me, Amelia is nice to me, once we're alone.

Chapter Twenty-two

STORIES

At night after we've blown out the lamp, Auntie talks about her life in Newcastle where she lives, a city by the sea a long way away, and she keeps mentioning someone called Olga. I think she must be a friend, but then she starts calling her "the old girl." "The old girl" goes through my things when I'm not there, you know," she says. Also, she tells us that "the old girl" is always wanting to raise the rent, and that once, she even asked for it twice. And when Auntie said she'd already paid, she pretended she'd made a mistake. And, every winter, she doesn't turn the heat on right away, saying that the heater needs fixing.

"But isn't Olga your friend?" I ask.

"Friend? That old cow? My God! She's a bloodsucking landlady. Whatever gave you the idea she's my friend? I'd never call an old cow like that my friend!"

Even though Auntie's a bit cranky with me, I don't worry because I know she loves me.

One night, she starts talking about her life when she was a young woman, keeping her voice even lower than usual to make sure my parents— whose bedroom is just across the hall—can't hear. Sitting in her bed with her arms locked around her drawn-up knees, she reminds me of a picture of a girl looking out to sea in one of Mummy's "Girls Own Annuals." Smoking cigarette after cigarette, she tells us how, one evening after she'd gone to live in Newcastle, a fellow she'd just met asked her to walk on the beach with him. "He said he wanted to look at the moon with me, and I thought that would be nice. But the next thing I knew, he'd ripped my panties off. He had me pinned down; he was a big chap, too. Well, I thought I was done for. Then, all of a sudden, I see this bobby standing there looking down at us. I couldn't believe my eyes."

"Bobby?" I ask.

"Sorry, a policeman. I forget sometimes—we used to call them "bob-bies." Anyway, you girls don't know Newcastle, but the beach is right at the end of the main street, and he must have been on his beat. 'Let the young lady up!' he yelled. Must have stood there till he knew for sure what was going on. The bloke got a shock, I can tell you. When he saw the uniform, he jumped like he'd been hit with a branding iron. *'Now get the hell out of here!'* the bobby shouted."

I don't understand. They were on the beach together, so... "Why didn't the fellow see the policeman?"

"He was on top of me, Pet..." Auntie pauses, sighs, and says to Amelia, "I keep forgetting she's only six. It's above her head." To me she says, "Don't worry about it, pet. It doesn't matter. One day you'll under-stand." She puffs on her cigarette.

"What happened then?" Amelia asks.

"I was shaking that much, I could hardly get up. The bloke—I've never been able to remember his name since—took off, and I didn't have any money for the bus. I'd gone on a date with him, so naturally I thought he'd see me home." There's a long pause. "Well, the only thing I could do was tell the bobby. So he paid my fare, and went with me on the bus all the way to my stop. Nice looking chap he was, too.

"But you know what the bugger did? He must have picked up my panties from where the bloke threw them and put them in his breast pocket. And all the way home, he kept pulling them out just enough to show the lace, with this silly grin on his face, and he'd wink. The bus was crowded, too—people going home from the movies. I was that embarrassed!"

Auntie takes a last puff of her cigarette and the ashtray clinks against the water glass on her night table as she grinds the butt out.

"Did the bobby give you your panties back?" I ask.

"Panties?" Auntie sounds puzzled.

That was the wrong thing to ask.

"No! He walked off with them. I was too ashamed to ask him for them."

"What happened to the bloke?" Amelia asks.

"I never saw him again." She pauses. *"Thank God."*

Amelia always knows the right thing to ask.

Auntie lights another cigarette and breathes in deeply.

"I felt like such a fool. Guilty, too. Once, I thought I saw him on the street, and this terrible feeling came over me. I crossed to the other side, and went into a shop and watched through the window. But it was just someone who looked a bit like him."

"But why did you feel guilty?" Amelia asks straight away."

Silent, Auntie puffs on her cigarette. "After what he did I knew I should never have gone to the beach with him in the first place. I tell you, I was damn careful where I went with boys I didn't know well after that. That's why I'm telling you girls—so you won't make the same mistake when you start going out with boys."

Going out with boys. She sees me as nearly grown up, too!

"Mum never told me anything about sex," Auntie continues, a sadness in her voice. "Not one thing." She pauses. "Anyway, you always want to stick to places where there are plenty of people the first time you go out with someone—and until you know him well. Men can easily get carried away, you know. They don't have the same controls we do."

The glowing spot of Auntie's cigarette disappears and as she grinds its butt out, I hear my parents' bedroom door open and Daddy's heavy footsteps pass our door and continue though the house to the outside. *Can he and Mummy hear what we talk about?*

"Nighty-night," Auntie whispers, wriggling down under the bedclothes. "Sleep tight."

"Goodnight, Auntie," Amelia and I say.

"I wish you girls would call me Charlotte. "Auntie" makes me feel old."

"But I like calling you Auntie," I say.

"I do too," says Amelia. "But we can call you Charlotte if you like."

"Well goodnight, again," Auntie says.

"OK then. Goodnight Charlotte," we both say.

But the next day we go back to calling her Auntie, and she doesn't seem to mind.

One night, she says. "Life is meant to be enjoyed, you know, and I don't see much of that on the horizon for you two if you stay up here. You might have wondered why I excused myself and went to bed early tonight. Well, I couldn't stand them going on about 'the workers and Russia any more."

Claude and Daddy had started talking about "the boot of big business" being "planted on the necks of the working class," and Daddy had said, "Well, they can't keep the workers down forever. One day they'll rise up

Figure 22.1: My dear Auntie.

just like they did in Russia. It'll come—mark my words." That's when Auntie yawned and said goodnight.

"My Dad's the same—always going on about *the workers*," she continues. "They remind me of old wethers.[1] The magazines they get from Russia may be full of pictures of happy, smiling people, but you can't tell me that things are that much better there, when all's said and done."

I've always thought that the things Claude and Dad say about the Soviet Union were true—but now I know there's another way of looking at them.

"You girls should think of going to the city and finding a job, when you're old enough," she says. "You could go nursing. Accommodation's provided, you know. The pay's good, too. Nurses have a great life. You get a lot of respect as a nurse. There was a lovely girl looking after me the last time I was in hospital. And you should see the nurses' home—it's right on the beach. When they're off duty, they spend their days sunbathing and surfing. And," she draws out the word, "you get to meet all these young, good-looking doctors! You might even end up marrying one."

"Mmmmm," says Amelia. "How could I find out about going nursing?"

"Well, let me see. You could write to the hospital. But I don't think they'll take you till you're seventeen. And that's what? Seven years away?"

At that moment, I decide that I'll go to work in the city—and maybe go nursing—as soon as I'm old enough.

The next morning, Mummy looks at us with a dark face. That afternoon, she and Auntie talk as they string beans together, Auntie asking questions. But their voices are high, as if they don't mean what they're saying.

While Auntie is resting that afternoon, Amelia and I go for a walk and talk about leaving. And she says how she hates Mummy's yelling and wishes she'd stop, and that she doesn't know why she yells at me and hits me so much. We talk and talk about all the things that are awful about living up here, like having to see chickens and animals killed. And we both say how much we love Auntie.

When Auntie and Daddy talk that evening as we're all sitting around the fire, it's different from how she and Mummy did: their voices sound normal, and they smile.

Most of the time, Amelia and I hardly talk to Mummy because she yells at us so much—which she never does to Claude; she hardly ever yells

---

[1] Castrated male sheep.

at Laurence, either, but she does give him the switch now and then. We make jokes with Auntie about Mum's anger. And when she starts rushing through the house with armfuls of washing, Auntie says, "You girls had better watch out—it's washday again, and your mother's on the warpath." And we all laugh.

Chapter Twenty-three

SCARLET WOMAN

As the days get hotter, people on the wireless talk a lot about something I've never heard of before—Christmas. One day I ask Mummy about it. She says that it's a religious holiday and we're not religious.

But Auntie tells us that you don't have to be religious to enjoy it, and that people usually give each other presents. So we ask Mummy whether we can do this, and after a while, she says she "sposes" we could. We decide that everyone will buy everyone else one present. And I look forward to having Auntie with us for our first Christmas.

But after we turn the light out that night, she says she has to go back to Newcastle soon.

It's as if I've fallen through a hole. "But what about Christmas?"

"Christmas!" she says in a pained voice. "It means very little by the time you're my age."

I'm shocked that things can get so bad, and that Auntie, who's always saying we should enjoy ourselves, and laughs so much, thinks like this. She must have forgotten about the presents. "You'll get a lot of Christmas presents if you stay," I tell her.

Auntie gives a funny little laugh. "No, Pet; I really do have to get back—there are things I have to attend to."

"What do you have to do?"

"Things. I can't stay here forever, you know. And, truly, I can't stay for Christmas. Much as I love you both."

She draws on her cigarette, making a red glow around her face. "Do you know what I feel when Christmas is coming? I just want to crawl into a hollow log till it's over." She sounds really sad.

Amelia says, "But why, Auntie?"

Auntie's voice is strong again. "It's not much fun when you're on the pension."

I don't understand. "Why?" I ask.

Auntie sighs. She sounds almost angry. "After the *old girl* gets her money for the rent, there's not much left." She puffs on her cigarette, and then adds, "I'm looking forward to confronting the old bitch when I get back." She explains that Olga steals tobacco from her jar; she brought "tailor-mades" with her, but at home she smokes "roll-your-owns." Before she came away, she glued a hair across the lid of the jar so she'd know if it had been opened; she also glued hairs over all her cupboard drawers. "She's clever, I'll give her that—I've never been able to prove she's been into my things till now. But I'll have her this time." She puffs again. "Anyway, as far as Christmas goes, I just don't have the money to buy presents. And that's the truth of the matter." Talking about Olga seems to have cheered her up—she no longer sounds sad.

Amelia's voice is gentle. "You wouldn't have to buy us presents if you stayed."

I'm disappointed, but I say, "No—you wouldn't have to buy me anything."

"Oh yes I would! I'd have to buy presents for everyone. Your parents have been extremely generous to me. I've been here nearly three months. It would be very bad form not to buy presents. I'd—well, I'd feel humiliated." She wriggles down under the covers and says goodnight.

I don't go to sleep right away, staring at the window above the dark miniature mountain range that's her lying on her side, and feeling sad at the thought of her not being here. The window becomes a tiny square of light very far away, my body feels huge and my arms seem too big and heavy to lift. At first, the strange feelings are interesting, but then I decide I've had enough of them. I squint, look at the window from different angles, and then sit up. The fatness has disappeared, but the window stays far away and won't come back to its normal size. But eventually, I go to sleep.

***

As the time for Auntie to leave gets nearer, I feel sadder and sadder. And what's really awful is that, ever since she told Amelia and me she's not staying for Christmas, she's stopped telling us stories at night and hardly talks to us at all. One night, she just mumbles goodnight, turns over and goes to sleep, and I lie in the dark with the sound of a blowfly buzzing round and round and hitting the walls. And I begin to think that she has come to see me as Mummy does, and no longer loves me.

The next night, Auntie excuses herself and goes to bed as soon as tea is over. I don't want to be in there with her, so I sit by the fire drawing one of our chairs. The pencil moves lightly over the paper, as if it doesn't know how heavy I feel inside. Amelia is reading; she and I haven't talked about how things have changed with Auntie, but she isn't hurrying to our room, either. Finally, Mummy tells us to go to bed like she used to. *Did all those nice things with Auntie really happen?*

In our room, Auntie is already under the covers and doesn't move. *She must be asleep like I hoped she'd be.* But, as Amelia and I are getting undressed, she suddenly sits up, lights a cigarette and says, "I have something to say to you girls. I've noticed that things aren't the same between us. You two have changed towards me."

"But Auntie— " Amelia begins.

"Please don't interrupt, Amelia—I know you don't feel the same as you did. And it's time to clear the air. No doubt you've learned certain things about me."

Certain things? What can she mean?"

She draws on her cigarette. "About what happened when I was young, I mean. You had to find out, sooner or later, I suppose. But I'm disappointed that you've taken the attitude you have after all we've shared." She sounds as if she might cry, but takes another puff and continues, "I want to tell you both my side of the story. It's only fair." She pauses. "I didn't want to, you know. He—he forced me. I was too embarrassed to call out or anything. I-I couldn't stop him—he was too strong."

"Auntie— "

"No, Amelia—please!"

"But Auntie—*we have no idea what you're talking about.*"

"You *really* don't know? Nobody has told you? But why are you treating me the way you are?"

"What way? We're not treating you any differently—you're the one who stopped talking to us."

"I did? You mean to tell me that you don't know about the baby? Well, that puts a whole different complexion on things. But let me get this straight—you know nothing at all?"

"We don't know anything about a baby," Amelia says.

"No we don't," I say.

"I thought your mother and father must have told you, and that was why you weren't talking to me. The people in the Upper Hunter never stopped gossiping about me after it happened. As far as they're concerned, I'm still the *scarlet woman.*"

"Wait a minute," Amelia says. "Maybe we didn't talk to you as much as we did before, after you told us you weren't staying for Christmas. We were disappointed, that's all. We don't want you to go. And you're not a "scarlet woman" to us—you're our dear Auntie. So can you tell us what this is about?"

"I have to tell you now, that's for sure. Where to begin?" She starts and stops a couple of times, and then says, "Well, when I was very young— nineteen, to be exact—I had a baby. I wasn't even engaged, let alone married."

The three of us are silent while Auntie puffs on her cigarette, and then Amelia says, "It doesn't make any difference to us, Auntie." She gets out of her bed, goes over and hugs her. "It doesn't matter at all to us. We don't think anything bad about you. We love you."

Then I get up and go to Auntie and hug her and tell her I love her, too.

"I love you both very, very much, too," Auntie says. And then we're all crying.

When Amelia and I are back in our own beds, Auntie takes a deep breath. "Now that I've let the possum out of the bag, I'd better fill in the gaps. As I said, I was only nineteen. I'd been seeing a bit of this chap, and one night, we were kissing on the couch at home—Mum and Dad had gone to bed. We'd never done much more than kiss." She lights another cigarette. "He was a big chap, and I didn't have a hope of stopping him.

"Afterwards, I couldn't believe it had happened with Mum and Dad right there in the house. I was unlucky. When my period didn't come, I had to tell Mum. *That was the hardest thing I've ever had to do in my life. My God!*" She pauses. "Mum took me to the doctor, and he confirmed what I knew. We kept it as quiet as we could. The relatives and friends we told thought I should give the baby up for adoption, but I refused. And once he was born, he was such a beautiful baby, I simply couldn't. Keeping him was really hard, but I'm very glad I did. Phil's a fine young man."

Amelia says, "I thought you'd been married."

"Oh I was—later—and divorced. Jan's his daughter. But Phil's not his son."

"Who—who's Phil's father?" Amelia asks.

"That was Bob Green. Not that it's going to help you girls to know. He was a good dancer, and considered quite a catch. But I wouldn't have married him even if he'd asked me, after what he did. We had to take him to court to make him pay, you know, so who he is is a matter of public record."

Later that night, before we go to sleep, she says, "After I'm gone, you'll see something fluttering over here in this corner one night and it'll be me." She chuckles. "I've told Phil and Jan they won't have to pay for a funeral—I've willed my body to the university. I like the idea of all those handsome young doctors picking over my bones."

Chapter Twenty-four

UNDER THE MISTLETOE

The next day, Auntie tells my parents she's going home, then telephones her daughter Jan and arranges for her to come and pick her up in a few days.

That night when we're in bed, Auntie says, "I suppose you'll start decorating the house, soon."

What's she talking about?

"Decorating the house?" Amelia asks.

"Yes, don't you put up streamers and things for Christmas? And have a Christmas tree?" She pauses, and then says, "Oh, I'm sorry—I forgot that you've never celebrated Christmas."

At breakfast the next morning, she mentions the Christmas decorations and tree, and Mummy says she thinks there's a tin of Christmas stuff that her mother left somewhere. She also says that she knows what kind of tree would be good—a "wild cherry" from up on the hill in the reserve.

Some time later, she appears with a big blue tin. "Guess what I found in the wardrobe?" She says, easing the lid off. "Christmas decorations!" Inside are red balls and silver icicles for the tree, scalloped leaves with red berries she calls "holly," folded up sheets of red and green crepe paper, and a big red crepe paper bell.

She shows us how to cut the paper into strips, attach one end of each strip to a picture rail, twist and twist it, and attach the other to the opposite rail. We hang the bell where the streamers cross in the centre of the room. Auntie admires our work, and then says, "But something's missing."

"We're going up the hill to get the tree later," I say.

"That's not it. Do *you* know what's missing, Amelia? You're, what—ten, now—so it'll be of more interest to you, though you're not quite there

154

yet, either."

"*I'm* nearly seven now, you know," I say.

"I know, Pet," Auntie says.

Amelia looks puzzled.

"Mistletoe!" Auntie calls, doubling over with laughter. "You can't have Christmas without mistletoe!"

"Mistletoe!" Mummy sounds disgusted.

When Mummy leaves the room for a moment, Auntie whispers, "Your mother doesn't approve. But what you do is, if there's a Christmas party, you put some above the door, and if a nice gentleman—for me, or boy for you, Amelia—happens to be under it at the same time as you, he has to kiss you." We all giggle.

"There's plenty in the bush—we can get some when we're up there," I say. Mummy has pointed it out to me, and told me how it's spread by the little mistletoe birds that eat the berries. The seeds in them are covered in sticky stuff, and the birds wipe it off their beaks onto the limb of whatever tree they land on next, and the seeds grow, sending their roots into the tree, and living off it. And if enough mistletoe grows on a tree, it dies.

The next afternoon, Amelia, Laurence and I, and Mummy carrying the axe, go up the hill. The *wild cherry* trees are light green with needles instead of leaves, and Mummy says they're the same shape as Christmas trees. She chooses one about as tall as Amelia, and chops it down.

On the way back with the tree, I point to some mistletoe.

Mummy stops. "Yes, it's a parasite—it's already killed part of the tree. See?" And again she tells us about the mistletoe birds.

"Let's take some home," I say.

Mummy looks puzzled. "What on earth for?"

"So we can put it up."

She frowns. "Just because Charlotte said you should! It doesn't matter what *I* say. Why anyone would want to hang that stuff up, I wouldn't know. And that business about kissing strangers! When I was staying at her place over New Year once, she had a party—she's a great one for parties—and when midnight came, everyone started slobbering on everyone else. God, it was awful. I hated it. You'd never know what germs you'd catch. Thew!"

While she's talking, I climb up on a log underneath the mistletoe and break a branch off.

Back in the house, we stand the wild cherry tree in a bucket in front of the fireplace—it's too warm to have a fire at night now—and pack stones around it. After we've decorated it, Amelia and I tack the mistletoe above the door to the verandah, where everyone goes in and out.

When Daddy and Claude get home, I say, "We've put mistletoe up!"

Mummy sighs. "Charlotte's been telling them about it."

Daddy grins. "She'd better watch out for old George, then. He's coming round this evening for a drink." George is an old man with a big moustache who lives a few miles down the road.

Mummy's voice is sharp. "Old George? Who invited him?"

"I did, when I seen him round the road this morning. He's a good neighbour, and he lives alone. Thought it would be nice for him to come over."

Old George arrives smoking his pipe as usual, but looking very neat in a jacket and tie. I smell shoe polish, and notice that his shoes are really shiny; and there's another scent—maybe hair oil. Dad introduces him to Auntie, and gives him a glass of sherry, and, as soon as he sits down, Auntie springs up, and, smiling, holds out the plate of fruitcake. "Won't you have some cake, Mr. Simpson?"

He looks into her eyes and smiles back. "Don't mind if I do. George is the name."

Daddy clears his throat. "Well, George, those seed potatoes you gave us are growing really well. Looks like we'll have a great crop."

But old George doesn't seem to hear him. "And how have you been enjoying your stay, Mrs. Warnock?" he asks Auntie.

"Please do call me Charlotte."

"Charlotte."

"Thank you for enquiring, George. Joe and Gwen have treated me like Royalty. But, as I was telling the children, unfortunately, I have to get back before Christmas. I do miss my own house—one gets so used to a view. And I have my little dog to consider."

"What type of dog do you have?"

"But Auntie," I say. "You said Olga—"

Frowning at me, Auntie snaps, "Don't interrupt when grown-ups are speaking, Pet!" She looks back at George. "Olga is my neighbour, George. She's been looking after my little dog. But I hear he's pining."

Surprised, I ask, "Do you have a dog, Auntie?" Again the frown, and this time no answer.

"Well, I've had quite a few dogs in my time, but I couldn't say what type most of them were, aside from the blue heelers.[1] I'm sure you know

---

[1] Australian dogs with bluish fur that are part dingo—a wild dog in Australia, but thought

them. Wonderful for cattle work—think just like a man." He pauses to sip his sherry. "But you didn't tell me what type of dog yours is."

"Oh, it's just one of those little cocker spaniels. It wouldn't be the sort of dog to interest a man such as yourself, George. But us widows get lonely, you know."

George stares at her for a moment.

"Joe was telling me what a beautiful property you have," Auntie says now. "And a very fine flock of sheep, too, I believe. Perhaps I could come and visit sometime?"

Old George gives her another long look. "Oh, by all means. By all means. Come for a cup of tea. Or a drink. Anytime. Just phone first, to make sure I'm not out in the paddocks."

"Well, regretfully, I don't think I'll have time on this visit. I'm leaving in a few days, you see. But perhaps next time I'm here?" She looks at my parents. "If Joe and Gwen will have me again, of course."

Daddy grins and mutters, "Course you'll be here again," and Mummy clears her throat and smiles.

Old George says, "Oh, I see. That's too bad. Well, please do try to fit me in, anyway. I'd be... delighted."

"Oh I will. I will, you can rest assured."

I've never seen old George smile so much—he looks almost young.

Auntie is up again, filling his glass and offering him more cake. "Really, I *will* be sorry if I can't come sometime. I can't think of anything more delightful than... afternoon tea with a gentleman such as yourself." She also is smiling a lot, and is all flutters and glides. They look at each other for another long moment.

That's when a little devil gets into me. "We've got mistletoe, you know," I say, pointing. "Over there, above the door." Nobody seems to hear, even though I say it and point several times.

When old George finally stands up to go, Auntie walks alongside of him, the rest of us following. When they get to the door, he suddenly grabs her and kisses her. Daddy and Claude guffaw and the rest of us giggle.

But almost as soon as the door has closed behind old George, Auntie's smile disappears. "Silly old goat," she mutters, then excuses herself and goes to our room.

---

to be descended from domesticated dogs; they nip the heels of the cattle they are bred to herd.

Mummy screws up her face and whispers to Daddy, "Imagine being kissed by that moustache! Thew! Filthy things! She led him on. Never changes." Daddy and Claude laugh again.

That night, as we're undressing in our room, Auntie says, "That old fool! Thought he'd made a conquest. All men are after the same thing, no matter how old they are."

"You don't really have a house, do you, Auntie?" I ask.

"Listen, Pet, when I tell somebody something, don't contradict me. It's very bad form." She pauses. "But I admit that was a white lie."

"What about the dog?" *I really hope she does have one.*

"The sort of people who live on the harbour in Newcastle all have those little dogs. Personally, I hate them, but I could tell George was impressed. However, did you hear what I said just now about bad form?"

***

Late one morning the following week, Jan arrives in her VW; she's pretty with fair hair, but I leave her talking to Mummy and Daddy and go into the bedroom where Auntie's packing. When she's finished, she puts her arms around me and holds me close. "Listen, my dear little girl, I want you to know that I'll be watching over you. Always. I'll be your guardian angel. And remember what you promised about going to your father if your mother ever tries to hit you again like she did." Crying a little bit, I nod.

After the midday meal, Daddy carries Auntie's suitcase out to the car. As she kisses me goodbye, she says she'll wave her hankie out of the car window, and to watch for it. It sounds like something people just say, but when the VW is climbing the hill, a white spot does appear on the end of her arm reaching out of the window.

Everyone else goes off in different directions, but I return to the bedroom where we all slept. In the rubbish basket, there's an empty cigarette carton, fragrant with her tobacco. I open a drawer, and inside is one of her powder boxes, covered in pale pink paper. The lid eases off with squeaks and puffs of air, and inside, there's a little bit of pink powder, like the gold that's left in the prospecting dish after all the dirt and gravel have been washed away. I breathe in the scent of her dear face. And I remember all the things she said to me, and her warm hand on my back that terrible and wonderful day after the beating when she first told me she loved me. The red mark from the strap is still on my thigh, though it isn't raised any more.

I put the powder box next to the cigarette carton in my drawer. Then I search everywhere again, including under her bed and in the wardrobe where she kept her things, but I don't find anything else of hers.

I go to bed right after tea, and cry for a long time. Then I hear rain tapping on the roof, as if the whole place is crying with me.

***

My first Christmas ever is really nice. Amelia and I get a doll and a book each, and pieces of material for dresses—though I don't find these very interesting. We have ham with new potatoes with mint and salt and pepper for Christmas dinner, and afterwards a Christmas pudding Mum made—I've decided to call her Mum from now on, and Daddy, Dad, like Amelia does. The pudding has a lot of dried fruit in it and is boiled, and I don't like it much. Claude and Amelia wanted her to put threepences in it, but she wouldn't, because she said someone might break a tooth.

When Mum yells at me, I continue to tune her out with Auntie's words. And once I'm alone, I whisper to Auntie—I always feel she's near.

Chapter Twenty-five

NARROW ESCAPES

When my parents decide to pick up a plough from a big property a long way away, taking Claude and Laurence with them and staying overnight, Dad looks at Amelia and me and says, "You fullahs'll be alright on your own here for one night, won't you?"

Mum clicks her tongue and sighs. "What on earth do you imagine could happen to them?"

I don't care about being on our own, and Amelia doesn't seem to, either, and we tell him we'll be OK.

The lorry starting up wakes me around daylight, but I go back to sleep after it drives away. When I wake again, it's one of those perfect sunny days, quiet except for the occasional cough of a gillbird[1] in the orchard. As I wander around later, I think how nice it is to have nobody telling me what to do, or what I've done wrong.

In the afternoon, though, our being the only ones here starts to feel a bit strange. About two o'clock, Amelia fills the Tilley lamp with kerosene from the tin on the back verandah and puts it on the kitchen table ready to light. "So we won't have to go out there in the dark later," she explains. Something prickles through me.

She also says we should tie the dogs up early. Someone—usually Claude—ties them up every night around dark, to stop them from running off after foxes and maybe ending up on someone else's place, where they might be mistaken for dingoes[2] and shot. Many dingoes don't look very different from ordinary dogs, and sheep farmers—like the people in the

---

[1] A large grey bird, also called a wattlebird, found in Australia, with red eyes and wattles; it eats honey and insects and makes a sound like coughing or barking.

[2] A wild dog in Australia, which is hunted because it eats sheep, etc.; thought to be descended from domesticated dogs.

white house—are always on the lookout for them because their favourite food is lamb. When we clip the kennel chains to our dogs' collars while the sun is still shining, they look up at us with sad eyes, wag their tales and whimper.

We feed the chooks earlier than usual, too—and I'm waiting for the last of them to wander into the fowl house where we lock them up at night so they'll be safe from foxes, when I notice the woman who lives in the white house at the other end of the valley with her black poodle, Roger. We know his name because we hear her calling him. My parents and their friends on the mountain make fun of Roger because he isn't a respectable working dog, and say he's a "lap dog," like the ones the Queen and toffs have.

We aren't going to milk the cows in the morning, so we don't lock the calves up for the night as we usually do. But, late in the afternoon, all the cattle wander into the yard, and stand around, as if they've come to see what's wrong. Besides Nancy, we have two other milking cows now, as well as a bull (who's not very scary) and a couple of bullocks for meat, or "killers," as my father calls them.

Just before dark, the lights go on in the white house. I think how strange it is that they don't even know that Amelia, ten, and me, six, will be all by ourselves here tonight.

Once we have the Tilley lamp pumped up and fizzing away in the kitchen, its brightness makes me feel better; but I'm aware of the vast darkness that starts in the next room and goes on forever.

After we've loaded our plates up with leftovers and sat down to eat, we keep hearing strange sounds we've never heard before—scratchings, squeaks and bumps—and stop chewing to listen, but we can't figure out what's making most of them. I also hear memories of sounds—the voices of Dad, Mum and Claude talking to, or yelling at, the dogs, cows, cats, each other or us, Laurence talking or buzzing or chirping, footsteps on the verandah, the sound of an axe chopping wood.

Tea over, we can't think of anything to do. The idea of falling asleep in a cozy bed and not waking till tomorrow, when, later, the others will be home, is appealing. We take the Tilley out onto the front verandah, where we're sleeping now that the weather is warm—Claude seems happy in the little room off the back verandah. Tonight, we wee in the front garden just beyond the lamp's shine, feeling naughty, but to go to the lavatory at the back is too frightening.

Not long after we've turned the lamp out, we hear more sounds, this

time outside, hold our breaths and listen. We decide that they were just
the noises the cattle make as they move around, and their little creaks
and groans when they get up or lie down.

Just when things seem to have quietened down, we both think we hear
voices outside, and again strain our ears, but only the sounds we heard
before come to us. A little later, though, we're certain we hear voices, but
too low to make out what they're saying.

"Maybe they've come to steal the cattle," Amelia whispers.

"They must think nobody's here," I whisper back. I'm shaking.

The voices get louder. "They're coming to the house," Amelia whispers.

*To steal things? We should pretend we're not here—keep totally silent—
or they might kill us.*

Knocking on the back door. The wire under our mattresses makes little
squeaks with our shaking.

More knocking, louder.

Amelia whispers, "Maybe someone's hurt. We'd better see who's there—
they might need help. Or to make a phone call."

We get up, and pull sweaters over our pyjamas. Amelia picks up the
Tilley. "My weapon," she says in a shaky voice.

Teeth clattering, we go inside through the front door. Just before the
back door, Amelia asks who's there, and I'm surprised how strong her
voice sounds.

"Willy and Max."

We've met them when we were with our parents many times, and they
aren't scary. We open the door, and there stands Willy, who's nearly as
old as Dad and works on a property round about, and Max, who's about
Claude's age, and lives on the Gloucester side of the mountain.

Her voice shaky now, Amelia tells them that our parents are away, but
asks them in and offers them a cup of tea, like Dad does when anyone
calls. In the kitchen, Willy takes a chair, and Max sits on the floor. The
stove is still alight, and we clumsily stoke it up, put the kettle on, get out
cups, biscuits, etc.

"You two seem a bit shaky. Scared you, did we?" Willy asks as we all
drink our tea. "Sorry."

After a while, Max says, "We've been poisoning dogs."

"Poisoning dogs?" we both echo.

"Yeah. Down at your friendly neighbours," Willy says. Their dogs—
like ours, and everybody else's in the countryside round about—are tied

up outside at night. "Only thing is, we didn't get Roger."

"He'd be in the house," says Max. "That's why."

Despite their weird story, the presence of these men we're comfortable with, and the hot tea, gradually relaxes us. After about an hour, they say they'd better go, thank us, and leave.

When my parents get back, we tell them what happened and how scared we were. They don't seem particularly surprised about the dog-poisoning story, and as I'm leaving the room I hear Dad say, "Well, we can't be blamed."

I hear nothing more about the dog-poisoning, and don't understand why they did it. And sometimes I wonder if they just imagined the whole thing. If they did do it, I feel sorry for the poor dogs.

***

A couple of rifles hang on the door to the little room off the back verandah where Claude sleeps; he and my parents shoot foxes, birds that raid the orchard, and rabbits, kangaroos and wombats because they eat our grass, or to feed the dogs.

One day, when Claude, Amelia and I are alone in the house for a few hours, we discover that Midnight, a stray black cat that came to live with us not long ago, has messed in a corner—which he does every now and then, even though Mum has rubbed his nose in it to cure him.

After we've cleaned his mess up, I go out the back door, and see him sitting on the grass, as if nothing's wrong. "Why can't you be a nice clean cat?" I ask him. At that moment, there's a gunshot, the cat jumps into the air, and falls down dead, blood running from his head.

Not far away, Claude lowers a rifle. "Damn thing deserved to be shot. Health hazard."

He finds a shovel, scoops up the cat's body, carries it up to the reserve, and throws it somewhere.

When I tell Amelia what he did, her eyes get big. "I thought he was just target shooting. Why would he want to kill the poor thing, just like that?" She sounds sad.

***

My parents have told us over and over never to point a gun at anyone, even if you think it isn't loaded, because "a lot of people have been shot that way by mistake." Once, Laurence pointed a stick at one of us, pretending it was a gun, and Dad took it from him, and told him in a loud voice that he wasn't allowed to point even a pretend gun at anyone. "That's how people learn to be careless with real ones," he said.

Later on the same day he shot Midnight, Claude comes in with the rifle and starts pointing it at various things. "Stop doing that!" she says.

Swinging around, he aims it at her.

"Stop! Right now!" Amelia orders, bending down and moving away; but he keeps it trained on her.

"I told you to stop doing that!" she yells. "You know Dad says never to point a gun at anyone. If I tell him, you'll be in big trouble!"

"Ah, what are you worried about? It's not loaded."

"He says you shouldn't point a gun at anyone, even if you *think* it isn't loaded."

"That's just for stupid people. I told you, it isn't loaded. I *know* it isn't. I'll prove it." He swings around, points it at the window, and pulls the trigger. There's an explosion and the loud jangling of falling glass. The window has a jagged hole in it.

We all stare open mouthed, and then Amelia stamps her foot, leans towards him and yells into his face, "You bloody well nearly killed me!" She collapses on the couch and bursts into tears. Then she takes a breath, and yells at him some more.

Tears thickening my throat, images flash... her, splattered... blood everywhere... But then I think that now, at last, my parents will find out what Claude gets up to when they're not around.

After a while, Amelia stops yelling, and then—I don't know why—she helps him clean up the glass, and together they make up a story to explain the broken window. Noticing an old cricket ball on the mantle shelf—Mum used to play the game with her brother—they decide they'll say that they were playing with it outside and it went through the window.

When my parents come home, they frown when they hear the story, and peer at the ball, and then the broken window a number of times. But eventually, they seem to believe it.

Chapter Twenty-six

BLIGHT

Dad arrives home from town with a tractor on the lorry, backs up to the side of the hill, and drives it off. Now he won't have to dig with the mattock and potato fork any more.

Not long afterwards, it starts raining, and continues for weeks and weeks. Bogs form in many places on the road above the Black Cutting and, coming back from Scone one night, the lorry gets bogged on the last hill, and Dad only just manages to get it out by packing stones and sticks in the wheel tracks. After this, he puts chains on the wheels whenever he needs to drive on the road.

People make detours around the bogs by clearing away the rocks, logs and small trees, and when the detours get boggy, they make others around *them*—until there's no space left. That's when the bogs get so deep that chains no longer work, and we can't get to Scone at all.

After we haven't been able to get out for a couple of months, every time Mum creaks the lid of our big bin open, she says we need "more supplies." So Dad gets Claude to drive the tractor ahead of the lorry and pull us through the bogs, and to meet us below where they start and do the same thing when we're coming home.

A few days later, Dad calls us outside and shows us a large wooden platform he's built onto the tractor. "There'll be room for us all on there," he tells us. After this, we leave the lorry at old George's place, which is just below the last bog on the way to town, and ride back and forth on the platform. But we still have to worry about Dicky Dan's Crossing—though we've always managed to get through it so far—and there are many scary rides over the Black Cutting. It's three months before we can get to Scone in the usual way.

Figure 26.1: Left to right: Amelia, my father, Claude, my mother and Dave Ogle on the contraption my father built onto the tractor to take us over the bogs.

***

I go into the kitchen late one afternoon to find Dad sitting at the table with his head in his hands, Mum beside him. "Whole bloody lot's ruined. Whole bloody lot," he keeps saying. He looks up with watery eyes, then says angrily, "But those potato plants were completely healthy! I'd never seen a better looking crop. You saw them, Gwen. Lovely new potatoes for Christmas, and the next lot I dug up were good, too."

He folds his arms and stares at the floor. "Black rot—that's all that's

Figure 26.2: A potato patch near the house at Hunter's Springs

left under most of them. Checked them all over the paddock. Well, there's the odd one with decent potatoes—but who knows how long they'll last. Blight[1]—that's what's done it. Curse of the bloody Irish!"

As we eat that evening, he says, "I'd noticed some spots on the leaves

---

[1]A disease of potato plants that rots the potatoes under the ground while the tops look healthy; it contributed significantly to the great Irish famine.

of a few plants a while back, but it's been that wet, I didn't take much notice."

Next day, we all go to the potato field. Like Dad said, under nearly every plant is black, stinky rot. At tea that night, Dad says, "I guess we'll just have to wait and see what's there in the autumn. But it'll be a miracle if we get more than a few bags."

***

A week or so later, Dad announces that he's decided to sell timber from the bush up on the hill. Next time we're in Scone, he buys a Newcastle Herald, and answers ads for men wanting work. And one day he tells us that "a couple of fullahs" are coming to cut down trees in the back paddock, and that jinkers like the ones I fear meeting on the Black Cutting will haul the logs away so they can be sold. One of the men who's coming lives in Newcastle and is called Dave, and the other is James, a New Zealander.

Mum tells me that New Zealand is a country made up of two islands, and between them and Australia there's a big lot of salty water called the sea, or ocean. I ask if I'd be able to see New Zealand from our side of the water, but Mum says it's too far away. I don't say so, but I'm sure that I'd be able to see it if I tried really, really hard. Dad says that James and Dave will eat with us, but there's nowhere in the house for them to sleep, so he'll build them a bark hut on the hill where they'll be working.

After breakfast the next morning, he ruffles my hair when he gets up from the table. "If you get your boots on quick and lively, you can come up the bush with me; I'm going to cut down a stringybark to build that hut. There are nettles and ants and Gawd knows what up there, so you can't go barefoot."

He drives through the bush on a track he's cleared except for saplings, which scrape and screech along underneath the lorry and pop back up behind it, their broken ends making them look like strange paintbrushes. When we stop, he carries the axe over his shoulder, and our boots crunch over dry leaves as he searches the bush for a suitable stringybark tree. The one he chooses is huge, and, as they all do, it has bark as brown and hairy as a wombat. He has me sit on a log close enough to watch him cut it down, but far enough away so I'll be safe when it falls.

His strong arms swing the axe wide, and as it cuts into the tree, a deep huh comes out of him like it used to when he was digging up the potato patch. Chips of yellow wood as big as plates fly through the air, rattle into bushes, or thump onto the ground, and two dark patches appear on the back of his shirt, grow and join into one. Cutting the tree down takes a long time, and, bored, I find a stick and bang on the log I'm sitting on, look for interesting stones and leaves, or watch the Pet ants.

A creaking makes me look up. The huge stringybark is tilting. Halfway down, the trunk above the cut twists and breaks off. The tree hits the ground with an explosion, everything shudders, leaves rattle, three rainbow lorikeet parrots screech up into the sky and disappear, and bits of bark rain down onto the lake of leaves the tree has become.

Puffing, Dad comes to where I am, fills a pint with water from the water bag, and gulps it down. He grins. "Big bugger. Smell the sap."

We walk closer to the tree. Twisted limbs have dug into the black earth, and ants race over the trunk and limbs—small black ones, Pet ants and big Bull ants with their nasty pincers. I feel sad for the ones who've lost their homes.

Dark clouds are boiling up into the sky, and Dad says, "I'd better get back to work; it looks like rain."

Using the axe, he makes cuts around the tree trunk every eight feet or so, and then with an adze,[2] separates off pieces of bark as big as the kitchen table. With its hairy covering, the bark is almost as thick as his arm. "That'll keep any storm out," he says. He piles the sheets up and covers them with a tarp. Just then, raindrops start hitting the leaves and we run under a big tree and wait till it stops enough for us to get back to the lorry.

***

Dad takes us all to see the finished hut. A log is stuck in the ground at each corner, the sides and roof are bark, and two beds and a table are made of pieces of limbs stuck in the ground, with bark, smooth side up, laid on top. Around the table are chopped-off pieces of the bigger limbs to sit on.

Dad goes to town and brings the two men back in the early afternoon. Dave has pale hair and wears glasses, and James has brown eyes, a beard and a nice voice. Ever since we've had the wireless, we've been listening every morning to a fellow called James, who talks as if he knows us and plays music before the news comes on, and, as soon as I meet James, I tell him that we listen to him on the wireless all the time. Everyone laughs,

---

[2] A large implement with a sharp blade at a ninety degree angle to the handle, used for woodwork.

Figure 26.3: Left to right: Me around six, Dave Ogle, Claude, Laurence, my father, my mother and Amelia with her doll.

and I don't understand why, until Mum explains that this isn't the same one. I didn't know before that two people could have the same name.

Dad shows the men around, and they all go up to the shed with a bottle of rum, where they stay until Mum calls them for the evening meal. As we start on our soup, James's spoon clatters onto his plate and his head falls to his chest; he's asleep, and the others have to wake him and help him into the lorry, so they get him to the hut.

***

When we dig up the potatoes, we get only a few bags, but Dad makes sure he saves as many of them as he can for seed; by doing this, he says, we'll eventually have potatoes that are blight resistant.

Chapter Twenty-seven

THE NEW GAME

When my parents and Laurence go to Scone one day, leaving the rest of us at home, Claude shows Amelia a drawing book he says is James's. In it is a strange drawing of a woman and man without any clothes on, the man peeing on the woman, who's lying on the ground. After he's put it away, he goes into my parents' bedroom and comes back with a book with a dark red cover, and he and Amelia read bits aloud about periods, men's penises, and how babies are made. Claude has already told me some of this in his horrible way, and he and Amelia giggle at the diagrams.

Awhile after he puts the book back, they start watching something through the window. "Look at his penis," says Claude, and I see Norman the bull climbing onto Nancy's back and sticking his long tap into her— we've always called it this before because his wee runs out of it like water from a tap. The bull and cow are "doing it," just like people do, they say.

One afternoon not long afterwards, I'm on the front veranda drawing one of the dead trees. Claude and Amelia are down the other end, talking about a story in a newspaper some city people left.

She reads aloud, "In Newcastle today, a twenty-eight-year-old man received a sentence of ten years for rape. Clifford Martins, a labourer, admitted that he had seen the victim, a thirteen-year-old girl, walking along the Pacific Highway. He persuaded her to get into his car by saying that her father had asked him to pick her up. Martins admitted that he raped the girl in the back of the car. Fortunately, a man who happened to be walking his dog nearby, heard her cries, and came to her aid. The examining doctor stated that the girl had been a virgin before the attack. A member of a respectable family, she is a student at a Catholic school. The judge said..." She trails off.

"I told you, *Rape* is when the woman doesn't want to do it," Claude says.

"But how can you be sure that's what it means?"

"It just does, that's all."

"I know—I'll look in the dictionary." Amelia comes back with a large book. "Forced intercourse." "Intercourse without consent." Now we'll have to look up intercourse." A little while later, she says, "Yeah. You were right. It *does* mean *doing it when the woman doesn't want to.*"

***

Thinking about rape, I start worrying about Laurence; he's only a little boy now, but if somebody doesn't tell him about it, he could rape somebody when he's older without knowing it's wrong, and go to jail.

One day when I'm alone with him, I try to explain all this to him. I start by talking about what *doing it* is, mentioning his little grub thing. But he doesn't understand at all, and I give up.

That night, he, Mum, Amelia and I are by the fire when he starts talking to Amelia about his little grub. I can't really hear what he's saying, but Amelia looks uncomfortable, and I think he's talking about what I told him.

My mother looks at me suspiciously, then asks him, "Who's been telling you these things?"

I'm scared he'll say it was me, but he doesn't.

***

Late one afternoon, my mother is sewing in the hallway with the front door open, Amelia is somewhere else, and I'm squatting in the garden watching a strange yellow spider building its web in a bush, when Claude comes around the side of the house.

He stops. "What are you doing?"

"Watching a spider. Look—it's yellow and it has a tail."

He doesn't bother to look. "I can show you a new game, if you like."

Wanting to stay where I am, I don't answer.

"Come on—it'll be fun."

Still I don't move. "Aw, come on." Then, pleased that someone wants to play with me, I get up.

"You'll have to come up on the verandah." He puts his finger on his lips. "Shhhh. It's a secret."

My mother can't see the steps from the hallway where she's sewing, but I can hear her treadling on the machine, as, making as little noise as possible, I follow him up the steps and to the middle of the veranda. He stands behind the little red chair that's always there.

"You've got to get up on this chair," he whispers.

I sit on it.

He shakes his head. "Not like that!" Then he says more gently, "I'll show you."

He arranges me upside-down—my head and neck on the seat, my thighs resting on the chair's back, my knees bent over its top and my lower legs dangling behind it. The skirt of my floral dress has fallen over my head, and it's as if I'm in a little flowered tent. Then, close by, a whispery sound I've never heard before begins, and goes on and on. The chair pinches the backs of my knees, and I move a little to get comfortable.

The whispery sound continuing, Claude orders in a breathless whisper, "Keep still! I'll show you now."

One of his hands moves my legs apart, and something as hard as wood slips under the elastic in the leg of my panties, and tries to push into the centre of me. Burning pain. I cry out. The pushing and pain stop.

As I slide off the chair onto the floor, I see Claude racing down the steps stuffing something pale into his trousers.

A moment later, the treadling of the sewing machine stops and I see Mum's head as she leans back in her seat and peers through the door. "What are you up to?" she asks suspiciously.

Seeing me sitting quietly on the floor, her head disappears and the treadling starts up again.

A strange light plays through the garden till the sun goes down and I start to feel cold. The treadling stops, the machine squeaks as it's lowered into its cabinet, and the lid thumps shut. My mother's boots stamp away down the hallway, and then I hear her in the kitchen talking to Laurence.

Chapter Twenty-eight

STORIES ABOUT NAN AND GRANDFATHER

One day, Mum tells us that her parents, who live near Sydney, are coming to visit. She brings out the photo album. In one photograph, her mother—stout like Mrs. Rose, with a little smile and wearing glasses—has a baby in her arms. "That's your uncle Geoff," Mum says. "Two years younger than me."

Behind them is a clothes line, and higher up, a tree. "When Geoff was a baby," she tells us, "Mum used to leave him on a rug in the shade of that tree while she hung the clothes out. I was about three, and one day, I saw something on the hill above where he was. Mum used to hold a spoonful of honey above my toast and make it wriggle across it. Shining in the sun, it was moving like the honey. We had plenty—Dad always kept bees. 'Look,' I said pointing. 'Honey.' I was always asking her to look at something, and this day she turned, frowning, and glanced up to where I was pointing. Next thing, she grabbed the rifle propped against the clothes line post, and fired. Then she raced up to Geoff, who was screaming, and picked him up. 'That wasn't honey,' she said to me. 'That was a snake. A big bitey. It can't hurt anyone any more, though.'

"In the shadow of the tree, the bits were pale brown. And she told me that if I ever saw another one, to get away from it and call someone. Lucky the rifle was nearby. Dad had taught her to shoot, and made her promise to keep it close whenever she was outside. She hated guns and hadn't wanted to learn."

On another page, there's a photograph of a man in a field with white boxes behind him. "There's Dad with his hives," she says, a thickness in her voice. His face is shadowed by a hat—but with a smaller brim than the one my Dad wears. Peering into its shadow, I see a thin face.

"He never wore anything to protect himself when he robbed the bees. And he *never* got stung."

"Robbed?" I ask.

Amelia grins. "Stole the honey they had in their little wax jars."

"It's dreadful what people do to bees," Mum says. "Some people just let them starve and get a new lot every spring. But your grandfather believed in fair play, even when it came to bees. 'That's the English way,' he used to say."

"Is he from England?" Amelia asks.

"Well, he was born there, and so were his parents. Anyway, whether he was dealing with people, animals, or other creatures, he believed in fair play. He never hurt or killed anything unless he had to. He always made sure he left the bees enough honey to see them through the winter." She's quiet for a while, and then continues, "And he reckoned that's why they didn't sting him. He was fair to them, and they were fair to him. When he robbed those bees he didn't even roll his shirt sleeves down—and he never got stung. Most people have to wear overalls and gloves and hats and veils."

As she's telling us these things, I think of all the bee stings I've had.

"He *never* got stung?" asks Claude. "Not once?"

"Well... He did once, I think, but he reckoned he must have brushed against the bee by mistake and hurt it."

She turns back to the photograph. "His poor old right arm isn't much good."

I see now that his left hand is under his right elbow. "He was always exercising that wretched arm, but it never got very strong, and it stayed smaller than the other one."

We ask what was wrong with his arm.

"Some damn fool let him fire a shotgun when he was only eight, and it gave such a kick his arm was injured for life," she says in a scratchy voice. "I don't know how many operations the doctors put him through. Altogether, he must have been in hospital for months. They kept saying they could fix it. But for all the good the operations did, they might as well not have bothered. Useless buggers. Then they had the hide to tell his parents he'd be a cripple the rest of his life."

She pauses. "They didn't know the sort of person he was," she says, her voice strong. "That arm could only kind of anchor things, but he figured out ways to work around it. People were always amazed at how much he got done—a lot more than most people." She gazes into the distance.

"All he wanted was to make a living from running cattle on his own land. Ten healthy young men couldn't have cleared this place, and by the time he and Mum bought it, he wasn't young any more."

She turns the pages until she finds a photograph of her mother and father in front of the house we live in. "This was taken after the house was built. Mum had just bought this lounge suite we're sitting on, and she was very proud of it."

I look at the chairs and couch, and wonder what she'll think when she sees how dirty they are now.

"There wasn't enough cleared land to run many cattle. He and Geoff did their best to get things going, but Mum kept getting sick, and after Geoff won a bit of money in the lottery, she persuaded them all to move closer to the city."

"Are there any other pictures of your mother?" I ask.

"*Nan*, she says she wants you kids to call her, so you might as well start now. Well—she was usually the one taking the pictures." She pauses. "Anyway, I was telling you about why they left. It wasn't for the want of hard work that he couldn't make a go of this place. He could do everything just as well as anyone else." She's quiet for a moment, and then says, "But sometimes of a night, after a hard day's work, when he thought nobody was looking, I'd see him holding that arm and screwing up his face in pain. But he never complained. And he never took time off because of the pain—or any other sickness, either."

She shows us another photograph of Grandfather next to a small table piled with vegetables. "He had a big vegetable garden. Look at the size of those parsnips! I never saw anybody who could grow vegetables like him. And those are tomatoes. The most delicious ones I've ever tasted."

She sighs. "He had a lot to do. I helped him as much as I could. Course, I'd always had jobs. When I was five, I had to find the horses in the afternoons and bring them in. It was a big paddock—a hundred acres. Mum would be lying on the couch, and I had to take Geoff with me. She was too sick to look after him by herself. He was three, so I had to help him along. She wouldn't let us go if it was foggy, but one day a thick fog came up after we left. I don't know how we found the horses, but *they* took *us* home."

"What was wrong with her? I mean Nan?" Amelia asks.

Mum shifts in her seat and shakes her head a couple of times. "I don't know. Women's troubles, she used to say."

I'm surprised. *Women have special sicknesses?*

She's told us before, but now tells us again of how Nan stayed away for months when she was twelve. "She went back to the city—to her mother in Sydney." Her voice is wavy. "Dad and I had to do everything. I had my lessons and Geoff's to supervise. And I had to learn how to run the telephone exchange.

"Some of the subscribers weren't very nice, either. One woman got that annoyed with me! I was trying to get her a trunk call,[1] and the lines were busy, as I told her. It was a party line, and when they were, there was nothing I could do except wait. But she went on and on about how inefficient I was.

"Well, Miss Hay's voice broke in; she was the postmistress at Moonan. 'Don't be so hard on her,' she said to the woman. 'She's only a little girl, you know.' The woman stopped complaining, but she didn't say she was sorry or anything."

"I did most of the cooking, too, and helped Dad with the outside work as much as I could." Her voice is scratchy again.

"But why was your mother—Nan—away for so long?" Amelia asks, though she knows what she'll say.

Several times, Mum starts to say something and stops; then she says, "I think she had to have some kind of an operation." She lies back in her chair and looks up at the ceiling. "She was a city girl."

Mum is always calling people from the city "useless." They call at the house every now and then and ask directions, and when they've gone, my parents talk about how they know nothing about the country. They're scared of things that won't hurt you, like garden spiders and the big brown tarantulas that are our friends, and the old milking cows. And they do dangerous things and don't know about things that could really hurt them—like that you shouldn't walk behind horses because they'll probably kick you if you do. They don't watch out for snakes when they're out in the paddocks, either, and they "shoot anything that moves," my parents always say.

But Mum is speaking again. "She never liked it up here. She was always wanting to get back to that damn city."

We move on to a photograph of Mum when she was fifteen, sitting on a wooden chair in front of a house.

---

[1] Formerly, a long distance telephone call within Australia.

Figure 28.1: Me at three, Nan, my maternal grandmother, and Amelia, seven.

Claude says, "That's taken at the station, isn't it?" He means a property a few miles away.

Mum nods. "Dad was manager there, then."

"What'll we call *him*?" Claude asks.

She thinks for a moment. "*Grandfather* should be alright. He's not the sort of person to worry about a thing like that. He wouldn't really care what you called him. No. As long as you show him proper respect and do what he tells you. He doesn't like kids that are disobedient or cheeky."

Some of the background of the photograph is blanked out, and Mum says it's fog. I look at the summer dress she's wearing in the photograph. "Weren't you cold?"

"Probably," she says. "That station was a cold damn place. It was supposed to be summer, and Mum wanted to take a picture of me in that dress—I'd just finished making it.

She shivers. "Talk about winters. One time I picked some violets and put them in a vase on the table by my bed—I used to sleep on the verandah. It was closed in with louvres, but they didn't help much. When I woke up, the flowers were sitting there in a column of ice—the vase had split clean in two, and the pieces were on either side of it. I'd liked that vase, too."

***

Dad smiles when Mum asks him to get some meat when he goes to town to pick Nan and Grandfather up. "Why don't I just shoot one of those old wombats up in the paddock?" he asks. We know he's joking about all the creatures Mum has told us they used to eat when they had no meat, and everyone laughs.

Like when Auntie was coming, Amelia, Mum and I tidy and shine the place up and put flowers everywhere. Amelia and I are giving Nan and Grandfather our room, and we're to sleep on the front verandah; Claude is still in the little room off the back verandah.

Chapter Twenty-nine

NAN AND GRANDFATHER VISIT

As soon as we see the lorry coming down the hill, Mum hurries outside, the rest of us following. She hugs the skinny old man who jumps down from the lorry's cab first. A plump woman with a pale face climbs down next, and stands looking at her hands, till Mum puts her arms around her. Grandfather grins at nobody in particular, and Nan puts her arms around me and draws me to her. "How are *you*, Darling?" Then she hugs and kisses everyone else, looking really happy to see us all.

Dad lifts two big suitcases down from the back of the lorry, and we all go into the house. Nan gets him to leave one suitcase in the loungeroom, and to take the other to their room, where she leaves her and Grandfather to get settled. When he comes back, Mum points to the suitcase, and says in a low voice, "Look at the size of that suitcase! She has so many dresses—I don't know how she'll have time to wear them all while she's here."

A little while later, I'm in the loungeroom with everyone except Nan and Grandfather, when the others start laughing. Turning, I see a weird face, and jump. Then I see that it's Grandfather, who's now laughing so much, he's doubled over. He straightens up, wipes his eyes and looks at me. "Only teasing you."

I don't feel like laughing.

Mum's voice is strong. "Don't be so silly, Leila. Grandfather didn't mean to frighten you."

"See?" he says. He hooks his forefingers into the corners of his mouth, stretches it wide, and lets his long, pink tongue hang down to his chin, then reaches it up and licks his brow, his eyes rolled back so they're mostly

white, and his ears wiggling. His face back to normal, he says, "Just pulling a funny face for you."

From the doorway, Nan glares at him. "Dick! The first time you see the child in years, and you frighten her. Why do you always have to do things like that?"

"I was just pulling a funny face for her." He looks at me, and holds his arms out wide with his head on one side. "Come and give your poor old Grandfather a hug."

I don't move, and Mum says, "He won't bite you."

"I was only playing with you. Don't be a silly cuss."

"Come on, Leila," Mum urges. "Give him a hug."

When I still don't move, Grandfather comes over, leans down, and brushes his prickly face against mine. "Only teasing."

After he moves away, Nan comes over, squats down and looks into my face. "Tell you what, Darling, I have something for you in my suitcase. I'll be right back."

She gives me a green parcel, and underneath tissue paper, in a cardboard box, is a little glass vase. I've never had one of my own, and I like that it's green, like the paper.

Nan pats my shoulder. "Do you feel better, now, dear?"

I feel myself smiling, and nod.

"OK, then. Put it somewhere safe."

She looks at Mum and points to the big suitcase. "I hope that's not in your way, Gwen—it's full of magazines for you. I've been saving them up ever since we knew we were coming. They're out-of-date, of course, but I didn't think you'd have read them. I'm sure you don't get many up here."

"Oh? Thanks very much, Mum. There's not always a lot in them, though."

Nan frowns. "Well, I like the recipes."

After everyone else has left the room to do different things, I follow Nan as she and Grandfather walk around looking at Mum's paintings on the walls, most done a long time ago, and some recent ones. They stop in front of one with cattle in it, and Nan says, "Look at Gwen's funny old cows!"

I somehow think I should tell Mum what she said, but don't have a chance till the next morning, when I find her in the kitchen by herself, cooking breakfast. When I tell her, she looks as if she's going to cry, but doesn't. Soon afterwards, Grandfather comes in for breakfast, gets a sharp knife and three glasses, and starts cutting and squeezing juice into a glass from two big yellow fruit they've brought. When Nan comes in, Mum, with a crack in her voice, asks her what she meant about her cows.

"Your cows?"

"Leila told me you said 'Gwen's funny old cows.' "

"Ohhh. I see." Nan goes over to her. "Oh Gwen, dear, don't take it like that. I'm very sorry—I wouldn't hurt you for the world. It was just a silly remark I made to Dick. I don't know what I could have been thinking."

"Well, what *did* you mean?"

"Well, I just meant... that they're... unusual, that's all. Look, you paint very, very well. You're very talented—I've always said so."

Nan hugs Mum, who sniffles into her hankie.

"You *are* very talented, Gwen. I could see that from the the first paintings you ever did. I've always thought you were an amazing artist, and I still think you are."

While Mum is serving the bacon and eggs, Nan turns to me. "And you, young lady, have to learn not to repeat things you hear. See how much trouble you've caused?"

I keep my eyes on my plate.

Grandfather puts a glass of yellow juice next to Mum's place, and one next to Nan's and starts drinking from the other one. I ask him what the yellow stuff is. "It's grapefruit juice," he says. "Have some." He pours a little into a cup, and I taste it. It's horrible, and makes the inside of my mouth go all funny. I pull a face.

"Go on, drink it all. It's good for you," he keeps saying.

Nan keeps sighing loudly, and finally says, "Don't try to make her drink it if she doesn't like it, Dick. Please. You should know by now that children don't like bitter things."

He shrugs, but stops.

The next afternoon, when Nan and Grandfather are outside, Mum opens the suitcase Nan brought and is going through the piles of magazines when Dad comes in.

"Useless *Women's Weeklies*, most of them. Royalty, fashion, make-up, weddings," she says to him, dropping them back into the suitcase. "And more weddings."

"Marvellous the money people waste on weddings, isn't it?" Dad says. "Go into debt for years, some of them. People love to put on a big show. Aping the rich. They've done away with all that in the Soviet Union."

"And most of the presents people get they'd never use in a blue moon. Things they put in the china cabinet in the front parlour, and there they stay, gathering dust."

"The only reason people go to weddings is to have a good feed. In Russia they have special *marriage palaces*."

"Well, we have registry offices."

"What's a registry office?" I ask.

"It's a place where people who aren't religious get married," Mum says. "Your father and I got married in one, didn't we Joe?"

"Yeah, we did."

***

After the evening meal, when we're all sitting around talking, and James is drawing in his sketch book, as he often does, something makes me cry. But then I notice that he keeps glancing at me as he's sketching. *He's drawing me.* When he stops, he shows the drawing to my parents, and they laugh. I go and look over their shoulders. The girl in the sketch has an ugly face with tears flying everywhere, and I burst into tears again.

Mum laughs. "Oh heavens, she doesn't like it."

Dad folds his arms, and he and Claude look at one another and laugh a bit. But Nan gets up, comes over and puts her arms around me. "It's alright, Darling," she says. "Don't worry—it doesn't look at all like you. You're a very pretty girl." To James and the others, she says, "You've hurt her feelings. And she's such a dear little thing."

Mum looks over at me. "James didn't mean to upset you."

"No," says James, "I didn't. It's a cartoon." He puts the drawing away.

Nan stays planted next to me, solid and strong, and soon I'm feeling alright again. And, from that moment, I really, really like her. But too soon, she and Grandfather go back to Grose Vale. Then, James and Dave leave, and Trevor comes back to work with Dad.

Chapter Thirty

THE BRIDE IN THE GARDEN AND OTHER CREATURES

Every night after Amelia and I go to bed, we look at the *Women's Weeklies*. Like Mum said, there's a lot about brides and weddings in them.

"Why do people get married?" I ask.

Amelia stares into the distance. "When a man falls in love with you, he asks you to marry him. Then you find a church and invite all your friends and family, and you promise to love each other forever."

"Mum and Dad reckon weddings are stupid."

"I know. But *I* think it'd be nice to have a wedding in a church." She shows me a full-page picture of a bride standing half-way up a curved staircase, looking back over one shoulder. "I want a long white dress like this one." The dress flows down the steps behind her like a waterfall. "That's the *train*—it says here it's six feet long." She looks up. "When you get married, you wear white for purity. And a veil."

"What's *purity*?"

"It means you're—you're a—a *virgin*. That you haven't done anything... wrong."

"Oh."

Opposite, are pictures of flowers. "And you carry a bouquet."

In another magazine, a bride in white stands next to a coloured glass window, its colours on her skirt, only paler. Amelia sighs, and lies back with her eyes closed and the magazine over her tummy. "I can almost hear the organ music. Claude and I sneaked into a church in Scone once and watched a couple get married. There was a window just like that, and when the bride and groom came out, the organ played."

The next afternoon, Mum is squatting down weeding in the front garden, and I'm picking flowers for a wedding bouquet. My bouquet becomes as beautiful as the ones in the Weekly; all it needs is trailing bits, so I add long pieces from the mint plant. *One day, I'll find a man who loves me, and we'll get married.* I walk slowly along the garden path, eyes half closed. *I'm in a church, in a long, white dress with a train, coloured light on the skirt. Somewhere nearby is the dark-haired man I'm marrying.*

Mum's voice. "You've got your new cap on, Claude." She's standing there admiring him in the khaki army cap shaped like a boat Mum's cousin gave him. "I'll get the camera and take a snap.[1]"

I manage to stay in the church as she goes into the house and comes out again, and, the camera in her hand, tells Amelia to stand next to Claude.

Amelia asks, "Isn't Leila going to be in the picture?"

Mum says, "Oh I spose she could be. Leila, come over here."

The dress, colours, flowers and church fade away, but the bouquet still in my hand, I stand next to Claude and Amelia, looking straight ahead like them, and feeling as beautiful as the brides in the Weekly.

***

Not long afterwards, I hear Dad tell Mum that Trevor is going to Newcastle for a holiday. "I bet he's got a girlfriend down there," he says. "Maybe he'll get married, and never come back."

"Girlfriend? He's never mentioned a *girlfriend*!"

Dad laughs. "Ah, men are pretty cagey when it comes to things like that. Course he'd have a girlfriend. It's only natural."

"Trevor would never go to live in a city. Don't be idiotic. And, anyway, he'd have told us if he was getting married."

***

A few days later I'm in the kitchen, next to the coloured glass doors of the cabinet where we keep the plates and cups and things, when Trevor comes in. I have to lean back to look up at his face. "Do you have a girlfriend?" I ask.

He picks up a *Weekly* someone has left on the table, and studies it, then glances down at me, and asks sharply, "What?"

"Do you have a girlfriend?"

---

[1] A photograph.

He scratches his head. "No," he says. "I don't." He goes back to reading the magazine.

"Can I be your girlfriend, then?"

He sets the magazine on the top of the cabinet miles above my head and stares down at me. "No, you can't."

"Why not?"

"Because you're just a little girl with big ideas."

I feel very, very little, and stupid, as he strides from the room. I worry he'll tell my parents; but they don't say anything about it so he couldn't have.

The next time we're in Scone, Mum drops the roll of film off at the chemist[2] to have it developed, and I can't wait to see the photo; I know I looked beautiful that day in the garden.

When the photos finally come back in the mail, we all crowd around to see them, and there we all are: Claude, his arms folded, and very grown-up looking in the army cap, and Amelia with her white hair and chin in the air. But next to her is a sad-looking little girl with pale, untidy hair and a bunch of scraggly flowers. *Can I really have looked that awful?*

***

But I'm soon distracted by the beauty all around me. When I go to get Nancy the next morning, she's a long way from the house. Now that her calf is big, she doesn't hang around when it's in the pen at night. The sun hasn't been up long, and, all around me, the clover looks silver with a mauve tint. I squat down to look at it, and silver balls of water roll off the leaves, purple and green lights spiking from them. As I push my bare feet through the plants, they feel like wet slippers, and when I stop and look back, I see I've left a dark green path.

***

My mother leaves Amelia and me to clean up the breakfast things, saying she's going to saddle *Locket*, the mare she has now, and ride around the paddocks. But a few moments later I hear her step back onto the veranda; she bursts through the kitchen door, eyes bright. "Come up the shed with me and see what I've found!"

We follow her across the sunny yard, and, as we're about to go inside the shed, she shooshes us, and we follow her on tip-toe past the saddles on their pole, to a dark corner.

---

[2] A pharmacy where medications are sold, and other goods and services may also be offered.

Figure 30.1: Me at six in the garden with Claude, thirteen, and Amelia, ten.

"There! On the old horse collar."

She means the collar grandfather had for his draft horse, and, in the dimness, I gradually make out what looks like a very large, furry moth.

"I haven't seen a bat this close since my father..." Her voice catches. "showed me one when I was a kid."

Now I see a body, a head, folded, leathery wings.

Smiling, she says, "Isn't it a *dear* little thing? She reaches out a forefinger, and strokes the creature's back. "So soft. Feel its fur."

Amelia also strokes it, and my hand reaches out, hesitates.

"Oh for heaven's sake! Touch it—it won't hurt you."

It's really soft.

"See its dear little face?"

I peer. Its eyes are like tiny drops of brown liquid.

She carefully unhooks a claw, lifts what looks like a hefty spider's leg from the collar's worn leather, and lets it curl over the tip of her little finger. "See its long thumb?"

The creature's eyes move, and it doesn't seem afraid at all. My mother takes the edge of a wing between her thumb and forefinger and draws it out; shiny grey ridges separate islands of spidery red lines. "See its red blood vessels?"

***

One afternoon a week or so later, Dad calls us all into the kitchen. Eyes shining, he holds a cornbag by its top, something heavy in it resting on the floor. He looks around at us, grinning, then opens the top and stands back. The bulge doesn't move until he gently nudges it with the toe of his boot. Then out walks what looks, at first, like a tussock blackened by fire, and then I see that it's an animal covered with dark spines and with a beak.

Happiness spreads across my mother's face. "Oh for heaven's sake!"

Dad looks at me. "It's a porcupine. I found it up in the paddock, and I thought you fullahs would like to see it."

"Echidna is the correct name," my mother says quietly.

As the animal strolls across the floor on stubby little legs, and then stops and looks at us, I let my eyes turn it from porcupine to burned tussock and back again.

"I'd better take it back to its home—its family might be worried," Dad says. He opens the bag and holds it in front of the animal, and it walks right back in.

Chapter Thirty-one

STARTING SCHOOL

"I'm nearly seven, and I'm starting school soon," I tell Arn, an old man who lives down near Scone and has called in for a cup of tea on the way to somewhere else.

He sighs. "And you reckon that's a *good* thing, do you?" He looks at Mum. "I was the same. Kept asking me poor old Mum, 'When can I start school?' 'When can I start school?' 'You won't like it,' she kept saying. But I wouldn't have any of it." He shakes his head and gulps his tea. "About a week after I'd started, I was crying and asking her to take me out again." he sighs. "They all want to start school, and then you can't keep them there."

Mum throws him a look. "I liked school. But I did correspondence, which is very good—and that's what she'll be doing."

"Why didn't you like it?" I ask Arn.

"It's so long ago, I can't hardly remember. All I know is I didn't. You'll see."

"Well, what was it like?"

"Well, course you won't have no other kids to worry about—that's one good thing."

Mum nods. "Kids can be cruel."

"It wasn't just the kids." Arn pauses. "I didn't like being stuck inside all day. I wanted to be out working. And the teacher just about broke a cane on me a couple of times."

"Oh, some of those teachers are damn useless! Claude and Amelia didn't learn a thing the year they spent at Stewarts Brook School."

"Oh this bloke knew what he was on about, I reckon. He'd try and explain." He puts his cup down and scratches his head. "I left the first

190

chance I got. Went droving[1]."

He laughs. "Nah, nobody likes school."

Mum clears her throat. "I'm not sure it's a good idea for her to hear things like that, Arn."

"Eh? Oh. Yes. Yes, course that's so, Gwen." He takes another mouthful of tea, then says. "Truth is, many's the time I've wished I hadn't been such a stubborn little beggar. I dunno why I didn't like it, young lady. Course there was a lot of caning in them days, as I said." He looks at me. "Now, that's not something you'd have to worry about with your mother here teaching you. And the bigger kids were that mean... But that's another thing you won't have to worry about.

"When the droving was finished, I went to work for me uncle. He had a big dairy farm." He laughs. "Worst time of me life. Worked me like a dog, he did. Of a night, me whole body'd be aching. So tired, half the times I couldn't hardly finish me tea. And there wasn't much of that, either. I tell you, when I had to go out there and milk them cows at daylight on a frosty morning, I'd've been glad to be back in school, canings and all."

He sure changed his tune when he saw Mum didn't like what he was saying.

"Did you go back?" I ask.

"Go back? Where—to school? No. I couldn't. I'd got to be a man by then, see."

Nobody is going to turn me off school. "Well, I still want to start, anyway."

Mum frowns at me. "Don't be cheeky to Mr. Martin!"

When Dad comes home that night, Mum says, "That old Arn doesn't have much sense. He went on and on to Leila about hating school."

***

When the yellow envelope with my first set of lessons in it arrives, Mum shows me how to undo the brass clip that closes it. Inside, there's a thin book with a green cover—her favourite colour. "Look at the cover, Mum! It's a lovely green."

"That's the exercise book you'll be writing in."

Me—writing. I feel a little thrill.

---

[1]Cattle are usually taken to market by road transport these days, but in the past, they were driven in a mob by a person on horseback called a "drover," and this occupation was called "droving."

The first lines of the book have red writing on them. "'A very warm welcome to Blackfriars, Leila,"' Mum reads aloud. "'I am to be your first teacher, and I look forward to receiving your work. I know you will be a good pupil."'

Stamped on the same page, are purple outlines of a hen and an egg, the same size, and I wonder if they've ever seen a real hen and egg.

Then there's a wad of paper with printing on it. "'Instructions for the Supervisor,'" Mum reads in a sharp voice.

Amelia does her lessons in the kitchen, and after breakfast the next Monday, we clear off the loungeroom table so I can do mine there. I sit down, and Mum begins to read the instructions aloud, then trails off. "They must think a person's an idiot." She tells me to fill in the shapes of the hen and egg with slanted lines, and shows me the angle. "That's to get you ready to start writing," she says. "Your letters will have the same slope."

I finish the exercise in no time. Then she reads me a story about a dog that gets lost, but ends up doing an act in a circus. "I hope you kids get a chance to see a circus one day."

My first day of school is over too quickly. Outside, I notice dark red apples on a tree in the back yard, and pull one off and eat it. It's the nicest apple I've ever tasted, and when I tell Mum about it, she says it's a "Red Gravenstein."

As the weeks continue, if it's a sunny day, Mum reads the instructions aloud, and then goes and gardens. If she finds out she has to stay and teach me something new, she stands alongside my chair, staring outside, and says in a scratchy voice, "Look at that! Just look at that! A beautiful sunny day, and a person's stuck inside."

When I do something right, she kind of grunts, and sometimes she says, "That's good." But her voice always rises up at the end, as if she's surprised, or I could do better.

After a few months, I'm to do my first test, and the instructions say, "If you cheat, you cheat only yourself." She goes outside as usual, but I don't want to cheat—I want to see how well I can do. When the test comes back, the red writing tells me I've done well, and I'm pleased.

But after a while, I start making a lot of mistakes. When I have to write the same thing over and over, it's so boring that I tell my hand to keep doing it while my thoughts roam around, but my hand always forgets. Also, if Mum, Dad and Claude, and whoever else is working here, are inside because it's raining, say, there's a lot of talk, and sometimes they listen to the news on the wireless and people talking about the news as well, and I make even more mistakes. I'm not allowed to use an eraser—I'm supposed to cross out any mistake and write the correct thing above it.

Sometimes I make so many mistakes my lessons look really messy. Then Mum sighs and says, "Do try to be tidier. I don't know why you have so much trouble keeping your book neat. You should have seen mine—I hardly ever made a mistake. And I didn't need someone to help me all the time like you do, either."

She finds one of her old schoolbooks and shows it to me, and it's true—there's not one mistake. She reads aloud from her teacher's red writing. *Good work, Gwen! It's wonderful to have you for my pupil.* And she writes, *Love,* before she signs her name.

***

One day, I ask Mum to pass me the apricot jam. We always buy tins of IXL jam, and sit them on the table after we've opened them. She sighs. "You can reach it. You ought to be able to read enough to find it yourself by now." IXL is in big letters, but she points to the name, which is in small letters.

"But I've only just started school."

"Amelia could read all the labels *before* she started." *She pauses. " She used to read newspaper headlines, too, and the signs on the road to Scone.* You never make the least effort."

Though it's exciting to think of really being able to read, reading labels and road signs seems boring to me.

Chapter Thirty-two

A WHITE APHID IN A WHITE FLOWER

The nicest Mum's been to me for a while was on my seventh birthday when she came into our room, picked up one of my dresses from the floor and said in a soft voice, "I do wish you'd learn to be more tidy." Amelia made me a birthday cake with pink icing.

Dad is almost always really kind. One night, I wake crying in his arms as he carries me through the dark to to a huge crackling fire in the loungeroom, and sits with me on his lap in front of it. "You were crying in your sleep," he says. "You have an earache. I thought you might need warming up."

So this pain spiking through my head is an earache. He heard me and got up in the middle of the night, and made this fire just for me.

My head rests on his arm, which is curved around me like a surface root of one of the big trees we use for pillows on picnics. He asks which ear hurts, and moves my head carefully so that this earhole is at the top. He lifts a chipped enamel jug from the hearth. "This is warm castor oil; it'll make it better."

The first drops tickle, and I wriggle.

"Hold still, Pet."

A warm stream fills my earhole, a little bit spilling into my hair, and soon the pain stops.

Setting the jug down, he begins rocking, and making shooshing sounds, and as I start to drift back to sleep, points of light on the hairs of his arms become golden bubbles.

***

194

I get earaches quite often, and we all get a lot of colds. Mum says this is strange because we're so far from germy cities. Trevor thinks the germs come with the coastal mists, and he reckons that a teaspoon of sugar with a few drops of kerosene will stop them. Mum doesn't like the idea, but I take some, anyway, without telling her. It doesn't seem to make any difference, though.

When I get a cold, usually my throat gets so sore I can hardly talk, and then thick yellow stuff comes out of my nose and I have to cough it into my hanky. When I use up all the ones I have, Mum shows me how to make new ones by tearing square pieces off the old sheets we keep in a cupboard on the verandah.

On the wireless, people keep talking about kids who have a lot of colds needing to have their tonsils or adenoids—or both—out, and she decides to take Amelia and Claude to the doctor in Scone so they can be checked.

When the nurse calls, "Mrs. Wright," we all follow her into a room where the doctor with the yellow eyes—the same one I saw when I burned my foot at the rabbiting camp—sits. Mum has him look at Amelia and Claude, and he says they're OK. We're about to leave, when he nods towards me. "What about her?"

Mum smiles. "Her? Oh, *she's* alright."

"Nevertheless, I'll take a look in her throat, too."

He presses on my tongue with one of the flat wooden things like the one Mum used to use to put ointment on my foot after I burned it, shines a torch[1] into my mouth, squints, and asks me to say *Ahhh* a couple of times. He looks at Mum. "This child *does* need to have her tonsils out."

***

Mum gets me ready to go to the hospital in Scone. She tells me they'll give me *anesthetic* to put me to sleep for the operation, so I won't feel anything. "It smells awful, but it's good stuff," she says. "After that, there'll be nice nurses to look after you, and if you need something all you have to do is call, 'Nurse,' and one will come."

She and Dad take me to the hospital; she's to stay with her cousin, Jenny while I'm there, and before Dad leaves to go home, he says, "Remember that after the operation you can eat all the ice cream you want. It'll help your throat heal." He loves ice cream, and is so happy telling me this that I don't say I don't like it much.

---

[1] A flashlight.

A nurse in a white uniform with a winged hat puts me in a white bed in a big white room with a lot of other beds, all empty, and then Mum says she'd better get back to Jenny's. Leaving my two books on the table next to my bed, she kisses me, saying she'll be back the next day at 3 o'clock when the visiting hour begins. She makes sure I can read the time on the big clock on the wall at the end of the room.

I feel as if she's dragging part of me with her when she goes, and I have to tighten up my whole body and keep very still so as not to cry. But then, through the window, she reappears from behind shrubs shaped like big, green balls, sees me, and smiles and waves, and I feel alright again.

Early the next morning a nurse helps me into a white pyjamas and white cotton socks for the operation. I don't know why, but I'm shaking and I wet myself a bit. When the nurse notices, she's really kind. "Never mind," she says, "Don't worry about that," and she brings me clean pyjama pants. Then she helps me onto a bed with wheels.

The man who usually sweeps the floor comes in and says he's taking me to the theatre. He grins and gives the bed a shove, shouting, "Wheee!" as it spins around, making my tummy do a lovely whirly thing, and we both giggle.

In the operating theatre, the nurses and doctors all wear white masks over the bottom halves of their faces, but their eyes look at me kindly, like Auntie's, and their voices are soft. Above one of the masks are the yellow eyes of the doctor who's to do the operation. Then a man tells me he's going to put a mask over my face, and that, when he does, I'm to count to ten. I smell something strange and strong. "You can smell the anesthetic," he says. I only get to three.

Mum is by my bed when I wake in the room where I was before. My throat is the sorest it's ever been, and my tongue hurts too. Mum says they must have pressed on it with a spoon to keep me from swallowing it.

I tell her I only got to three with the counting. But I don't tell her something very interesting. I've seen lots of things die—blowflies, ants, spiders, rabbits, sheep and Midnight. Dad and Mum always say it's OK to kill things for food—and that killing them doesn't hurt them if it's quick. I know people die too—if a snake bites them, or they're very old; and when Dad goes to town and is late coming home, I'm frightened he's fallen over the edge of the Black Cutting and died. But when I woke up, I had the thought that dying must be like going under anesthetic. No pain. Sudden nothingness. That's all. And I'm not afraid of it any more.

Mum hands me a spoon and opens a screw-topped jar she's brought;

in it is something red that looks like thick blood mixed with white stuff. She looks surprised at my face. "It'll help your throat to get better. It's jelly and ice cream. You *like* jelly."

I don't want to eat it, but she keeps saying, "Jenny made it for you." *I like jelly but I don't want it all mixed up with ice cream like that.* But she's holding the spoon out with some in it and saying, "Please try some." I eat a spoonful or two, but the ice cream is all melted and it doesn't make my throat feel better at all.

In no time, the big clock shows it's four, and she has to leave again. She kisses me goodbye. "I know your throat's really sore now, but it'll be better soon."

I have the same feeling of being dragged out the door with her as I did before, but again she waves from the other side of the green ball bushes.

The nurses are always hurrying to somewhere else. But every time the man who took me to the theatre comes to clean the floor, he makes the bed spin round, and I giggle and feel happy. The wet floorboards smell like the ones on the verandah at home when they're washed, and afterwards, he spins the bed back into place, and we giggle some more.

One afternoon they put an old lady into the bed next to me; she smiles and says hello, and I'm pleased there's someone else in the room. But after this, she seems to get very sick, and sleeps all the time. That night, I'm woken by voices; people are around her bed behind a curtain and I can't see what's happening. In the morning, she's gone; and I'm the only one in the ward again. I think she died.

Everything is white except the floors—the nurses' uniforms, the walls, the sheets, the covers, and my pyjamas. When I see nurses walking by, I wave but they usually don't seem to notice. I'm as hard to see as a white aphid in a white flower. If I call, "Nurse," usually, they say "Hello," and keep going, as if something is pulling them. But one day one stops and stands there making little movements like a horse wanting to gallop off.

"What's the matter?" she asks.

"Nothing."

"Why don't you read one of your books?"

"I've read them."

"Oh." She goes away again.

Soon my throat isn't nearly as sore as it was, but the days are very long and there's nobody to talk to and nothing to do; I just want to go home. From the time I wake up, I watch the clock till its three, and, often, the hands seem stuck. Right at three, Mum walks in and stands alongside my bed like a flower. Once she's there, the hands of the clock race, and in no time she's gathering up her things and kissing me goodbye. Then I wait for her wave after she's passed the round bushes.

One day, she doesn't wave—or even look in my direction. I burst into tears, and a nurse does come to my bed. "What's the matter?" she asks, as if she really wants to know.

I can hardly believe someone is asking why I'm crying. It's hard to explain, but finally she understands; and she puts her arms around me. It feels nice, but funny because I don't know her. "It'll be alright, dear," she keeps saying. "Don't cry. Your mother loves you. She just forgot."

The next day, this same nurse stops Mum when she comes into the ward, and they keep glancing in my direction as she talks to her in a low voice. *She thinks Mum would want to know that I cried because she didn't wave. Is this the sort of thing mothers usually want to know?* I'm afraid *Mum* will think I'm acting like a baby; she might even get angry. I see her laugh, though, and hear her say, "Oh, for heaven's sake! Kids are funny." But the nurse's face stays serious as she talks to her some more. Mum doesn't forget to wave again.

Soon my parents take me home. Mum has been really nice to me, and didn't get cranky once while I was in hospital, and I think things will be better from now on.

On my first day home, she lets me stay in bed. But after a couple of days she's yelling as much as ever, and I can hardly believe I was silly enough to think she'd be different.

***

Early one spring morning, I'm in the front garden when I see a kookaburra dive down from a high limb and fly back up to where it was, with a snake about a foot long wriggling in its beak. It drops the snake, dives down, picks it up, and does the same thing several more times, then flies back up with the snake hanging long and still in its beak, and swallows it, after which it breaks into loud laughter. When I tell my mother what I saw, she says that kookaburras drop snakes like this to break their backs.

I love birds, and when my cousin Phil, Auntie's son, comes to stay, I notice a red breasted robin with wriggling worms in its beak and point it out to him. I overheard Mum mention that he's nearly twenty, so he talks mostly to my father and Claude, but he looks pleased, and tells me he'll teach me how to find birds' nests.

Figure 32.1: A kookaburra in the garden.

We watch the robin from a distance, and as soon as it flies off, we follow it, but not too close. It keeps stopping and peering at us as if it's wondering what we're doing and wishing we'd leave it alone. But it's not long before it flies straight to its nest—wanting to get back to its chicks and feed them, Phil says. We sit on the grass a little way away, hear them squawking, and watch them being fed. The babies are ugly, with no feathers, round heads and yellow beaks. Phil reminds me never to touch nests because if you do, the bird might abandon them—something I already knew from Mum.

After Phil has gone home, my mother and I are walking near the swamp, when a pair of plovers start diving at us; she says they must have a nest nearby. We search the ground underneath the spot where they seem the most agitated, and find a speckled egg in a little hollow out in the open.

Not long afterwards, my mother discovers a robin's nest with chicks in it in the rose trellis in the back garden. But, sadly, the next day, Mummy Cat presents us with the body of a grey female robin, and we notice that the mother bird is missing from the nest. We're all sad, and worried about the babies. Mum says we should watch to see if the father feeds them; she, Amelia and I take turns watching, and he does.

My mother says the next test will be whether he'll sit on the nest at night to keep them warm. As soon as it gets dark, we shine a flashlight on the nest and see the father sitting on a branch nearby, and when we check awhile later he's still in the same place.

My mother gets an idea: she makes a wad of cotton wool, and, using a pair of kitchen tongs, lays it carefully over the babies. When we check again before we go to bed, the "eiderdown" is still in place, and the next morning, it's on the ground, where the father has apparently thrown it.

So every night, we cover the chicks, and in the morning the eiderdown is on the ground. When the chicks are old enough, the father teaches them to fly.

Chapter Thirty-three

FOXES

We have many hens now and two roosters, one young and one old. The fowls roam around in the yard next to the house, and in what's called "the reserve" beyond our boundary fence, which is made of strands of wire only, and is easy to get through. The reserve is a piece of land set aside for drovers to let the cattle they're droving to market rest overnight. When a mob is coming along the road, we hear their sad bellows before we see them, and they're so tired they walk very slowly.

Locked in their coop,[1] or little house, at night so they'll be safe from foxes, the fowls sleep perched on long sticks that go from one side to the other. Also in the coop are wooden boxes lined with straw where the hens lay their eggs.

One morning, before he leaves to do his work, Dad says to Mum, "I was thinking we could have some chicken for tea. If we don't kill that old rooster soon, there'll be trouble between him and the young one."

"It'd be nice to have a bit of chicken," says Mum. "Alright, then—we'll have him for tea."

Later, she throws a handful of wheat on the ground and calls, "Here, chook, chook, chook," and they all come running. As they peck away, she sneaks up behind the old rooster, grabs him, and carries him upside down by his legs to the woodheap, his wings hanging away from his body and showing the secret white fluff underneath.

She lays his head on a log, and his golden eye looks up at her as if he's not afraid at all. But I can see her fumbling behind herself for the axe. Chop! It slices through his neck and into the log, his head, with its frill of orange feathers, and pink eyelids now covering his eyes, landing on the

---

[1] A cage or pen such as that in which fowls sleep at night, and where they may also lay their eggs.

chips. Mum struggles to keep hold of the bucking, headless body, and, once it's still, she twists a wire around the legs and hooks this onto the fence so that the body is upside down and the blood can drain out.

She shows us kids how to pluck a chicken. She puts the rooster's body in the round tub we used to bathe in, and, as she pours saucepans and kettles of hot water over it, an ugly smell rises up. She sniffs the air. "Thew! Wet feathers." Everyone helps pull the bigger feathers out by hand, but many little ones remain, and when we pull these out with tweezers, they have fat, grey ends. There are still many like hairs left, though. Making a gash in his flesh, she pushes her hand inside the body, and drags out the innards with squelching noises, and an even more horrible smell rises up. She shows us the liver and gizzard and saves these to cook, washing the bird inside and out with clean water. Lastly, she carries it outside, lights pieces of screwed up newspaper, and burns off the hair-like feathers, making another horrible smell.

But soon the house is full of the pleasant aroma of the bird baking. At tea, everyone keeps saying how wonderful the rooster tastes, and having second helpings, but the image of that trusting eye still in my mind, I eat only what's on my plate.

***

It's autumn, Dad doesn't have anybody working for him who needs to stay in the house, and Claude is again sleeping on the front verandah, instead of in the little back room, so I decide to sleep there. But alone in that room at night, after we've listened to "True Crimes from the Files of the New South Wales Police" on the wireless—often about bad men murdering people after they've broken into houses—the dogs start barking. My parents are still up, and I hear Mum say, "There must be a fox hanging around."

If the barking goes on too long, Dad stomps out to the back steps, and roars, "Peggy! Jock! Settle down or I'll come up there and beat the living daylights out of you!" I shrink down in my bed, and, the dogs, after a whimper or two, become silent. I know they don't understand what he's said, but I wish he wouldn't talk to them like that. In the daytime, they jump up on us, wanting us to pat them, but we hardly ever do. If we touch them, we have to wash our hands right away afterwards because our parents have told us over and over that if we don't, we'll catch a horrible disease they call Hydatids, which makes cysts grow everywhere inside your body and kills you. They say that the dogs get the germs from eating "offal"—the insides of the sheep we kill—but that we can't catch it from eating the meat.

Usually, long after I've fallen asleep, I'm woken by more barking, which goes on and on. Being so far from cities, we never lock the doors, and I imagine a man sneaking onto the verandah, stealing one of the rifles that hang on the outside of the door of the room I'm in, and shooting us all. And I think of a family like mine hearing what happened on *True Crimes*, long afterwards.

***

One morning, I notice that the low limbs of the Rainier apple trees, now with only a few apples here and there, are strangely reddish, and call Mum. She peers at the limbs, and the ground underneath, then points to something on the ground, like crumpled chamois leather encrusted with the wings of beetles and black seeds like little eyes. "Foxes," she says. "See the apple seeds in their jobby?" She pauses, and then adds, "These Rainiers have short trunks, so it's easy for them to climb up." And I notice that the reddish limbs are the low, thick ones that are level with the ground for some distance before they turn upwards. She looks around, and points to a recently falllen dead tree in a patch of red earth on the side of the hill, its roots looking like a giant, red spider. There, a faint red track begins, crosses the orchard and ends at the Rainiers. "The red on the limbs is from that dirt on their feet," she says.

But foxes eating apples? "They must be starving," I say.

"Starving! It's just that the damn things'll eat anything! There's nothing *poor* about them."

Then, as always, she says how "the English toffs brought them for their damn hunting," and today she adds that they "cleaned up the brolgas,[2]" which she says are big bluish birds that dance, and "were all over the mountain, once."

A week or so later, I'm woken by Mum's voice outside, "What on earth's happened, Joe?"

"Rotten bloody foxes have killed half the chooks!"

I dress quickly and hurry outside; Claude and Amelia are already there. Dad's arms dangle helplessly at his sides as he stares through the netting wall of the fowl house at the heaps of bloodied feathers on the hardened

---

[2] Also known as "native companions," large grey-blue birds and members of the crane family, found in Australia and New Guinea.

manure of the floor. "I can't understand why their squawking didn't wake a man up."

Mum's hands don't seem to know what to do. "Oh my poor hens," she keeps saying. "And where's the rooster?" she asks. But a little while later, we all hear the young rooster calling the hens because he's found something to eat.

Dad continues to examine the coop. "Reckon the mongrels found a little hole a bloke missed, and scratched and pushed till it was big enough to squirm through." He points to a bit of orange fur stuck at the edge of a hole in the netting below a rotted-off post. Then he goes up the hill and staggers back with a boulder, which shakes the ground as he lets it crash over the hole. Several other posts have rotted off, too, and he drops boulders over these places as well. "I'll have to build a new coop as soon as I get a chance. There's always something to torment a man!"

A couple of days later, I notice a shiny map-like thing edged with fur on the outside wall of the shed, and ask him what it is. "That's the skin of a fox I shot up on the hill yesterday."

Late that afternoon, when the trees on the hill across the swamp are half golden and half dark, Mum picks up a rifle, "I'm going out into the paddocks to see if I can find a fox to shoot," she says, and asks me to go with her.

An empty corn bag is draped over her shoulder. "It's time you learned about safety with guns," she says. "The first rule is, *never, ever* carry a loaded gun—always check to make certain there are no bullets in it before you set off." Pointing the barrel towards the sky, she clicks the trigger. "And even if you think it isn't loaded, like your father has told you, never, ever point a gun at another person. Or at anything you don't want to shoot, for that matter." I've heard all these things before, but it feels nice that she's teaching *me*.

When we get to the first fence, she doesn't climb through it right away. "You wouldn't believe how many people've been shot getting through fences, so watch how I do it." Laying the rifle on the ground with the barrel pointed away from us, she climbs through, then reaches between the wires and gets it, keeping the barrel pointing away.

I'm following her around the side of a hill when she stops and turns slowly, her forefinger over her lips, then nods slightly towards the field below. A fox's long tail and body is flowing over it. It looks as beautiful as the one we saw at the rabbiting place when we went around the traps. Silently, she puts a bullet in the rifle, and trains it on the fox. It stops, turns its head, and looks in our direction. A shot cracks and echoes away, the fox twists, leaps into the air, and falls.

I follow her as she hurries down the hill to where it's stretched out, it's head bent on its neck and blood trickling from its nose. But its side moves. "Mum, it's still alive."

The toe of her boot nuzzles the fur. "No, it's dead alright. That's just the breeze moving its fur."

She takes her pocket knife and slits the skin around each leg, and soon the blade is whisking through the glistening cobwebby stuff between skin and body. The fox smell, and thoughts of the beauty of the living animal make me feel sick, and I stumble over to some tussocks, and rub the dry straws between my palms till I feel better.

A strange, sucking sound makes me look again at what she's doing. Teeth clamped shut, she's gathered up in one hand the skin she's already cut free, and, gripping the body with the other, is pulling the skin off. When the body is naked, she hacks the skin off around the neck, making the black-tipped ears jiggle. She stuffs the skin into the corn bag, and heaves the body into some logs and ferns. "Something'll find it and eat it. Remember the crows when we were rabbiting? Not nearly as many here. But maybe a dingo will come by. Or another fox."

I walk home behind her, the bag moving on her back as if the live fox is inside. At the shed, she tacks the skin on the wall beside the other one.

Chapter Thirty-four

FISHING FOR SPIDERS

On a warm autumn afternoon, we set about harvesting the potatoes Dad has grown from the ones that didn't get the blight; the crop is small, but Trevor and old George lend a hand, and Uncle Bill, who's again visiting, keeps an eye on Laurence.

I'm walking along a furrow, the chocolate earth cool on my bare feet, when, a few yards away, Dad shouts, "Get off me!" I see him stamp and grind his boot, and then he looks closely at his hand. He leans down and stands up with something on a flat stick. "Reckon me hard old hands saved me," he calls, holding out the piece of wood. "Nasty little bugger of a spider tried to bite me."

We all go to him, and peer at a squashed spider about an inch across.

Claude says,. "Look at the size of its fangs!"

Trevor nods. "Quite a pair of hooks for a little bloke."

Stroking his moustache, old George says, "You've done a good job smashing him up, Joe. But I reckon he's the same as the ones I've seen around these parts for years. Usually a lot bigger, though. Never seen one this close before—or seen its fangs. Haven't heard of anyone being bitten, though."

"Nasty-looking customer," Uncle Bill says. "I'd steer clear of the likes of him in future, if I were you, Joe."

Dad frowns. "I'll be alright. But with your eyesight, Bill, you'd better not go poking around in the dirt with your fingers."

That night, Dad says in a serious voice, "I have something important to say to you kids. From now on, I want you all to make sure you wear shoes and socks when you're walking over any ground that's been dug up. Ten to one that spider was deadly. And you can be sure there are plenty more around."

Mum mentions the holes that are in the garden and paddocks—lined with web and about an inch across, which her father had suspected were the holes of nasty spiders, and she wonders if the one that tried to bite Dad was the same kind. In the days that follow, we walk around looking carefully at any spider holes we notice, sometimes catching a twinkle of disappearing legs.

Then one day, old George arrives with a Sydney newspaper in which there's an article about a spider called a "Sydney Funnel Web." A photograph shows one the size of a saucer, with fangs like curved daggers. "Looks like the same spider to me," he says.

"That big?" I ask.

Everyone laughs. "They show them that size to make the story more dramatic," Mum explains.

Dad studies the photograph and reads bits of the article aloud. "Kill you in fifteen minutes. No antidote. Only on Sydney's North Shore... Hmmm..." Everyone agrees that nobody would know whether the spiders were anywhere else or not. "Treat like a snake bite...[1]"

My parents have already taught us about snake bites, but Mum reads this part aloud, anyway. " 'Put a tourniquet on the arm or leg above the bite... You can use a shoelace.. or a belt... or tear a strip from your clothing... Twist it tight... Now wash where you've been bitten—with spit if there's no water... Don't suck the poison out—if you happen to have a hollow tooth, it could get into your bloodstream that way and kill you... Once you've washed the place where you've been bitten, scratch it to make it bleed... Release the tourniquet every twenty minutes... If you don't have a watch, count slowly.... '"

"A bloke can only hope the bite isn't on his head—I don't fancy a tourniquet round me neck," says Uncle Bill. "And they never say what you're supposed to do if it's on your body, either."

Mum continues, "Ah yes, 'Go to the nearest hospital.'" That being at least four hours away—if you don't get bogged or stopped by a flooded river—everyone laughs.

Dad and Claude decide to catch one of the spiders from the holes in the garden to send to the museum in Sydney so it can be identified, and we all gather to watch.

---

[1]This remote region treatment is no longer recommended for snake or spider bites; my research suggests that the preferred treatment is now the application of a pressure bandage and immobilization.

Trevor brings kitchen chairs from the house. He grins. "So these blokes've decided to go spider fishin'. Reckon I'll stick to trout." He and Uncle Bill sit close to where Laurence is playing on a patch of grass.

The picture from the newspaper article in her hand, Mum stands near the place where the holes are, and, next to her, Dad holds a wide jar filled with clear liquid. "Metho, to preserve the spider in," he says when I ask him what's in it.

"Methylated spirits," says Mum.

Claude arrives in shorts, and places a short, wide board on the ground.

Dad says loudly, "Like I said, Son, we'll have to dig to find them. The burrows'll go down yards."

Claude clears his throat. "Look, Dad. I see the spiders' legs poking out of these holes all the time. I tell you, the best way to catch them is to jiggle a straw in the entrance."

Dad gives a short laugh. "The spiders aren't sitting around near the top waiting for you to put them in metho for a trip to Sydney, you know."

Mum smiles at Claude. "You're probably right, Son. I've seen their legs poking out, too."

Claude says to Dad, "If we try to dig them up, we'll lose them in the dirt." He pauses. "Or damage them."

"Damage them? How in God's name would you damage them?"

"With all that dirt, we wouldn't be able to see what we were doing, that's how. They're no use to the museum damaged. Might as well..." He jerks his head to the side. "*throw them in the garbage.*"

"I'm telling you, you'll never find them if you don't dig." He looks from Claude to Mum, but seeing their hard looks, he shrugs. "Well, have it your way, then."

Mum looks pleadingly at Claude. "In case they *are* Funnel Webs, you want to be damn careful, Son."

"The chance they're funnel webs is ninety-nine to one," Claude says airily.

"Then jiggling a straw sounds too damn dangerous." She puts her arms around him and looks into his face, nodding her head as she speaks. "Fifteen minutes! I want a live son, not a dead one."

Claude turns red, laughs, and ducks out of her arms. "Tell you what, Mother. I'll get Leila to bring the axe."

"The axe?"

"So if one bites me, you can chop me leg off. Or me arm. Wherever I've been bit." He sways with see-saw laughter.

Smiling, Mum pretends to hit him. "You're a *bad son*! A person ought to give you a hiding!"

"Just relax, Mother. Coaxing them out with a straw is no more dangerous than digging. If it comes to that, I'd rather be able to see where they are than be scratching around in the dirt looking for them."

I hear Uncle Bill ask Trevor, his voice a squeak, "How does he reckon he's going to get them out?"

"He reckons they have that bad of a temper that if he jiggles a straw in the hole, they'll latch onto it, and he'll be able to haul them out. I'm not so sure meself." He shakes his head. "Used to catch crayfish that way when we were kids, though."

"Well, someone'd better keep the lorry warmed up in case we have to make a dash for the hospital."

Claude calls to them, "If I get bit—and I won't—I'll treat it meself, like a snake bite."

Uncle Bill raises an eyebrow. "Course there is the odd bloke who's no longer with us because he got bitten by a snake, despite tourniquets and all the rest of it."

"Probably didn't do it right," Claude says in a high voice. "There are a lot of stupid people."

Dad has walked over to the holes, and now points to little piles of red clay near them. "See that, Claude? That's come from way down in the subsoil."

"Maybe," Claude says. "But anyway, they hang around near the top. Let's get started. And if my method doesn't work, we'll try yours."

Dad shrugs.

Claude chooses a thick straw about ten inches long from a tussock, glances at Mum's worried face and gives a laugh. "Now Mother, I'll have one of them spiders out before you can say *fang*."

Mum clicks her tongue. "You be damn careful, Son."

Claude lays the board he brought next to one of the holes. "Keep the open jar of metho close," he tells Dad, "Give it to me when I nod, and be ready to hand me the lid." He squats, dark hair falling over half his face, and his left hand begins to jiggle the straw in the hole. Imagining the spider so close to his bare hand and leg, I shudder.

For a while, nothing happens. Bill and Trevor yawn, and Dad smiles to himself.

Then Claude says softly, "Got a bite." A big black spider appears, clinging to the straw, only to drop back into its hole.

Claude's hand keeps jiggling. "Biting again," he says. Again the spider appears and disappears. He keeps jiggling. The next time the spider emerges, he quickly but smoothly moves it on the straw a little way away from the hole. The spider drops to the ground, its dark body as big as a peach seed sticking up at an angle, and makes little jumping movements towards his bare leg. I hold my breath.

Mum's voice is low and trembly. "Careful, Son!"

"Yes, watch out for the mongrel!" Dad echoes. "Move your leg further away."

He doesn't, and the spider leaps an inch or two closer.

"Look out!" Dad says again.

Claude wriggles the straw in front of the creature's head till it grabs it again. He nods at Dad, takes the jar of metho with his free hand and brings it up behind the spider, then suddenly lets go of the straw, picks up the board, and sweeps the spider into the bottle. "Lid," he calls, grabs it from Dad and screws it on. "I could see the poison dripping from its fangs," he growls.

Mum peers at the spider in the jar. "My God!"

Claude holds the bottle up. With its legs, the spider is perhaps three inches across, and still very much alive, it dashes back and forth in the metho, and tries to climb the glass sides, but he keeps knocking the jar to make it fall back in.

The spider's movements get clumsier and smaller, and part of me feels sad for it. Soon, it becomes still, except for spasms, and when these stop, it floats to the top of the liquid. Stretched-out, it's as wide as my hand, and the liquid outlines its legs and body in silver, making it it look like a weird Christmas tree decoration.

Everyone stands up and stretches in the sunshine, but Claude continues to stare at the spider in the bottle, his nose almost on the glass. "Look at those fangs!" he keeps saying. When I happen to be near him, he suddenly shoves the bottle towards my face, making me jump back. He laughs. "What's the matter? One thing's for sure—this spider ain't bitin' no one no more."

Taking the newspaper article from Mum, he compares picture with spider. "Spittin' image," he says, handing jar and picture to Dad.

Dad compares them. "You're right. If it wasn't for me hard old hands, I *would* be dead." He looks around at us. "My God—and you kids walking around with bare feet!"

Jar and picture get passed around. Next to me, Trevor looks and pulls

Figure 34.1: About twice its normal size—the body of the living spider being up to two inches long— one of the several species of funnel web spiders, Atrax robustus, the most deadly spider in the world.

a face, then goes to hand the jar to me, but I can't bear to touch the glass with the spider inside, and get him to hold it while I look. The fangs are like the sharp horns of a tiny cow, but point downwards.

"Fangs are hollow," Mum explains. "The poison flows through them, from sacs." She turns to Claude and hugs him. "I'm glad that's over, Son. I didn't like it being so close to your hand and leg."

His face goes red, and he again escapes from her arms. He rubs his hands together "Well, we've still got one or two more to get."

Mum's eyes widen. "Son, don't you think capturing one of the dangerous damn things is enough?"

"Course one isn't enough. The museum'll want both a male and female."

Dad says, "You're right, Son. But first I think we need a cuppa tea."

Claude puts the jar among the cakes and bread and biscuits on the table, but as we drink and eat, he picks it up three or four more times, comparing the spider to the picture, and repeating, "Spittin' image." Then he says, "Actually, there's no need to send it to the museum. It's a Funnel Web, alright. *Only on Sydney's North Shore!* They know *nothing* about anything outside that damn city."

"Well, let's see what the museum people have to say, anyway," Dad says firmly. "We need to be certain. Only problem is finding someone to take it down to Sydney. Can't send it in the mail."

I'm remembering walking in the furrows. *The feel of the dirt under my feet... The spider biting... like being stung by a bee, but a thousand times worse. And worse than when I stepped in the boiling water. Violent spasms. Bigger and bigger... Then... nothing.*

"What'll I do if they are funnel webs, Son?" Mum groans. "The garden's full of their holes."

"No need to worry, Mother."

"But how'll I get rid of the damn things? I can't have a garden full of deadly spiders!"

"Easy," he says. "Boil the kettle, and pour the water down the holes."

Dad stands up. "We'd better get back at it if we're going to catch some more."

Mum goes back outside with everyone else, leaving Amelia and me to clear up. We want the spider off the table, but neither of us can bear to touch the jar. She uses the oven cloth to carry it into the loungeroom, putting it on a shelf far from where people sit.

It's nearly dark by the time they bring in two more spiders in jars—smaller, and females, they think. They demand to know where the first one is, and sit all three jars in a row on the loungeroom table. I'm glad when Mum wraps the jars up, and packs them in a box with a letter to the museum.

A week or so later, some people call in on their way back to Sydney after a camping trip, and, in exchange for a box of apples, agree to deliver the parcel for us. Eventually, a letter arrives from the museum telling us that the spiders are close relatives of Funnel Webs, and just as deadly. They mention that, at night, Funnel Webs leave their holes and crawl on the ground, and that these ones also probably do this. We never have walked barefoot at night—it's usually too cold—but now we'll be sure not to. Funnel Webs also crawl into houses without steps, they mention, but our place has front and back steps so we don't think this will be a problem.

Mum takes Claude's advice, and pours boiling water down the holes, but new ones keep appearing, as they do when she tries to get rid of them by digging and squashing them. But now that we know more or less how to protect ourselves from them, they no longer worry us much.

Chapter Thirty-five

THE SHIRT TAIL

When I'm eight, Mum sees an ad for a circus in the local paper. "It's Riccolo's, and Dad always said their circuses are the best." She looks around at us. "I'd like to take you kids."

"Joe? Riccolo's circus is coming to Scone," she says to my father. "We should take the kids."

"There's not a lot of money to spare at the moment, and it would probably be dear."

"It might be a bit dear, Mum says. "But they've never been to a circus. And I haven't been for years."

"But it probably wouldn't finish till all hours, and I don't fancy driving up the mountain at midnight."

Mum thinks for a moment, and then brightens. "We could stay in town with Elaine and Henry—Elaine said we could in her letter, remember? They've got plenty of room, she told me." They're friends of my parents I've never met who've just moved to Scone.

"Well, I suppose it'd be alright if we could stay with them."

Mum phones Elaine, who says they'd love to have us. And so it's decided.

We set off in the lorry, Laurence on Mum's lap, and Claude, Amelia and I take turns riding in the front. Dad has laid corn bags on the back to sit on, but we like standing up and holding onto the boards behind the cab.

At the edge of Scone, Claude points to a strange light brown hill thing. "The big top!" he yells. And when I ask, "What?" he says, "The circus tent."

I'd thought of the tent they kept talking about as smaller and white like our rabbiting tents, but this one's three times bigger than our house.

Elaine is plump and smiley, with long, blond hair, and Henry, thin and dark. "How about a rum, Joe?" he asks, and the two of them go to the kitchen, while the rest of us drink tea in the sitting room.

When it's time to go to the circus, we leave Laurence with Elaine, and the rest of us set off. The tent in the distance, we hear music and smell the animals. We stop at a lion's cage, and Mum looks angry and sad. "Just look at the size of the cage that poor animal's in! It can hardly turn round," she says. "They ought to be shot!"

Wanting to see the lion better, I start to move closer, but Dad grabs my shoulder and stops me. "Stay here!" he orders. "It's not safe."

"But it's in a cage."

"It don't matter." He turns to Mum. "Trevor was telling me that McInnes fullah got it all over him. *Nice cat, nice cat,* he was saying. *Nice cat* let him have it!" He screws up his face, and makes wiping movements over his jacket.

Mum sounds tired. "That's enough Joe! Let's just keep going."

He doesn't stop. "Dripping all down his front, Trevor reckons. His best suit—had to throw it away."

"Throw it away? Why couldn't they clean it?"

"You'd never get the smell out."

After we set off again, I'm still trying to understand just what he was talking about when we hear loud plinkety-plonk music, and children clinging to white pretend horses swing way out in the air.

Dad leans down and looks into my face. "Would you like a ride on the merry-go-round?"

"Merry-go - ?"

He points. "That's what it's called."

I nod.

When the horses stop, I almost get knocked down by the crowd of kids getting off, but then he lifts me onto a horse. Faster and faster it goes till I'm flying way out, everything blurring past, and I have to lie down with my arms squeezed tight round the horse's neck so I don't fall off.

I'm glad when it stops and Dad lifts me down. Things are spinning, and I almost fall over, but his arm is around me. "Did you like that?" he asks, and I nod.

As we continue walking, things flash and glitter everywhere, men with leathery faces call out, and I think I hear my name.

Mum looks at me. "You? Why on earth would they be calling you?"

Inside huts, people play games for prizes. In one, you have to get a ball in the mouth of a clown—there's a row of clown's heads, turning half way round and back again. In another, you have to shoot, with pretend guns, cut-outs of rabbits and foxes moving across a screen. Claude tries both, but doesn't win anything.

"Don't worry, Son. It's all rigged," Dad says.

Near a stall where a woman is selling fairy dolls on long sticks, Dad sees a friend, Frank, goes over and talks briefly with him. I ask Mum if I can have a doll, but she says they're too dear.

Finally, the tent is towering into the sky above us, and we find our seats inside; the crowd is full of children making more noise than Mr. Rose's cages of birds, and women's brooches sparkle back and forth as if they're signaling one another. The big space in the centre is the ring, Mum says.

A man in a tall hat appears, and the crowd falls silent, except for a few little children. "The Ringmaster," Mum whispers. He bows, welcomes everyone, then says, "Many of the acts you will see here tonight have never been attempted before."

First, elephants lumber in, and the Ringmaster makes them sit down on their bottoms, their front legs bent, and women in glittering costumes come and sit against their tummies, as if they're huge armchairs. Then the women jump up and stand in a circle, and the elephants walk around them, the trunk of each hanging onto the tail of the one in front.

Groans and giggles come from the crowd, and then I see, swinging from side to side below one of the elephants, a tap thing like the bull has, only huge. I'm glad when they all leave the tent.

After a sprinkling of clapping, I hear Mum say irritably, "Why do you have to leave now? We came to see the circus."

"Well, I promised Frank I'd have a drink with him," Dad mumbles.

"But how will I find you when it's over? I don't want to have to walk back to Elaine's with the kids on my own."

"I told you—I'll meet you outside the tent. And if we miss each other, you turn left outside the gates, then right, and—"

"Left and then right—what use is that?" She's searching through her handbag. "Did I give the address to you?"

"I don't think so." He searches his pockets, but then Mum finds it.

The Ringmaster has appeared again and people nearby start shushing us. "If you're goin' mate, for Gawd's sake go," a man behind us says.

Dad stands up, swings round, and stares at him.

The man shrinks down. "Sorry, mate, no worries."

Dad turns back to Mum, who whispers something to him.

"Promised, didn't I?" he says. "Christ, can't you ever trust a man!" He jambs his hat on his head, pushes past the other people in the row and goes down the steps and out the door.

A woman in a glittering costume stands next to the Ringmaster. "Ladies and Gentlemen," he says, "the act you are about to see has never been performed until now, and I ask you to cooperate by being *completely silent. Any sound whatsoever* could put the performers at grave risk."

"But Mum," I whisper. "What about the little kids? They won't keep quiet!"

She shushes me.

One might squawk at any moment! I'm glad Laurence isn't here. My toes scrunch up.

"Mum? They've forgotten about the little kids!" I whisper.

"Shhhhh. It'll be alright," she whispers back.

The lions are in the ring now, and the Ringmaster makes the first one stand on its hind legs. As the woman walks towards it, it swipes at the air. The Ringmaster cracks his whip, and it becomes still again. The woman shakes one of its paws, and then shakes a paw of each of the others. Halfway through, somebody coughs; I take a big breath in, but the lions don't seem to have heard. Then a child cries out, but, again, nothing terrible happens. At the end, the people clap so hard it sounds like hail on our iron roof.

The clowns in their bright, baggy trousers and pompoms are my favourite act. One, pretending to be a customer, gives his clothes to another pretending to be a laundry man, who washes the clothes in a machine. But they shrink to the size of dolls' clothes, making the *customer* so angry that he pushes the *laundry man* into the machine and turns it on. When he opens the door, out tumbles a dwarf! Everyone claps like mad, and there's yelling and whistling.

I wish the circus would never end, but it does. Everyone tries to leave at the same time and it takes quite a while to get down the steps and outside. We can't see Dad anywhere, but I feel so happy I don't care. Mum keeps saying, "I knew this would happen." The crowd around us thins, and she looks at her watch. "I guess we ought to go to the main gates and see if he's there."

We haven't gone far when we spot him ahead of us, standing up very straight, arms folded. Now I walk alongside of him, with Mum, Claude and Amelia on his other side. But a few moments later, only Dad is next to me. I tug at his sleeve. "Where are Mum and them?"

"Don't worry—we'll meet them back at Elaine's," he calls down to me, in an odd voice.

For a while, the crowd is so thick we creep along. When we start moving faster, I glance up, but instead of Dad's face, I see a stranger's! I search all around, but can't see him. The crowd is now so thick that I'm in the dark among the strange skirts and trousers, handbags hitting my head. My chest aches till I think I'll burst. Then the crowd moves off fast and my feet hardly touch the ground.

A long time later, a space opens up around me, and I stop. Squinting against the glare of the floodlights on high poles near the exit gates, I search in front of me, then turn and look behind, and to the sides. The space around me grows. Not far ahead, people are going out the gates. *To their warm homes.* I'm shivering. I don't know where Elaine and Henry's house is. Soon, I'll be all alone. I remember Mum telling me, *If you're ever lost in a town, find a policeman.* I look around, but can't see one. *Where do I find one? I wish Mum hadn't stopped Dad telling her how to get to Elaine's.*

Everything's wobbling, and a see-saw wail starts coming out of me. *What'll I do when everyone else has gone?* A warning from Mum, *"Never go anywhere with a stranger."* So I can't ask anyone to help me. I have to keep looking for Dad. The crowd closes around me again. I wait. When there's enough space, I peer at the silhouettes up ahead.

A broad-brimmed hat, above the crowd. It's him!

And through me surges a river of love for him. Huge. Bigger than even my love for Auntie. I fight past the people and handbags till he's walking right in front of me, though he doesn't know I'm behind him. I try to will my arms to stretch so they can reach him. And then I yell, "D-a-d!"

People stare at me. *I sound like a baby.* He keeps walking. I call again, louder. He stops, twists around, sees me. Waits. When I'm nearly there, he points to his blue shirt-tail, which is hanging out. "Grab onto that and hang on for your life," he says in a thick voice.

I take it in both hands, and love flows through me, down my arms and through the shirt to him. Making our way like this, soon we're through the gates and on the street. Now I'm one of the people going to a warm place. But people give us peculiar looks, and I feel silly hanging onto his shirt. I wish he'd stop and let me walk beside him, but he just keeps striding along, sometimes wobbling a bit. *I have to hang on, or I might lose him again.* Soon we, and our peculiar shadow, are the only things moving along the footpath.

When he knocks on Elaine and Henry's door, it flies open, and Mum stands there, glaring. "What on earth took you so long?"

"Oh, well..." he says, as we go into the sitting room. Henry steps forward. "How about a drink, Joe?"

"He's had more than enough already," Mum snaps, but Dad turns to Henry. "That'd be good, mate. Thanks." And again they go to the kitchen together.

Mum says quietly, "I'm sorry he's got himself into such a state, Elaine."

"Look, Gwen, everyone has to let off steam once in a while. Don't give it another thought. Henry and I aren't upset. He's home now, and everything'll be just fine." She pauses. "How about a cup of tea?"

"Mum smiles. "That would be nice."

Elaine goes to the kitchen to get it, and Dad comes back with his drink.

"Fine promises you make!" Mum says in a low voice.

I wish she'd stop. I want to keep feeling the love for him.

"Fancy coming back to Elaine's in that condition! You went back to the bar after you left us, didn't you?"

"No. Leila got lost."

"*Lost?* What do you mean? How?"

"One minute she was alongside of me, and the next she was gone."

"Well, if you hadn't been half sozzled... Anything could've happened to her." She turns to me. "And how come you didn't stay with your father?"

I try to explain, but can't, and stare at the leaves on the carpet.

"If you don't learn to keep your wits about you, something really bad'll happen to you one of these days."

If only the leaves would cover me up...

***

Even though it ended badly, the excitement of the circus stays with us, and we all talk about it for weeks—everyone except Dad, that is. He tries to join in one day when we're arguing about one of the acts. But Mum looks him in the eye. "How would you know? You weren't there." He looks down, then turns and drifts out of the house.

Chapter Thirty-six

MISSING PAGES

These days, Amelia does her lessons at a desk in our bedroom, so I use the kitchen table. Usually, I don't find Arithmetic hard, but one day I don't understand how to do a new exercise. Mum tries to explain, and then starts demanding the answers to the exercises. She grabs the strap from it's nail by the stove, raises it in the air ready to hit me, and eyes like glass, yells through clenched teeth, "What's the answer?" I can't think, and blurt out the first number that comes into my head. It's wrong, and she belts me.

Soon after this, the whole school thing begins to go wrong. The teacher starts writing more and more angry comments in my book, until I begin to dread receiving the corrected lessons back.

In the beginning, school was boring, but so easy that I finished everything by midday. But now, half-way through second class, the work is still boring, but I'm at it all day. At first, the teacher used to write things like, "Not your best work, Leila. Please strive to improve." or, "Strive"— she seems to love that word—"to do better next time." Then one day, a set comes back with one-word comments like, "Untidy!!" and "Messy!! I think of exclamation marks as frown marks. Mum slams the book on the table. "I've had about enough of this," she shouts. "You're nothing but a lazy little mongrel! If you don't pull your socks up, you'll get a taste of the horsewhip."

Today I have to copy "Quick" and "Fox" in running writing, over and over. Mum explains that to make perfect letters you hardly let the pencil touch the paper on the upstrokes, and press it down hard on the downstrokes. Capital Q is one of my favourite letters; it's like a big "two" except it starts with a dot, and the capital F is another one I really like—it starts with a wavy line that's the same as the smoke I draw coming out of a chimney. The first words I write look good, and the next ones even better. Many lines wait to be filled, and I sharpen my pencil, and look at my hand, willing it to keep writing properly while I think about more interesting things. I glance around the room. Sunlight comes through the holes in the blind for the strings. *A beautiful glowing yellow, it looks solid. Like the butter icing shells on the cakes in the food tent at rodeos. Or the white hot metal I saw once in the blacksmith's shop in Gundy. The CLINK, CLINK, CLINK as he hit it... the metal going from white to red, to black.* I glance back at my writing. *Oh no! more mistakes!*

Practicing! Practicing! Always practicing. I hate practicing. Mustn't use an eraser. Have to draw a line through the mistake and write the correct word above. Before I had an eraser, Mum would give me a bit of bread to rub things out with... I could use bread—it's not a real eraser. I get some from the middle of the freshest loaf we have. Ugh! A smudge of dough on the page. Start again. This time, focus on the writing. But more and more mistakes happen.

When this set of lessons comes back, my mother reads aloud a note to her from the teacher. "For some time, now, Leila has been returning work of an unsatisfactory quality. It shows a careless and slovenly attitude, and I am very disappointed in her. If she is to obtain a passing grade this year, she will have to make a real effort to keep her book neat and tidy."

Mum stamps her foot and slams the book on the table. "What stops you from keeping your book tidy?"

"I try to."

"Try? If you *tried* the book would *be* tidy. *You're not trying.* That's the problem. I always kept *my* book perfectly neat. You're lazy. You never do anything properly. You're bloody useless."

She disappears, rushes back with one of her switches. Yells a word with every hit. "From-now-on-you-will-keep-your-bloody-book-tidy! That's-an-order!"

One day, after I've made many mistakes, I notice that the pages of the book I write in are held together by large staples, and get the idea of tearing the page out. But it's joined to another page in the other half of the book, so I'd have to take that one out, too. I turn the pages back and forth, looking at the horrible mistakes and wondering if I should do it.

I don't know why I have to write in a stupid book, anyway. Amelia, who's in high school, uses loose pages.

I tear the page and its other half out, and then—cleverly—notice and remove the little three-cornered pieces of paper caught in the staples. I'm pleased with myself. *If they'd seen those...* I think of keeping the clean page to draw on, but, wisely, decide to burn it with the used one, in the stove.

By the end of the day, I've removed several pages. But my book is clean and neat, and when Mum sees it, her eyes widen. "I told you you could keep your book tidy if you tried."

Every day, I remove more pages. And when the yellow packet arrives back in the mail, Mum reads comments to me like, "Well done!" and "Splendid!" That's another word teachers seem to love. And at the end of this set of lessons, the teacher writes, "Congratulations, Leila. This is excellent work. I knew that you could do it!"

As we read these comments, Mum looks as pleased as I begin to feel, and I almost believe I'm on my way to being a star pupil.

But one day when I go to remove yet another messy page, I find that I can't—it's attached to one I've already written on, and the teacher would notice. I sit there wondering what to do, all the nice things she's said swirling around me. Then I start believing that, somehow, I really have learned to keep my book tidy, and that I'll make no more mistakes. But it's not long before I make another one, and soon the pages I've just completed look as bad as they used to. But luckily Mum doesn't check my book, and it goes off without her knowing.

I don't have to think about the set of lessons coming back for two whole weeks, so I concentrate on doing the next set well. It ends up like the ones before I started removing the pages, though, and on the day I expect the terrible set of lessons back—I drag myself around feeling awful, and make more mistakes than ever.

Then I have to do a drawing of "The Place Where I Live." It goes well and is almost finished when Mum stamps into the kitchen. "Get that table cleared," she snaps. "The men need their afternoon tea."

Now she says "the men" when she's talking about only Claude and Dad; before, she used it only for Dad and Trevor or Old George or James or Dave. I'll just finish my drawing—it'll only take a few minutes.

She fills the kettle and puts it on the stove, opens the firebox, pokes at the fire, and hurries outside to get more wood.

I'm still working on the drawing when she comes back into the room, glances at me, and leaves again. Dad comes into the kitchen, and is checking that the kettle has been filled when she comes back, drags my chair with me on it out from the table, and beats me. "When-I-tell-you-to-get-the-bloody-table-cleared-it-means NOW!"

I screech and jump with pain as the switch bites into my legs.

"That'll-teach-you-to-be-disobedient!" She leaves the room again.

My legs crisscrossed and stinging, I cry as I try to gather up my things. Books and leaflets slip onto the floor as I move them to the sideboard, and I have to squat to pick them up.

A part of me watches Dad calmly rinsing out the teapot, adding tea leaves, pouring in boiling water. He opens a cupboard door, and puts the tin of biscuits on the table without even looking in my direction, his face calm and smooth. He's only ever hit me once, and is mostly sweet and kind, but I'm remembering Auntie telling me to run to him if Mum ever tried to beat me again like she did that day, though I also remember him and Mum agreeing that parents must back each other up when it comes to "discipline." I decide to test him.

Just loud enough for him to hear, I say, "Mongrel."

He spins around. Spits out, "What did you just say?"

"I... "

He glares. "Don't lie because I heard you. When your mother comes back in that door, you're going to apologize to her!"

I don't want to. Why should I? "But she hit me."

His voice booms, "Don't talk back to me."

Just then, Mum walks back in.

"Now, tell her what I told you to say." In answer to her questioning look, he says, "She swore at you."

I look down. Wait a moment. *I have to do it.* His huge hand grabs my shoulder. "Say it! Apologize to your mother. Or do you want another hiding?"

"I apologize," I murmur.

"Louder."

"I apologize," I say clearly.

They go back to getting afternoon tea ready.

When Claude comes in with the bag of mail and tips everything on the sideboard, I don't even think of the yellow envelope till it lands. Hands reach out and take things, and I find it and open it slowly.

Red writing covers half a page.

Just then, Mum happens to pass behind my chair. "What's this?" She grabs the book and reads aloud what the teacher has written.

"Dear Mrs. Wright, As I began to correct this set of Leila's work, I was disappointed to find that her recent improvement had not been maintained. Then, I couldn't help noticing how thin her workbook seemed.

Upon counting the pages, I discovered that over twenty pages are missing. This is a very serious matter, and I expect that, as her Supervisor, you will want to bring up the question of these missing pages with her without delay, as well as the continuing poor quality of her work. Thank you for your attention to this matter."

She reads the note and then stares at me, wild-eyed. "What do you have to say for yourself?"

I'm silent.

"What happened to the pages?"

I don't know what to say, but it comes out bit by bit, with long pauses, until she understands. Not seeming to know what to do or say, she sits down and doesn't move, looking sad and angry at the same time.

For the rest of the day, everything seems kind of dark, and she pays little attention to me as I do my school work. I feel very bad, but I still don't think it's fair that I have to write in a book so they can see every mistake I make. *When I start high school, I'll be allowed to use loose pages like Amelia, and I'll be able to throw pages away if I need to. I can't wait.*

When the next set of lessons is ready to be sent off, Mum writes a letter to the teacher, and reads it to me.

"Leila has been a problem from the beginning of her life. The difficulty is in many areas besides her school work. I am sorry for what has happened. I cannot imagine what she could have been thinking. She seems to be going through a particularly difficult stage at present. However, I shall endeavour to make sure she presents better work in the future."

"A problem from the beginning of her life." That really hurts. I don't understand why she thinks that. The teacher will see me as weird now, like the puppy that was born with part of its innards hanging out. That Dad killed by bashing it with a shovel.

Nevertheless, as time goes on, things begin to change for the better. I want to show Mum and the teacher that I'm not as useless and stupid as they think. And the good thing is that most of the boring copying gradually ends, and, as well, the things I have to read for school become more interesting. I start writing compositions, which I love doing, and making more paintings and drawings, and I get high marks and praise for these. My book starts to look tidier, though Mum doesn't notice; she seems fed up with the whole supervising thing. But more positive comments start coming back from the teacher.

Chapter Thirty-seven

TOOTS

We're half way up the mountain on our way back from Scone late one afternoon, with Claude and Amelia riding on the back of the lorry, when we see kangaroos bounding around the side of the hill above us. Claude bangs on the roof, and jumps down as soon as Dad stops. "I'll see if I can get a roo for the dogs," he says, grabbing the rifle from behind the seat and hurrying up the hill.

The rest of us get out and wander around near the lorry, me with the horrible feeling that always comes when some poor animal is to be killed.

A shot echoes, and the next thing, I see Claude coming back. But why is he carrying an armful of sticks?

"Wait till you see what I've got," he calls.

The sticks are thin grey legs, a long grey tail, dark feet and paws, and, in the middle, a dear little animal face, wide-eyed, nose twitching.

Claude sounds sorry. "I shot the mother. Didn't know she had a joey[1] in her pouch."

At least he hasn't brought her back for the dogs.

Mum's face shines as she takes the little animal in her arms, and then we're all smiling and stroking him. She holds him on her lap as we continue home, Laurence and I stroking him.

As soon as we get to the house, we find one of Laurence's old baby bottles, and warm up milk. He drinks two full bottles.

Dad says he's going to make a pouch for the little fellow to sleep in. He finds a corn bag, cuts it into pieces and stitches them together using a packing needle and string. "Do you know," he says, "when he was born, he was only as big as a peanut?"

---

[1] A baby kangaroo.

I can hardly believe it. *"A peanut?"*

"Yeah. Well, the size of a shell with peanuts in it. He had to crawl up his mother's fur all by himself, and find his way into the pocket at the front of her body. That's where the teat is, so maybe the smell of her milk guided him."

He hangs the completed pouch from a nail in a post on the back verandah. When it's time for Toots to go to bed, we carry him to the pouch and stand him in front of it. He sniffs it, puts his head inside, raises himself onto his tip-toes, jumps, somersaults, and ends up in the pouch on his back, his legs on either side of his head. We close the back door to keep him safe.

He's asleep in the same position when we take him a bottle of milk the next morning. He wakes, nose twitching, and makes a soft, stuttering t-t-t-t sound. We've never heard the sound a kangaroo makes before. Amelia says it sounds like "t-o-o-t-s," and that's what we decide to call him.

He quickly learns his name, answers with the same sound when we call him, and comes to where we are.

**

We love Toots, but he develops his first bad habit—eating paper. Mum says maybe it tastes like dry grass. At the table doing my lessons one day, I finish the first of several Arithmetic exercises on a loose sheet, and look for the sheet to do the next one. A rustling and tearing of paper makes me look under the table, and there sits Toots, chewing, the sheet at his feet with a bite out of it. Arithmetic being my least favourite subject, instead of rescuing what's left of the sheet, I tear it up and feed it all to him. When Mum comes to check on what I'm doing, she asks why I've done only one exercise, so I tell her the truth—that Toots ate the paper with the other exercises on it.

"How come you left the sheet where he could get at it?" she snaps, and tells me I'd better write a note to the teacher.

I write, "I can't do all my sums because the kangaroo ate the numbers."

When this set of lessons comes back a couple of weeks later, the red writing says, "Naughty girl for making up stories." Then I realize how what I wrote must have seemed to a teacher in Sydney who doesn't know that pet kangaroos eat paper. I show the note to Mum, who writes saying I've told the truth. And I have... except for a little whispery bit.

Figure 37.1: Amelia with Toots the Kangaroo and Blacky the cat.

One day after we've had Toots for a few weeks, Dad says he's going to start building a new fowl house, adding that, if he doesn't do it soon, the foxes will get in again. He digs the holes for the posts not far from the coop we have now, then takes the lorry up into the bush, and comes back with a load of posts he throws into a pile near the holes. The next morning, he and Claude go to town to get a roll of netting so they can finish the job.

After Toots has had his bottle, as usual, we let him out to hop around the big yard near our house until it's time for his evening meal. Later, we notice a family picnicking in the reserve next to our place not far from our fence. Around mid-afternoon, Amelia and I see Toots near them but on our side, with two children talking to him. We go up, and find them trying to feed him sugar cubes.

"He only eats milk and grass and things," I say. "Sugar's bad for his teeth."

They throw the cubes away, and ask what sort of animal he is. I can hardly believe that they don't know, and we tell them. They wish they had a pet like him, they say. When we leave, we call Toots, and he follows us back to the house, where we leave him when we go inside. Later on, I notice the family packing up and leaving.

Just before dark, I call Toots for his milk, but he doesn't come. I tell Mum and Amelia, and we decide that he must be too far away to hear, so the three of us walk through the outside yards and orchard, calling, every few minutes, "Toots. Too-oots" as loudly as we can, and listening for his answering "T-t-t-t-t." We even search behind the bales of hay in the shed, in case he went in there when the door was open and got locked in.

Outside again, we look around the kennels, and ask Ben the dog if he knows what's happened to Toots; he's been known to chase kangaroos, but we'd thought he'd accepted Toots as part of our family. He flattens himself out, slaps his tail on the ground, and looks up at us with big, sad eyes. We pass the chicken coop, and, nearby, the post holes and pile of posts. Then we search in the reserve, in case he got through the fence.

When Dad and Claude get home, they're sad to hear that Toots is missing. As we eat tea, I keep thinking of the poor little fellow outside somewhere, hungry and frightened. And several times, I get a flash of him in the corner where he usually stands, dark paws hanging at his sides.

"I hope those people that were in the reserve didn't take him," Mum says. "I'd hate to think of him going to live in a city."

It's dark when we finish dinner, and Amelia and I take torches to look for him again. The sight of his pouch as we cross the verandah makes me feel like crying. Round and round the yard we go again, calling and calling, and when we come to the pile of posts, we both sit down on them and cry.

That's when I think I hear his "T-t-t-t-t," and Amelia thinks she hears it, too. We both sit up and listen. Nothing. We stand up and call him. And then we hear his little stuttering sound clearly. Close. We shine our torches all around. And suddenly we both know where he must be, and run to the post holes. And there he is, in one of them! He's on his back, stuck and unable to move, his little face sad and frightened.

We kneel down and reach in. He's jammed in there so tightly, it's hard to squeeze our hands past his body to ease him out, but finally we manage to. He's shivering, and I cuddle him close to warm him up. He's so hungry he sucks at my fingers as I carry him home.

When we take him inside, everyone comes over smiling, and we all stroke him and talk to him as we wrap him in a blanket, and warm up milk. Like when we first brought him home, he drinks two full bottles.

***

Toots grows big, stops having his bottle, and eats mainly grass. But he develops his second—and worst—habit. One washday I catch him attacking Mum's long, white petticoat as it's drying on the clothesline, and chase him away; but his claws have already left several rips in it.

Mum is almost in tears. "My poor petticoat," she says, and then adds, sounding less upset. "He probably thought it was another kangaroo." She reminds us that, in the wild, male kangaroos "box" one another, using their front paws.

After this, we keep a close eye on him on washdays, but he still manages to make rips in other things.

"Why on earth he has to fight every damn thing, I don't know," Mum says, after he's destroyed Amelia's nightie.

Later, when we're all inside the house, she tells Amelia and me, "We've had Toots a long time, but we mustn't forget he's a wild animal. I think it's time that he was with his own kind." And then she says something I don't want to hear, "I think we're going to have to let him go."

"But people shoot kangaroos," Amelia says.

"Claude shot his mother," I remind her.

"Well, I think I know a place where he'll be safe. There's a property down in the valley where they don't allow shooting."

Figure 37.2: Laurence with Toots.

Dad and Claude rig up a cage on the back of the lorry, and with Toots inside it, we drive down the mountain, all of us in the truck. We stop when we come to the property where we're going to leave him. On the gate is a sign reading, "Wildlife Sanctuary. No Hunting or Fishing Allowed." Inside the property, we open the cage and let Toots hop down. We quickly say goodbye, and get back in the lorry. Sadness big inside me, I twist around to watch him as we drive away. Looking smaller than he's seemed lately, he's trying to get through the fence to follow us. I think we're all crying.

We do get used to being without him, but the image of him trying to get through that fence keeps returning and makes me very sad.

Chapter Thirty-eight

NASTY BOYS

When I'm nine, my father decides to visit his parents and sister, my dear Auntie, who lives with them, at Warners Bay; it's the summer school holidays and he asks if I'd like to go with him.

When we get to the little house where they all live, Auntie hugs me tight, and Grandfather seems full of life; I haven't met Grandma before, and she's very sweet with a beautiful, delicate-looking face.

In the afternoon of the next day, Auntie is out somewhere, Dad has gone with Grandfather to the "dorgs"—as he calls the dog races—and Grandma and I sit by the coal fire. Even though I'm only nine, she pours us both a glass of sherry, and I feel very grown up as we sip it and she tells me stories from her life. Like Auntie did when she stayed with us, she smokes cigarette after cigarette, the ash usually growing till it's as long as my little finger, before it falls on the hearth.

The day before we're to go home, Auntie asks Dad if I can stay for a couple of weeks. I want to, so he phones Mum, and although it's hard to hear her because of static—it's raining up there—she says I can.

The kitchen walls are papered with many pictures of the same man, cut from magazines, and after Dad leaves, I ask Auntie who he is. "Goodness—don't you know? That's Grandma's lover boy."

Grandma giggles. "Charlotte!"

"That's Johnny Ray," says Auntie. "Just a Walkin' in the Rain..." she sings in a scratchy voice, and Grandma laughs.

Auntie tells me that Uncle Bill, who's staying not far away with some cousins, will take me to the ocean one day soon. Right away, I ask whether I'll be able to see New Zealand. She laughs and says it's too far away, but I'm still sure I'll be able to.

Grandfather has his own room, and I sleep in the one Auntie and

232

Grandma share. After Grandma gets into bed, she plays with what I think is a necklace, and murmurs, and later, after they've put the light out, they smoke and talk.

The next day, I ask Auntie about the necklace and the murmuring, and she explains that Grandma "says the Rosary," every night—the necklace thing is to help her say her prayers to God.

One night, as they're talking in the dark, Auntie asks, "Have you ever heard of anyone having their periods through their mouth, Mum?"

I know what periods are, and I prick up my ears, but Grandma says she hasn't.

A few days later, Uncle Bill picks me up and we take a ferry across a lake. On the way, out of a paper bag, he pulls what look like yellow sausages with pointy ends, and asks, "Would you like a banana?"

I hesitate.

"It's a fruit."

We have apples, cherries and pears and plums at home, and oranges come in boxes from my mother's family, who have an orange orchard now, but I've never seen or heard of a banana. Uncle Bill hands me one and shows me how to peel it. It tastes really nice.

We get off the ferry and walk till we come to some yellow sand, with blue water rolling in and crashing. Uncle Bill looks at me. "Well, this is what I brought you to see."

I stare hard. "Where's New Zealand?"

He laughs. "It's a way over on the other side."

"But why can't we see it?"

"It's too far away, Pet." I still don't believe him, and stare and stare.

"The earth curves, too," he adds. "That's what really makes the difference." And when he explains what he means, I understand.

***

Auntie introduces me to Anna, who's the same age as me, with straight, dark hair, and lives down the street. "I'll take you to the bush, if you like," she says, and we arrange to meet the next day.

I live in the bush, so this doesn't sound very interesting. But when we get there, I find that it isn't the same as ours. It has no big trees, or flowers, or clean, soft grass—the trees are small and twisty. The ground is mostly trodden down, and there's quite a bit of rubbish, like broken bottles, that you have to be careful not to step on. Also, dogs and people go to the toilet here, and I nearly step in a pile of stinking brown jobby, making Anna giggle. The only thing I like about this bush is the bark of the trees they call "Paperbarks," which is like layers of tissue paper.

Anna takes me to a place she calls "the canyon," we sail sticks and leaves down a stream that runs through it, and it's fun.

After this, we go to the canyon every day. One morning, it's cool and misty, and I put on my new blue cardigan with the yellow fish buttons my mother just made me. We're sending more sticks down the stream, when we hear voices. Two older boys are watching us. Their names are Bruce and Lester, and they're 12 and 13, and much taller than we are. We chase each other around for awhile, and then play hide 'n' seek. But when you squat to hide, you're close to all the dirty ground, and I'm glad when the others say they don't want to play that game any more. I'm so hot I take off my cardigan, but keep it in my hand so I won't lose it.

Bruce whispers something to Lester and they giggle. One of them says that they know a better game, and will show us how to play it. They whisper and giggle some more, and, their hard little eyes watching our faces, Bruce says you have to take your panties off and lie down.

I know a new game...Burning pain. I've been caught like that before.

"What've we got to do?" Anna asks.

I take over. "We're going home. We don't want to play. Come on, Anna."

Anna looks surprised as I turn and start walking away. "Do we have to go?"

I keep walking. "Yes. I don't want to play any more."

The boys look surprised. "Why are you goin'?" Lester asks. "Come on. You'll like it. Don't be scaredy cats."

Anna hesitates, but I keep going, and call back to her, "Come on, Anna. Hurry up."

"Aw, come on," the boys say.

Anna follows me, kind of dragging her feet. I look back to see one of the boys hurrying after her. He grabs at her when he's close enough, but she steps sideways, suddenly looking frightened.

"Run!" I yell, taking off. Anna follows, and the boys chase us.

Close behind me, one of them grabs the sleeve of the cardigan I'm carrying. I keep going. Let it stretch out. Get ready to run even faster. When he's pulling really hard, I suddenly let go of the sweater. He falls onto the ground, and the other one stops to help him.

When we reach the highway, the boys are just emerging from the bush. They pause, but then disappear back into it.

When I get home, I don't have the words to tell Auntie what happened, even when she asks where my cardigan is. I know I was lucky to escape, but it's hard to explain. "I lost it," I say. But she keeps questioning me, and I finally tell her, "Some boys took it."

"Boys?"

"I lost it."

That night, I find myself thinking of picnics in the lovely bush back home, and, after eating, of snoozing with the others under a big tree. Of a little grey bird hopping up the tree's trunk singing it's one-note song. I think of my father, too, leaning against a log, his hat tilted over his face to shade his eyes, and Laurence playing nearby.

The next day, the doorbell rings, and I'm surprised to see Anna. Auntie leaves us alone. "Let's go to the bush," she says, as if yesterday didn't happen. I think of the weird little trees, the dirty ground, the jobby, the rubbish, and the nasty boys, and sort of shudder. I know it's not safe to go, and Anna isn't safe either. But she's looking at me and smiling. I look away. "No."

"Why not?"

"I dunno."

"But we like going to the bush. Come on."

"It's not real bush at all. It's horrible."

She looks hurt and soon leaves.

When I find Auntie, she asks, "Where's Anna gone? Aren't you going to play with her?"

"No."

"Why not?"

"I dunno."

She places her hand on my forehead. "Are you feeling unwell, Pet?"

I don't answer, but I let myself kind of sag. She's watching me, concerned. "That's alright, Pet. You'll feel better soon, and then you can play with her again."

I don't tell her that I never want to play with Anna, or go to that horrible bush, again.

That day, I follow Auntie and Grandma around, but, like always, they don't say much to me. It's rainy again, and everything seems grey. I begin to wish that I was home. I keep thinking of the lovely sunny days in summer on the mountain, and I feel as if the school holidays will be over before I get back. And, also, Mum said it was raining when Dad phoned her, and I imagine the pool in the swamp with all the mud washed out of it. I also think how sweet my mother is, and miss her.

The next day a letter arrives from her and Auntie encourages me to write back. So I do, telling her that I want to come home.

A few days later she telephones, and Auntie talks to her. She looks upset when she comes to get me. "Did you tell your mother you wanted to go home? She wants to talk to you."

I say I did, and then go to talk to her. After I hang up, I explain that I was worried that the school holidays would be over before I got back. Auntie looks surprised. "But there are weeks and weeks left, she says.

"Oh, are there? Then I can stay longer."

"No. You can't change your mind now. I told your mother you'd be back tomorrow, and she'll have booked your ticket by now. Everything's arranged."

I'm glad when Grandma says she'll come on the train with me and have a little holiday with us.

Chapter Thirty-nine

BAGS, BLASPHEMY AND SHELL SHOCK

On the train to Scone, Grandma says that when she was a girl, trains traveled so slowly that you could get off and pick flowers and get back on again. We stop at Maitland for a cup of tea, and she shows me how to pour your tea into the saucer and blow on it to make it cool enough to drink quickly.

Dad comes by himself to pick us up in Scone, and when we get home, Mum has made one of her lovely steamed meat pies for dinner. At the table, Dad says he's going to kill a pig the next afternoon.

Why does he have to say things like that when we're eating? I hope I don't have to see anything to do with it.

As Auntie did, Grandma shares the room with Amelia and me. While we're getting ready for bed, she talks about "her people" who lived in Ireland—her name was Fitzgerald before she married. In the old days, she says, they used to do a dance called "Bandy Legs."

"Show us," Amelia says.

She shrinks a bit and says she can't, but after we've both asked her a few times, she starts looking excited, and suddenly lifts her nightie and jigs about, singing "Bandy Legs, Bandy Legs..."

Amelia and I clap, and we all laugh.

The next afternoon is quite windy, and we hear the pigs up in their sty squealing. Grandma shakes her head. "Ah yes, they get upset on days like this. 'Pigs see wind as fire,' the old folks in Ireland used to say."

I like the idea, but I think they're probably squealing because Dad is trying to catch the one he's going to kill, though I don't say so. The squealing gets really loud, and through the window we see a pig with blood squirting from its neck racing past the house, Dad chasing it, a butcher's knife in his hand. After they're both out of sight, the noise stops suddenly, and I sit down and stare, trying to blank my thoughts out.

Dad looks upset when he comes inside, blood on his shirt and trousers. "Sorry for the terrible racket, Mum," he says to Grandma. "The poor fullah got away from me as I was trying to cut his throat."

Later, with everyone else at the back of the house helping with the butchering, Amelia and I walk around the front garden with Grandma, who talks about "the little people"—the fairies and elves she says the Irish believe in. Although I don't think they're real, from then on I start looking for them inside flowers and under leaves, in case they are.

Another cousin of Mum's, Charlie, and his wife Polly, have just moved to the Scone district, and a few days later, they visit us. Mum has often talked about Charlie, and how he was one of the "Rats of Tobruk"—he was imprisoned in the Middle East during the war—and she's told us that he and Dad used to work together. He's short, doesn't say much, and the way he stands with his powerful-looking arms hanging at an angle at his sides reminds me of a kangaroo. Polly is short and plump with white hair, and looks older than Mum, though she says they're almost exactly the same age. She tells me she visited Mum in hospital just after I was born, so she's known me since I was a baby. I like her right away, and I can see Amelia does, too; she's really nice, and laughs and jokes all the time.

Early that afternoon, Polly is feeling tired, and Amelia and I stay with her in the house while everyone else goes walking. We're all in our bedroom talking when Polly glances out the window, and says, "Oh me Gawd, Bags is in the potatoes." The bull has broken through a fence and is in a potato patch near the house. I always try not to look at the big white bag swinging between his legs, and we all burst out laughing. He's never charged at anyone, but Amelia and I keep our distance as we throw sticks to chase him out, yelling things like, "Get going, Bags," and roaring with laughter. Then we prop up the bit of the fence where he got through with sticks.

When the others get back, we tell Mum about the bull breaking into the potato patch, and, although I know it, I ask her what his name is.

"His name's Norman," she says primly.

Polly and Amelia and I all giggle.

Mum sighs. "What's so funny?"

"Nothing," I say, giggling some more. Amelia and I know that she wouldn't see the Bags story as funny.

Figure 39.1: My dear Polly.

Polly and Charlie leave after tea that night, and the next day I'm in the bedroom with Amelia and Grandma when, through the window, I see the bull in the potato patch again. Expecting to get a good laugh, I say, "Oh me Gawd, Bags is in the potatoes!"

But after a moment's silence, Grandma bursts into tears. "I can't believe it," she sobs. "My own flesh and blood!"

Amelia whispers that I'd better apologize. I'm not sure what's upset her, but I put my arms around her and give her a hug and kiss and say I'm sorry. Soon, she stops crying and hugs me, too. But then she draws back and looks into my eyes. "Promise me you'll never say anything like that again. Ever."

I promise, even though I'm not sure what I'm promising.

When Amelia and I are alone, she tells me I should be more careful what I say in front of Grandma.

"Why was she so upset?" I ask. "I thought she'd think it was funny, too."

"It wasn't that you called him Bags, she says. You see, Grandma's

Catholic, and when you say, "my God," it's called "blaspheming—taking the Lord's name in vain"—which religious people think is very bad.

I am more careful after this; but I still enjoy being with Grandma, and when it's time for her to go home, I'm sad to say goodbye.

***

It's a nice sunny day, and I start thinking about the waterhole in the swamp. As I walk towards it, the water looks beautifully clear. *The storms really have washed the mud away this time.* But as I wade in, the water is freezing and mud boils up around me like always.

Mum is on the verandah when I get home. Her eyes fix on my wet dress. "You've been in that bloody swamp again!" she yells, then grabs a switch and beats me with it. And I feel silly for thinking she was sweet when I was away.

***

My parents, Laurence and Claude go to Newcastle for a few days, and Uncle Bill comes to look after Amelia and me. The first day he's there, we set out the midday meal as usual: no tablecloth, various kinds of jam in the tins they came in, cold mutton on an enamel plate in a calico bag, a big lump of homemade butter in a basin, and beans and sardines in their cans.

After we've eaten, Uncle Bill says, "That was a nice lunch—thank you both very much. When I was young, we always called the midday meal "dinner" and the one in the evening "tea," but do you two realize that now most people call this meal "lunch," and the one at night "dinner?" It's funny how things change." We're surprised, but start referring to these meals in the new way.

He sits for a while, a dreamy look on his face. "I've been thinking about something. It might be a nice thing if you girls learned how to make the table look more attractive. For instance, I'm sure your mother has a tablecloth somewhere you could use. And you could put things like the beans and sardines and jam in dishes; I always think the tins don't look that nice. Do you see what I mean?"

I'm interested in what he's saying, and we both nod.

"And the mutton could go on it's own plate without the bag. Another thing is, we could have bread-and-butter plates—I see your mother has some in the cupboard. The butter would look nicer in small dishes, too." He pauses. "And, cups look better on saucers, you know."

He looks at us kindly. "I hope you don't mind me telling you these things. I think you'll find it's more pleasant to eat when the table looks nice. And this sort of stuff is good to know about now that you're both growing up." He pauses. "Another thing to avoid is chipped or cracked plates. They can harbour germs."

I've never thought about how we eat—we've always done it in the same way, unless we had a special visitor. But as I look around now I think the table looks like a garbage dump.

"If you like, next time we eat you could try setting things out the way I've described." He pauses. "Well, only if you want to, of course,"

Keen to follow his suggestions, we find Mum's fancyworked cloths in a drawer, put one on the table that night, and try to make everything look attractive. When Uncle Bill comes in, he stands for a while looking at our work, then takes off his glasses and peers with his head on the side, like he always does. He grins. "You two have done a great job. I'm really proud of you."

When we've finished eating, he says, "The meal was very good, and the way you set the table made it taste even better. But there's something else that would finish things off nicely. Do you know what it is?"

Puzzled, we look at each other.

"A vase of flowers! Maybe we could put one on the table next time."

Amelia and I notice the moon through the window, and when we've finished washing the dishes, we go outside. The moonlight is very bright, and soon we're running round, yelling, laughing, screaming, and pretending to frighten one another.

When we wander back inside, feeling excited and happy, we're surprised to find Uncle Bill in his chair with his head in his hands. Amelia asks him what's wrong. He looks up slowly, his face strangely pale, and stares at us. Then he says, as if talking is difficult, "Sorry... Feel really sick... The screaming... like wounded men in the war."

Amelia puts a hand on his shoulder. "But we were only playing, Uncle Bill. We're not hurt. See? There's nothing wrong with us."

He sounds sad. "I know, Pet... Don't worry... Go to bed... I'll sit here till I'm feeling better. It's... something called Shell Shock... I'll... I'll be alright by tomorrow."

Although we set the breakfast table carefully, he gives no sign that he's noticed, and goes back to his room to rest as soon as we've finished eating. It's the same at lunch, as we call it now, but afterwards he goes for a walk. The others are due back tonight, and while he's away, we start dinner, and put a pretty cloth on the table with a vase of flowers at its centre.

When he comes back, he smiles and tells us how wonderful the table looks. Then he says how sorry he is for getting sick the night before, and adds, "I couldn't help it—it just comes on me sometimes when I see or hear things that remind me of the war. A lot of soldiers were affected the same way, you know. But after a rest and a good walk, I'm feeling much better."

When the others get back, they stare at the table. Mum says, "My goodness, that looks very fancy! But I'm not sure we should be using my good cloths every day. I think there's a gingham one of Nan's somewhere."

Chapter Forty

MYTHS, AND A LUCKY FALL

The Argonauts' Club is on the wireless every week-day for an hour, and Amelia and I decide to join. It's run by a man they call Jason, after the one in the Greek myth. When you join, they give you the name of an Argonaut, and a number. Amelia gets Echo[1] 35, which sounds really nice, but I get Pauson[2] 2—which sounds boring.

You can earn marks by writing stories or essays, but I don't bother with those much.

I like listening to Tom the Naturalist, who gives a talk about the natural world on one afternoon. One day he tells how Shackleton took a bunch of Australian wildflowers to the Antarctic, and they remained in his hut when he left it. The next people to go inside it saw them looking as if they'd just been picked, but when someone reached out and touched them, they turned to dust—they had dried in the freezing air. It kind of feels like how it is with Mum when I imagine she's her old sweet self again, and then she yells at, or hits, me.

Phidias[3] teaches about the history of art. Argonauts can send in what they call "contributions" and earn marks towards a "Dragon's Tooth," which is then added to the name you've been given. I smooth papier mache over a pumpkin, with a potato for a nose to make a mask, and then paint it, and it wins a purple certificate—the highest one!

After Phidias talks about Leonardo da Vinci, I want to know more about him. We have few books, but I've read in the school magazine that Blackfriars School has a big library, so I write asking for a book about

---

[1] In Greek mythology, a mountain nymph who loved the sound of her own voice.

[2] An artist in ancient Greece who depicted what was defective or repulsive in his subjects.

[3] Named after a Greek sculptor, painter and architect, the man who spoke about art on the Argonaut's Club; in real life, he was Jeffrey Smart, who subsequently became a well-known artist.

him. When it arrives in the mail a few weeks later, I start reading it right away. The first line says that he was "illegitimate."

"Mum, what's illegitimate?"

"Why do you want to know?" she asks suspiciously, and I explain. She starts to speak several times and then says, "It means his parents weren't married."

I return to reading the book, but before long I'm stopped by another big word. After about the third time this happens, Mum and I agree that the book is too difficult for me, and she packs it up and sends it back, with a note. I don't understand why they didn't send me something at my reading level, and I feel that asking them for other books would be useless.

***

The news is always blaring during meals, and if anybody says anything, Dad snaps, "Can't a man listen to the news without people yapping?" So, mostly, we only ask for things to be passed. Once the news is over, Claude and Dad start sentences with, "The American Imperialists," or, "American propaganda," or, "In the Soviet Union," or "Old Joe Stalin," or "When the revolution comes."

I blank out what they're saying by staring—something I've always done—at the bread, say, till everything goes out of focus, and the colours and shapes and textures form patterns and images of landscapes or houses, people or creatures. I do the same thing when they're talking about what they've read in The Soviet Union, the magazine from there with photographs and articles about how well the people are doing, or The Tribune, a communist newspaper from Sydney that also comes in the mail.

One day, I stop staring after I hear Claude say, "Maybe we should hide the guns." They've just read an article in the Tribune saying that our government sees communists as a threat to Australia. "Maybe," says Dad. "The first thing they do if it looks like a revolution's coming, is take the people's guns." They discuss hiding them in the ceiling or under the floor of the shed, or up in the bush." The idea of a revolution is scary, but I don't believe it will happen, and the rifles stay on their hooks on the back verandah.

I'm alone in the house when I hear on the wireless that Stalin has died. They're always talking about him fondly, and certain that they'll want to know, I run over to the field where Dad and Claude are working.

"Stalin died!" I call to Dad. "I heard it on the news."

He straightens up and stares at me. "Well, I'll be damned," he says, then calls to Claude, a few furrows away, "Did you hear that, Claude? Old Joe Stalin's died."

And for a moment it's as if Stalin was a kind friend who lived far away.

***

Dad gets a call from his mother to say that his father is in hospital in Newcastle, so ill that the doctor says he won't live long. They'd wanted to send him home to die, but Grandma is not well enough to look after him, and Auntie is no longer living there. My parents agree that he should come up to our place to spend his last days. I'm again sharing the room with Amelia, Claude is sleeping on the front verandah, and nobody else is staying with us, so Mum decides he can sleep in the little room off the back verandah. Dad rigs up a tarpaulin over the back of the lorry, makes up a bed on the floor there, and goes to get him.

When the lorry arrives back, he helps Grandfather—who's so sick he scarcely notices the rest of us—into bed. He's as tall as Dad, and stretches from one wall of the tiny room to the other. With dark bushy eyebrows, his head seems too big for his body, and reminds me of one of those knobs on potatoes that develop after rain follows a dry spell.

He gets up only to go to the lavatory at the end of the stone pathway behind the house, and doesn't ask for much; but a couple of days after he's come, he complains of pain in his ear. Mum shines the torch in there but can't see anything. The pain gets worse. "It feels like something's in there," he keeps saying. Next, she fills his ear with warm Castor oil, puts an old towel on his pillow and has him turn over so the oil drains out; and there, wriggling on the towel, is a large maggot. A blowfly must have laid its egg in his ear while he was asleep, she says, as she shows it to him. Grandfather stares at it, then laughs for the first time since he's come. His earache stops.

A few mornings later, I learn that Mum has called the ambulance because Grandfather fell and hit his head on the way back from the lavatory last night. He has a red lump and a cut on his forehead, she says. He lies in his room with his head bandaged, talking to someone called Jim who isn't there.

The ambulance hasn't arrived by lunchtime, and we get a call from the driver to say it's broken down a few miles from Scone and that they're waiting for someone to come and fix it. We get two more calls—one to say a river is too high to cross and they're waiting for it to go down, and another to say it's shallow enough to cross now, and they're setting off again. They finally arrive just before dark, about ten hours after Mum called them, and, still confused, Grandfather is taken to Scone Hospital.

A few days later, Mum gets a call from the doctor looking after him to say that they've drained eighty ounces of fluid from his lungs, and that he's now doing well. Once he's recovered enough, Dad brings him back to finish his recovery before taking him back to Warners Bay, where he and Grandma live. Soon we get a letter from Grandma to say he's again going to the horse and dog races he loves so much. My parents boast that Scone Hospital cured him after the city one sent him home to die.

Chapter Forty-one

THE STRAPLESS DRESS

In Scone for the day with Dad, who has left us to do his chores, Amelia and I wander along Kelly Street, the main one, and named after Ned Kelly, the famous bushranger. We pause to look in the window of a dress shop, and a woman we hadn't noticed in the doorway calls, "Come on in and see—you don't have to buy!" Dark-haired and thick-set, she smiles broadly, flashing gold fillings.

Inside, a red evening dress catches my eye; I lift the net of its skirt, and sigh as it drifts back to its taffeta lining.

"You like? Tell your mother we're having a sale next week."

She thinks my mother would buy me a dress... But maybe she would?

"You can put it on lay-by—no extra cost."

"Our mother makes all our clothes," Amelia says.

The smile leaves the woman's face, but after a moment, she says, "Tell her anyway. She couldn't make dresses for what we'll be asking."

I point to the red one. "Will this one be on sale?"

"That one? Oh no! That's a *new season's.*"

I don't have the courage to ask how much the dress is. *But what good would it do to know, anyway?*

Amelia holds a strapless one, dark blue and with a sequined bodice, against herself and turns this way and that in front of a mirror.

It's nearly lunch time, and, through the window I see Dad passing, and hurry out. "Dad," I say, "We're in here," and he comes in.

The woman stands close to him. "Your father is very tall," she says, blinking up at him. "And very handsome."

A bit of a grin comes onto his face, but he folds his arms, and looks past her.

"These daughters of yours have found some dresses they like."

Amelia holds the blue one up.

He glances at it and shifts on his feet. "Very nice." He clears his throat. "Well, I've still got a lot to do, but it's time we had something to eat, so if you two can tear yourselves away, we'll go to the Vogue Cafe." Tipping his hat to the woman, he smiles slightly as we leave.

After lunch, Amelia and I call on Mrs. Rose, who lives in Scone now. Her house isn't nearly as nice as their place at Stewarts Brook with its lovely garden, but we love to see her. She has visitors, a woman and her son, Warren, from Tamworth, a city a hundred or so miles up the highway. Warren keeps mentioning his twenty-first birthday party which is coming up in a few weeks, and as we're leaving, he invites Amelia. She says she doesn't know how she could get there, and that she'll have to ask our mother if she can go. Mrs. Rose tells her that she and a neighbour are driving up, and invites her to go with them, and a happy look comes over her face. "That would be great!" she says. "But I'll still have to ask Mum."

As soon as we get home, she asks about the party, but all Mum will say is, "We'll see."

***

A week or so later, Dad says he's going into town to buy a few things, but won't be there long, so he says he might as well go on his own. Amelia, who's determined to go to Warren's party, asks him to get her three yards of blue see-through material and the same amount of matching taffeta so she can make herself a dress. He looks uncomfortable, but she writes down the exact names of the fabrics and where to buy them, and he puts the note in his wallet.

Around six, dinner made, the table set, and the house is full of the aroma of a casserole keeping warm in the oven as we wait in the lounge-room. "Your father will be home any minute," Mum says, getting out her crocheting. Claude lights the fire, Amelia and I look at magazines, and, half-lying in an arm chair, Laurence runs his red truck along one of its wooden arms, buzzing with his lips.

Raindrops scatter across the roof like a handful of gravel and then drum steadily.

Laurence interrupts his buzzing to say in a loud voice, meant to be Dad's, "Better put on the windscreen wipers!" Then he alternately buzzes and makes "Ee-errr" noises for the wipers, and spit for rain flies from his mouth onto the truck, making it shine. "Now, we're on the cutting," his loud voice says.

Mum looks out the window "I hope the rain doesn't make the road too slippery."

"'Hang on! We're slippin'!' Laurence's big voice says, his hand moving the red truck this way and that. Then with an, "Ohhhhhh!" the truck flies off the arm, crashes onto the floor, and comes to rest, upside down, against his sweet little dirty feet.

Mum says, "It's almost your bed-time, Laurence. Let's get those feet of yours washed, and then you can have your tea."

After she comes back, we keep thinking we hear a motor, and crowd around the window, watching for its headlights to shine into the sky as it approaches the top of the hill above the house. Sometimes what sounds like a vehicle ends in squeaks, as the wind blows the shrubs against the outside tin of the house, or it turns out to be only the burring of the fire.

When the rain stops, remembering someone saying that the aborigines could hear things from a long way off by putting an ear to the ground, I go outside without telling anyone why, put my ear against the wet grass and press down. But I continue to hear only crickets and frogs, the side of my head gets cold and wet, and, shivering, I go back to the fire inside.

"I hope to God he isn't stuck somewhere," Mum says. "Some of the rivers might be up. There hasn't been that much rain here, but there could have been more in other places." She sighs. "I don't know why he hasn't called. Unless he's stuck somewhere and can't get to a phone, or the lines are down." She calls the telephone operator, who isn't aware of anything like this.

I close my eyes, hoping magic will let me see where he is on the long road. But the image that keeps coming is of the lorry turned over below a slippery Black Cutting, and I pray silently.

Then there really is the sound of an engine. Two beams of light poke up into the sky above the hill, followed by headlights. But instead of the lorry, the dark shape of a car swings past our turnoff.

Mum looks at her watch. "It's nearly nine o'clock—time we had some food."

As we eat in the kitchen, which is on the side of the house away from the road, it's harder to hear engines and we can't watch the window for lights. Inside me, an awful feeling is growing. *What if I never see him alive again?*

But as we're finishing the washing-up, we really do hear the loud engine of the lorry, and soon my father's tall figure is black against the lights as he opens the gate to our place.

Mum's words march out as if she hasn't been worried at all. "There he is."

I want so much to run out and hug him, but we don't do such things in our family—we all wait by the fire for him to come in. Only when I hear his footsteps on the verandah, do I stand up. The doorknob rattles a few times before the door opens.

His hat is at an odd angle, and he has an armful of parcels. He looks down at me and grins. "How are you poppin' up, young lady?" His words sound kind of odd. He deposits the parcels on an empty chair and props a brown paper bag against the leg of the one he sits on.

My mother's voice flashes out, "Why don't you take your damn hat off?"

"Oh." He removes it and drops it on the floor. "Very sorry, my love." He reaches over, takes her hand and kisses it. "You're so beautiful," he says. He looks around. "Wonderful to be with me family. I love you all, you know. And I'm real proud of you, too. Real proud."

He's never said such lovely things before.

"It would be a lot nicer if you could say those things when you haven't been guzzling grog.[1]"

Why does she have to be like that?

"What do you mean?" He stares at her. "Surely you don't begrudge a man a bit of relaxation. Been working daylight to dark."

"Yes I suppose you have. But so have I, and I don't have to guzzle that stuff to relax."

From the paper bag he takes a bottle with an enamel mug over its top. "Show a fullah a bit of respect! I haven't drunk that much."

"Don't try to tell me that. I can smell how much you've drunk on your breath. It's no use telling a person lies."

He pours brown liquid from the bottle into the mug, and offers her a drink.

She takes a mouthful, coughs and pulls a face. "Rum! I don't know how you can drink that foul stuff."

Dad raises his eyebrows, swallows a mouthful and sits a moment. Then he reaches over to the pile of parcels and hands one to each of us. He gets my mother to open hers first. It's a silk scarf with violets on it. Claude

---

[1] Now Australian slang for any alcoholic drink, it originally meant a drink of rum and water.

gets a Swiss Army knife. Laurence gets a toy tractor, and I get a little box painted pink and orange.

All this time, Amelia has been sitting with a large, soft-looking parcel on her lap—it must be the material she asked him to get. She breaks the sticky tape, tears aside the tissue paper, and stares. It's dark blue with sequins! She jumps up and lets the evening dress she'd admired when we were last in town unfold. None of us has ever had a bought dress, let alone one like this.

Amelia's eyes are wide. "Dad, it's gorgeous!"

Mum screaches, "But it hasn't got any straps. What *on earth* were you thinking, Joe? The girl's only fourteen. *She can't wear a dress like that!*"

Dad grins and says nothing. For a moment, Amelia looks sad, but then a strong look comes onto her face.

"Why didn't you just buy the material she asked you to get?" Mum asks.

"Well, I know nothing about dress material, and I thought she'd like the dress."

Amelia puts her arms around him. "I do! Thank you, Dad. It's the most beautiful dress I've ever seen." She turns to my mother. "Maybe I could wear it to Warren's twenty-first. I *can* go, can't I Mum?"

"Hang on a minute. Just hold your horses. Firstly, you don't have anything to wear. A girl your age simply cannot wear a—" She nods at the gown. "a *thing* like that."

Amelia's eyes meet mine, and I know she'll fight to wear it.

We sit there until the fire is small, the rum bottle empty, and Dad is asleep, his chin on his chest.

Mum wakes him, and she and Claude help him down the hall to the bedroom. As they're coming back, I hear her say, "Why on earth did he have to get into such a state? And *driving* in that condition!"

My father stays in bed till late the next day, but that afternoon, when scarlet clouds criss-cross the sky, I'm squatting in the strawberry patch near the big corrugated iron water tank on it's low, wooden stand, my fingers searching among the leaves for the dark red, and very sweet, berries, when Mum and Dad come around the side of the house, his arm around her waist. But when they stop, she disentangles herself, and turns to face him. Her voice is low and tight. "If you don't stop drinking, I'm going to leave you."

I dare not move. Then I hear an odd sound, and a glance shows me Dad sitting on the tank stand sobbing, his head in his hands.

"I mean it," Mum says.

He takes a deep breath, and cries out, "A man ought to be horse-whipped!" Then he sobs some more, and after another deep breath, says in a strong voice, "I'll stop drinking. You have my word of honour."

***

When I tell Claude and Amelia what I overheard, they look frightened.

"What would happen to us?" Amelia asks.

"The kids usually go to live with the mother when people get divorced," Claude says.

They're quiet for a while, and then Amelia says, "I suppose we'd live with her." They wonder whether she'd stay on the farm or go to live somewhere else—like with her parents. We all agree that we can't imagine not being with Mum. The idea of my parents divorcing is terrible, but I feel a bit better now that Claude and Amelia know what I overheard.

But soon my parents are acting the same as they always have, and we forget about the threat.

***

When Polly visits a week or so later, Amelia mentions Warren's twenty-first party and shows her the dress. Again, Mum says she's too young to wear it, and adds, "And I can't imagine what on earth would keep a dress like that up!"

Polly laughs. "I know how you feel, Gwen," she says, "But all the young ladies are wearing strapless dresses these days. Only the other day, a woman I know who's always into the latest fashion was saying her daughter has one—and she's no older than Amelia. Apparently, they're all the rage."

"But what—" Mum begins again, but Polly holds up her hand and interrupts her. "Well, actually, I happen to know the secret of how they stay up, too. First of all, the bodices are so stiff they couldn't fall down if they tried. They're like those old corsets our grandmothers used to wear." She laughs, and gets Amelia to hand her the dress. "See? It's dem bones—or whatever they use now—that hold it up. Feel them."

My mother does. "I see what you mean."

"Strapless dresses are quite respectable," Polly continues in a soothing tone. "It's just a fashion, Gwen. That's *all* it is."

Mum still looks doubtful but I see that she's starting to relax, and Polly keeps talking to convince her. "Nobody's going to think badly of her for wearing a strapless dress—or of you because you let her wear one. They'll just think how nice she looks. The world's sure a different place from when we were girls, eh Gwen?" She pauses. "You know, I think it might be a really nice thing if Amelia *could* go to Warren's party; Charlie and I have known that family for years. Warren's a very nice young man."

Mum says, "Well, I spose it might be alright for her to go if she can get a lift up there and back with Violet."

Amelia jumps up. "Mum, that would be great!"

"Look, Gwen," says Polly, "in that dress, she'll be the belle of the ball."

Chapter Forty-two

NOTHING TO WORRY ABOUT

Many months after Dad has stopped drinking, he needs to take a load of potatoes to Scone, Mum has things to do at home, and Amelia and I decide to go with him. Farmers are supposed to sell potatoes through the Potato Board, which he calls "just another bloody bureaucracy that means the farmer gets less money," and he deals directly with the greengrocer, and sells them door-to-door by the bucketful as well, so he wants to get to town early when few people are about.

Easter is coming up, and we usually have roast pork, but we don't have a suitable pig to kill, so my parents talk about buying a butchered one. "But how on earth would we pay for it?" Mum asks. "There's no money." And she lists the expenses coming up.

Dad is quiet for a while, and then says, "I know! We could get a half off Mick. A lot of people don't want a whole one."

"Yeah, that'd work. I'll phone him and order it, then."

Dad looks around at us all. "We don't know how lucky we are. We're all healthy, and there's plenty of food, even without pork. When I was a young fullah tramping around with me brothers begging for work from the big landowners, half the times we didn't know where our next meal was coming from." He pauses. "Sometimes, I thought I was going to starve. And when we came to a property and asked for work, the bludgers that owned it looked at a fullah like he was some stray dog."

The night before our day in town, Amelia and I are up late, whitening our sandals, ironing our clothes and putting curlers in our hair—in my case, to make it straight. They're big and metal, and keep waking me up. I feel as if I've hardly slept when I hear my father's cheerful, "Time to rise and shine, you fullahs!" followed by the scratch and fizz of the match as he lights the lamp in our room."

Amelia, who's fourteen, sits up in bed and fastens her bra; being only ten, I don't need one. The days are still warm, but it's freezing cold this early in the morning, when we're usually asleep. Our dresses rest on the backs of kitchen chairs with our sandals on the floor below them, as if two invisible girls have swooned over backwards. So mine will stand out the way it's supposed to, I put on the full-circle petticoat I made out of unbleached calico, it's hem reinforced with thin rope, and starched very stiff. I can already feel it rubbing my legs as I walk down the hall to the fire crackling in the loungeroom. Dad, in his good shirt and trousers, and the daisy-patterned tie my mother made him because he likes flowers, sits on the couch with one hand in the black shoe he's polishing—making him look as if he has a hoof. He smiles. "Come over to the fire and warm yourselves." His voice has the sing-song rhythm I love that was always there when he read stories to us.

The streets are empty when we get to Scone. Our first stop is the greengrocer. Dad's back has been hurting lately, and he winces as he lifts the bags of potatoes off the lorry, and he climbs the steps into the building slowly. Then we drive around delivering buckets of potatoes to the people who've ordered them.

After tea and sandwiches at the Vogue Cafe, Amelia and I wander along Kelly Street like we always do. In the window of Campbell's department store, in a vase near some refrigerators, are strange and beautiful flowers we've never seen before. Wanting to be able to tell our mother about them, we go inside and ask what kind they are. At first the saleswoman doesn't understand, but then her face clears. "Oh those!" she laughs. "They're artificial—come and see."

We follow her to them. "They're foam plastic," she says. "It's new."

Close up, the material they're made from is shiny and thin with tiny bubbles—and ugly. Outside again, no matter how I squint at the flowers from different angles, I can't see them as I did before.

Farther down the street, in the window of the second-hand shop, is a vase made of bubbly orange glass. "Do you think Mum would like that for her birthday?" I ask Amelia.

"She might. She doesn't have one that size."

We go into the store, but she whispers something about not being able to stand the musty smell in there, and leaves to wait outside. I ask to see the vase, but instead of handing it to me, the man in the shop sits it on the counter. Picking it up, I see that a part of its base is missing. "It's broken," I say.

He stretches his face into a smile. "Let me show you something."
Taking it from me, he sets it down with the missing bit at the back, as
before. "Put some flowers in it and sit it like that, and nobody will be any
the wiser. *You* couldn't tell when you saw it in the window, now could
you?"

Through the doorway, I see Amelia looking irritated and shifting on
her feet. "I need a birthday present for my mother," I explain. "Do you
think this would be alright?"

"As I said, sit it how I did and put some flowers in it and she'll never
notice." I hesitate, but he adds, "It's a good price. You won't find anything
else for that."

Amelia is peering in the doorway and frowning. "OK," I say, "I'll take
it." But even as he's wrapping it up—in newspaper—I know I've made a
mistake.

As we continue up the street, the thick-set woman is again in the
doorway of her shop. "Your father must love you very much," she calls.

Amelia stops and looks at her. "What do you mean?"

"Well, he bought you that lovely dress, didn't he?"

After lunch with Dad at the Vogue Cafe, Amelia and I again walk up
and down the street, waiting for him to finish so we can go home. In
the morning, we kept seeing him, but now that we want to leave, he's
disappeared. The Autumn sun is hot, and there's not much shade, and,
several times, we go to the Niagara Cafe, where there's a fan going, for
cold drinks. Our feet ache from walking on cement, the backs of my legs
are sore from the rubbing of the starched petticoat, and as the afternoon
wears on, we move more and more slowly. I eye the edge of the footpath,
wishing I could sit there with my feet in the gutter; but girls in nice dresses
don't do that.

The town is golden in the last sun and the scent of roses from the
gardens in front of the buildings is strong when our father finds us and
says he's ready to go home.

The first few miles of the road home is asphalt,[1] and runs through an
enormous property owned by the Whites—the ones my parents say the
people in the white house know. Their land has clumps of dark trees instead of forests, and black cattle are scattered over the pale yellow grass
of the flats and hills. After this, the road is dirt or gravel, and we pass
through smaller properties, with houses, farm animals, tractors and other
machinery. In the distance are blue hills, and I ask Dad where our moun-

---

[1] In Australia, a surfaced highway—also called bitumen.

tain is, but he says you can't see it from anywhere on the road from Scone.
Just before Gundy, where we lived when Laurence was born, we clatter
over a wooden bridge and Dad parks next to the pub on the bank of the
river. "Got to have a word with Harry," he says. "Won't be long."

As he strides along the gravel path and climbs the steps to the bar,
something prickles inside me. *But that's silly—he promised. He really
does have to see Harry—he said so before we left home.*

After we've been waiting awhile, we start watching for him to emerge.
Each time the door to the bar opens, the murmur of voices from the men
crowded inside becomes as loud as the buzzing of blowflies at the gauze
door of our meat house[2] in summer when you're close to it.

But soon it's that lovely time of day when the sun has gone and the
crickets are singing, and we climb down from the lorry, and enjoy a little
time in a nearby paddock.

Back in the lorry's cab, I unwrap the vase, and show it to Amelia. She
picks it up. "It's broken."

"I know." I take it from her. "The—the man in the shop said nobody'd
notice if you put it around this way. See?"

"You shouldn't have bought it. She'll see it right away."

"I could put flowers in it and sit it somewhere with the broken bit at
the back."

"It's not a present unless it's wrapped."

I feel awful. "He reckoned nobody'd notice."

"You should return it. He's a crook."

I wrap it up again and put the parcel back where it was. After a while
I say, "He *is* a bloody crook."

Bored, I notice the brighter band at the bottom of my faded print
dress, where Mum let it down. She always doubles a three-inch hem so
my dresses can be let down as I grow. When I said the brighter band
looked odd, she assured me that people would think it was a decoration.
I didn't—and don't—believe her. "I wish Mum would buy *me* a dress," I
say.

"I'm looking forward to wearing my strapless," Amelia says airily.
"Good old Polly."

Is Mum really going to let her wear it?

We stretch out our legs, shift on our bottoms, rattle through the things
in the glovebox, and then start yawning. It's cool, now, but my skin is

---

[2]Before refrigeration, a small building for storing meat on a farm.

sticky from the day's heat, and we're both thirsty. We climb onto the back of the lorry, find the waterbag, and take long drinks.

Back in the cab, we talk on and on about food. After a silence, Amelia says, "I hope Dad hasn't started drinking again."

"But he's stopped," I say.

She gives an odd laugh. "Doesn't mean he can't start again."

A horrible feeling comes into my belly.

Once it's dark, every time the din tells us the bar door has opened, I search for him among the men inside. And when I hear someone coming along the gravel path, thinking we might have missed seeing him leave, I listen for the "one-two-pause, one-two-pause" rhythm of his footsteps. As it gets later, the door opens less often, and the crowd inside thins.

Suddenly, Amelia says in a strong voice, "If Dad's drunk, we'll get Ed Peters to drive us home." Ed is a taxi driver in Scone everyone knows, but we're half an hour from there, and we're three and a half hours from home.

"But how could we?" I ask.

"I could ring him up from the phone box over there." She points. "You just have to put money in—I have enough. The operator gets the number for you."

I've never made a call from a phone box. *How does she know these things?* "But how would we pay him?"

"Mum could give him a cheque when we get there."

"But Mum said there's no money."

She laughs. "When people say that, it doesn't mean they *literally* don't have any. You know Mum gets endowment money for each of us from the government? Well, she has some from that—I was with her when she put it in the bank."

"Has she?" I'm trying not to see the dark figure of a man by the fence or hear his stream of water hitting the ground. But suddenly, I *do* hear the rhythm of my father's footsteps, and his tall figure in his hat is walking towards us.

The door handle rattles, he slowly climbs up into the cab, and sits down with a thud and a clink from a bulky parcel he shoves behind the seat. He takes the keys from his pocket and puts them on his lap, and sits staring ahead, his arms draped over the wheel. Without looking our way, he asks in a thick voice, "You fullahs alright?"

Amelia says loudly. "You've been drinking, Dad. You can't drive."

"Ah, nothing to worry about." He scratches his ear, knocking his hat askew. "Few drinks. Thas all."

"You can't drive, Dad. We're not going home with you."

The lights of a turning car illuminate his face, staring at her. "Not coming with me?"

"I'm going to call Ed Peters from that phone box and get him to take us home," she says.

He folds his arms, and his head sags towards his chest.

"Oh well," he says in a falling tone.

That was easier than I expected. He understood, and everything's going to be alright! A good feeling begins to rise in me.

Amelia opens the door to get out, and I ready myself to follow her. *How exciting it'll be to go all the way home in a taxi!*

But suddenly there's a loud sob, and Dad's whole body is rocking. I freeze in horror. He's the one who rescues us. Cuddles me before a fire he's lit in the middle of the night when I have earache. Lifts huge bags of potatoes. Shifts logs off the road. Pushes the lorry out of bogs.

Amelia's hand is still on the half-open door. He takes a deep breath. "Ed Peters." he says, then sobs some more. "You-can't-go-with-him. He's not safe. Never forgive meself. Terrible driver. Can't even drive round town. Saw him nearly hit a kid on a bicycle." Then he says fiercely, *"I won't let you go with him!"*

Amelia closes the door, touches my shoulder, climbs over me, and puts her arms around him. "It's OK, Dad," she says. "I'm sorry. Don't cry. We'll go with you."

Why did she back down so quickly?

My father finds a handkerchief and blows his nose loudly. "Alright," he says. "It'll be OK. You'll see." His voice no longer sounds thick.

The keys have disappeared, but we find them on the floor. He starts the engine, puts the gear into reverse, and backs. There's a soft thud as the lorry nudges a fence post, but he changes gears, and we move off.

His driving seems the same as always, but whenever headlights are coming towards us, I watch to make sure he dims his lights and pulls to the edge of the road, which is, like everywhere else, only just wide enough for two vehicles to pass. But he keeps doing exactly what he's supposed to do. *There really is nothing to worry about.*

The moonlight is so bright that, through the side window, I can make out most of the details of the countryside, the colours as soft as chalk. The sky is pale blue with pinhole stars above the creamy grass. I can see the red of the tractors, and the brown, black and cream of the horses and cattle. Big blobs up ahead become dark green trees, their trunks hidden even when we're close to them, as if they're wearing dresses to the ground. Lights appear, and become the square windows of shadowy farmhouses.

Then we're on the Yellow Cutting—the road that runs around the sides of the steep hills just before Moonan Flat—and far below, winding through green flats, the silver worm of the river shines between willows.

"Dad!" Amelia screams.

We're heading for the edge!

"Dad!" we both yell. 'Turn the wheel, Dad! Turn the wheel."

"Say your prayers!" he yells, weird laughter see-sawing out of him.

"Stop, Dad!" we yell again. "Stop!"

He turns the wheel at the last moment, and we head for the hillside. More weird laughter. "Say your prayers! Say your prayers!"

He turns before we hit the bank, and then we're heading for the edge again, both of us crying and screaming at him. "Turn the wheel, Dad." "Stop it Dad!" "Please, Dad."

"Say you're prayers." More mad laughing. "Say your prayers."

He thinks he's just frightening us, but one mistake and we're dead.

"Say your prayers! Say your prayers!"

Now Amelia and I cling to one another, teeth clattering, unable to speak or sob. When at last the cutting ends, and there is ground on both sides, he silently drives straight along the road.

"Aw, don't be so silly," he says. "Only fooling around. Nothing to worry about."

Just before Moonan, we turn off the main road and climb towards two squares of light wobbling on a hillside. We stop in front of Mick's house where we're to pick up the half pig. All I want is to get away from him, but my legs won't work, and Amelia doesn't move, either. He looks at us. "Only playing with you fullahs."

After a while, Amelia opens the door, climbs down, and then helps me down. Clinging to one another, we scribble along the path towards the house. Behind us, my father's door slams, and the clink-clink of the parcel from behind the seat follows us.

Chapter Forty-three

HALF PIG AND THE MAGNOLIA

Mick opens the front door before we get to it, comes out, yells a greeting and hangs a lantern from the porch ceiling. Then I hear a giggle, and his brother appears. Very thin with red hair, he looks like a red ant, and Ant is what everyone calls him. The two men disappear round the side of the house, while my father sets his parcel down, climbs up onto the back of the lorry, spreads out the tarp, and puts an old, clean sheet on top of it.

Mick reappears first, the half pig's body resting on a shoulder, and the head wobbling above a leg in front of his chest. Behind him, Ant brings the pig's other end. Dad leans over the back of the truck, grasps the front legs and pulls. Mick scrambles up and helps, while Ant pushes. When the half pig is on the sheet, Dad lays another old sheet on top of it.

Mick and my father jump down. "Yeah, only killed this afternoon. Fat'll firm up nice once you're in the cool air of the Tops. Like a refrigerator up there, I reckon. Well, how about one for the road, Joe? Bring the girls in. Patty's home." Ant giggles, which is all he ever seems to do.

Mick's invitation is a relief. Amelia and I are still shaking, and the thought of going anywhere with Dad driving is terrifying. We go into a room with a fire and big brown armchairs, and the scent of fried food in the air, which makes my mouth water.

Mick says to a girl with straight brown hair leaning against a door-post. "Patty, take care of these young ladies will you? Joe's daughters." He nods to Amelia. "You two are about the same age, I reckon. I'll let you introduce yourselves." He pauses. "Oh, I should've asked—would any of you like something to eat? There are some sausages Patty can warm up."

Amelia and I say we'd like something, and in the kitchen, Patty pokes at several sausages stranded in white fat in a pan on the stove.

Then we remember our mother—we were supposed to be home for dinner—and Amelia asks if she can use the phone. When she gets through, she says, "We're still at Mick's, getting the pig... Dad—Dad's been drinking." After she hangs up, she says, "Mum said not to leave with him if he's drunk; she wishes she could drive." She pauses. "And she said to call again to let her know what's happening—it doesn't matter how late it is."

Patty's taking slices of white bread from a bag. "How about sausage sandwiches? We can take them outside if you like. I'll show you the magnolia tree."

We eat as we walk, leaning forward every now and then to let the juice from the sausages drip onto the ground. Never before have I known a night so bright and warm. Then we notice perfume, which grows stronger till, not far from the lorry, we're beside a tree with shining leaves and thick-petalled white flowers as big as dinner plates that seem to glow with their own light. Breathing in their perfume, I start to feel happy again. We walk around the tree, admiring it, and gathering speed till we're running, shrieking and giggling. When we stop, everything's spinning, and we let ourselves fall onto the grass around it.

We go to the lorry, climb onto the back, and peer at the pig under the sheet. It looks like a shallow canoe with a leg at each end and a head with bleary eyes and long, white eyelashes. But being near it is creepy, and we jump down again.

"I hate it when they kill them," Patty says. "I'm glad I'm not here all the time. Mum and Dad are divorced, and Mum and I live in Armidale, but she makes me come and stay with him once a year."

We say how bright the moonlight is, and Patty runs to the house and comes back with a newspaper. We can read the big print, but not the rest.

A giggle nearby makes me jump. Ant is there, and when we start running again, he runs with us. We decide to play hide-and-seek, and I hide in the back of the lorry, thinking nobody will look for me there because of the pig; but I climb down to get away from it again, and I'm trying to think of another place when the others find me. Everyone is thirsty, and Patty fetches bottles of Passiona, my favourite soft drink, made from passion fruit.[1] Then I notice Ant's gone and see him heading

---

[1] The purple Passiflora edulis edulis is a vine which thrives in many parts of Australia and produces edible purple fruit (genus Passiflora).

back to the house.

Patty tells us about her school, which sounds great; they put on plays, and go on what are called "excursions" to dams and museums and things. We try to tell her about our schooling, but she'd never heard of correspondence. Finally, she says, "Correspondence sounds *aw-ful.*"

In a silence, I think of telling her about our father's antics on the road, but decide that it would make us seem too weird. We talk a bit more about our lives up on the Tops, but everything we say seems to make us seem stranger. Yawning, Amelia points to the moon just above the horizon. "It'll be dark, soon."

Back inside, snoring comes from the loungeroom. Dad and Mick are asleep in their chairs, light from the lamp shining through the bottles in front of it flickering orange on their faces, and making them look very peculiar.

Once we're in the kitchen, Amelia says, "It's better to let them sleep it off."

"Right," Patty says. "Your Dad doesn't look like he'd be safe driving, even if you could get him going." She pauses. "That's another thing I hate about the pig business. He always gets on the grog with the blokes that come for meat."

She shows us a three-quarters bed we can sleep in, but noticing a clock showing three in the morning, Amelia claps her hand to her mouth. "Ohhh! We have to phone Mum again. After she tiptoes back to the kitchen and talks to her, she comes back saying Mum's glad we're OK and have somewhere to sleep.

Hot sunshine coming through the window wakes us; I have a headache. In the kitchen, Patty gives me aspirins, and then we eat cornflakes. Now awake, my father sits in the chair he slept in, his jacket over his head. Mick's chair is empty, and sounds of vomiting come from the bathroom.

Outside again, everywhere except for patches of green around the tank and underneath the magnolia tree, the red earth shows through the sparse yellow end-of-summer grass like the scalp of a balding man. The racket of cicadas[2] swells and fades, the grunts and squeals of pigs come faintly, and, in the distance, Ant's red hair moves among the pigs in their yard.

We girls are sitting on the grass under the magnolia, when Mick comes down the path from the house, gets into his car, and heads down the road. "Off for more grog," Patty says.

---

[2]Large flying insects, of which there are some 3,000 species, hatching and emerging from the ground at intervals of up to seventeen years; the males make a mating sound which becomes very loud when many sing in trees in hot weather.

Amelia stands up. "Let's see if we can get Dad to leave before he comes back."

She stands on one side of him and I on the other, but he doesn't notice us till she touches his shoulder. "Dad, we have to go. Mum's very worried," she says.

"Yeah, don't you fullahs go off anywhere," he mumbles. "We'll be leaving soon."

"Mum's *really* worried," she says. "We have to go *now*, Dad. Come on."

He peers up at her from under the jacket. "We can't just go without saying goodbye to Mick."

She looks at the clock. "It's already twelve, and, and—" She looks around the room. "The pig'll go bad in the heat."

"Oh, it'll be alright."

"What about the flies?"

"Flies?"

"Come on, Dad," I say.

Dad's hand goes to his head. "Can't you give a man a bit of peace?"

"We have to go *now*, Dad," Amelia repeats.

"Yes, Dad, we have to go *now*," I echo.

After awhile he says, "Well, praps we should." He sets his jaw, and rises slowly, swaying a little, steadies himself, grabs his hat and jambs it on his head. "Right you are, then. Come on."

We're almost at the lorry when Mick arrives back, gets out of his car and stands there looking upset, a bulky parcel under each arm. "You look like you're leaving, Joe. Can't let you go without a bit of a pick-me-up, mate."

Relief floods over my father's face. "Well, if you put it like that."

Amelia stamps her foot, and we both glare at him, but he doesn't seem to notice. "I'll just have the one, so don't you two go anywhere," he says. He follows Mick back into the house, and we stomp along behind them. On either side of his chair again, now with our arms folded, we swear under our breaths. When Mick pours a second drink for them both, we remind Dad that we have to go.

"Don't worry. Five minutes. Just give me five more minutes."

We give up when Mick pours a third, go outside and find Patty. She asks if we want to go to the river. "There's a nice swimming hole," she says. "It's not far away—you must see it every time you go past Moonan. I can loan you some shorts and tops."

The waterhole under the she-oaks on hot afternoons... People on towels on its pebble beach, or splashing through the water, and diving off the rocks.... Longing to swim there... My parents always saying we don't have time to stop.

Amelia and I go inside and ask our father, but, his voice firm, he says, "No. I don't want you two going anywhere. We have to get home."

Back outside, the air is thick and warm, even in the shade, everything seems boring, and the thought of my worried mother is constantly with me.

"I know," says Patty. "We can go to the cave."

"The cave?" we both say.

"Well—it's not really a cave. I mean, under the back of the house—it's dark and cool there, like a cave."

But soon we're hot again, and we go back to sitting under the magnolia tree. Patty makes us drinks with ice in them, and gives us some pork sandwiches.

Around two o'clock, we go back into the house. Noticing us, Dad says, his voice thick again, "Amelia! Leila! We're going. Right now."

We stare angrily at him. He raises his glass to Mick and finishes off his drink. "Cheerio, mate," he says. "They're good kids. Good kids."

Staggering to his feet, he heads down the steps, leaning on the railing, us behind him. Ant leans against the Magnolia tree, watching.

Close to the lorry, I can hear the buzz of flies. Dad slowly climbs up into the cab. "Come on," he says. "Get in." We don't move, and then he says, "Where the bloody hell are the keys?"

We hear him open the glove box, scratch around inside, and close it. His head disappears as he searches the floor. "Where the hell could they have got to?"

I see Ant raise an arm, a bunch of keys in his hand.

Amelia is watching my father. "I'd better help Dad."

I whisper, "Ant's got the keys—he just showed them to me."

"I'll pretend, then," she whispers back. "He'll get sick of looking in a minute, and we won't have to go."

Dad seems to be sobering up. "Where in God's name could those damn keys have got to? I could swear I left them in the ignition like I always do when we're at people's places." He pauses. "But maybe I did take them inside." He climbs down and we follow him back into the house. He looks around and asks Mick half-heartedly if he's seen them, then sits down and starts drinking again. We call Mum and give her an update.

That night, we're all too tired to run around, and go to bed as soon as we've eaten. We know that the pub is closed the next day, Sunday, so Mick won't be able to get more grog.

The next morning, Dad and Mick sleep till around eleven, then drink some more, and sleep all afternoon.

When we go inside around six, they're awake; they call for strong tea. We make them a big pot, and, after several cups, our father seems OK to drive. "Once I find those bloody keys, we'll be off," he keeps saying.

Ant comes in, and, making sure that only Amelia and I see him, pushes the keys under a chair, and nods in the direction of our father. We pretend to find them. Amelia phones Mum again, to say that we think Dad is alright to drive, and we're about to leave. She puts the phone down. "Mum was crying." Sad to say goodbye to Patty, we give her long hugs, and then, thunder growling and lightning flashing from a bank of dark clouds boiling up into the sky, we follow Dad to the lorry.

Chapter Forty-four

BACK IN THE FOLD

Rain flicks on the windscreen as we drive off. There's only one cutting on the way home, and that's the Black Cutting, and I'm terrified he'll re-start his nasty game on it. And heaven help us if it's slippery. I watch his every move and I know Amelia is doing the same. *If he does anything to frighten us, I'll force him to stop so we can get out.* But, looking half dead behind the wheel, he keeps going straight ahead.

I'm relieved when the rain stops as we start up the mountain. As well as my fear of the Black Cutting, I'm the one opening the gates.

In the dark behind the lorry as I close them, every rustle makes me jump.

He's fine on the Cutting, and I relax a little once we're over it, and our lights are sweeping across white tussocks and the moving backs of sheep on both sides of the road.

We lurch through the last stream, and climb the hill. From the top, I see Mum in the square of yellow light that's our front window, looking like an ant caught in honey.

Laurence already in bed, she and Claude hug Amelia and me—but not Dad. As soon as he's inside, he stumbles down the hall to my parents' bedroom. My mother's face is tight. "I spose I'll have to go and help him," she says, stomping off.

Once she's back, Amelia and I tell her a little of what we've been through, though something like shame stops us from telling the full story of how he frightened us on the yellow cutting. For once our anger at our father matches hers. "For God sake," she says, "if he ever gets drunk again when you're alone with him, don't go with him if he tries to drive."

I'm determined to, if there ever is a next time.

Amelia says she tried not to. And finally, we all decide that we shouldn't go to town alone with him ever again. "God I wish a person could drive," Mum says. "I hate the thought of learning in that big lorry, but I spose I'll have to."

Dad doesn't get up for breakfast the next morning, and eats only a spoonful or two of the porridge Mum gets me to take him.

A lot of work has piled up while we've been away, and now, as well, we have to bury the pig. "Nice bloody job that'll be," Mum says. "All that money wasted." There are tears in her eyes. "And we still don't have any nice meat for Easter."

It's as if we're a different family, and my tall, strong father, whose soft-voiced orders have always felt like iron, has become Laurence's age. I know he deserves to be punished, but it's as if he's no longer part of the family. My mother is kind and nice to everyone except him—even me, for a change. Now, we all decide things together, and if I say something, she listens. And the best part is, I can feel the love between us all.

Claude has been practicing driving on the farm, and we all follow the tractor as he drives it to a field, where he ploughs a short furrow. Then, he brings the lorry over, climbs up, and, coughing, clips a chain to the pig's hind leg. He jumps down. "Crawling with maggots." With the chain's other end attached to the tractor, he drives away till the half pig crashes into its grave. Then, everyone except Laurence works with shovels and mattocks to cover it over.

Dad isn't up when we arrive home, and Mum gets me to take him some soup. "Thanks, Love," he says. "Put it there. But I haven't much use for it." Tears are rolling down his cheeks as I turn and leave.

He's still in bed the next day, and that afternoon, I've just finished bringing the milking cows in and locking up their calves for the night when Mum rushes out of the house, Amelia hovering behind her, looking frightened. "Have you seen your father anywhere?"

Shaking my head, I tell her I haven't.

Claude comes out of the shed. "He isn't in there."

"Leila hasn't seen him, either," Mum yells. She goes back to the verandah and checks the rifles hanging there. "Oh no! One of the 22's is missing! God knows what he'll do in the state he's in."

Then I understand.

In minutes, we're spread out and moving across the paddocks. He could be anywhere on our seven hundred acres. Amelia walks with Laurence, who's six, helping him through rough or bushy parts and over logs.

We don't find Dad in the valley where the house is, though I wonder if we've missed him—he could be hidden by tall grass, bushes, logs, or little hillocks.

We continue in silence, walking as quickly as we can, and after squelching through a bog, and crossing a stream we're in the the big paddock. Laurence looks tired but doesn't complain.

Claude goes in a different direction to the rest of us, but when we rejoin, he hasn't found him. We hurry on, full of dread.

It's almost dark when Mum, who's ahead of the rest of us, stops and stares at something hidden from us by bushes. When we get to her, we see Dad sitting on a log, staring at a rifle lying on the ground with it's barrel pointing towards him, as if he's making a final bargain with it.

Seeing us, he bursts into tears, and, crying with him, we all try to hug him at once. We kiss his head and face and hands, and rub his back and shoulders and arms, and tell him we love him.

Surrounding and supporting him, we make our way home in the gathering gloom. Back inside the house, my mother and Claude help him back into bed and take him a cup of tea. After dinner, all our anger gone, we sit by the fire in quietness and peace.

By the end of the week, Dad is back working in the paddocks, and it's hard to believe that he's the same person who terrified us on the cutting. Everything in the family feels better than before, and my parents seem happier.

Even so, when we happen to be alone with Mum, she tells us again that we aren't to go to town alone with him ever again.

She makes him teach her how to drive the lorry. He looks uncomfortable in the passenger seat, but soon the vehicle is jumping across the front yard, Dad yelling things like, "Stop!" or "Brake! Brake!" The lorry makes horrible noises as Mum learns to change gears. "Push it right down to the floor or you'll strip the gears!" he yells. And Mum yells back, "Why don't you tell a person what to do in time?"

But soon, though she still seems nervous behind the wheel, she's driving smoothly all the way to the potato field and back. We're all pleased when she gets her license, though I'd still rather drive with Dad—when he's sober, at least.

He's sworn off the drink again, but if he goes somewhere alone and is late getting back, images of the lorry turned over below a cutting come more often than ever.

Chapter Forty-five

LAST DAY OF CHILDHOOD

When I'm twelve, Mum's cousin Jenny, her husband Dave and their children, telephone to say they're coming to visit the following Sunday. We've called on them quite a few times, and they're very polite—and really boring.

The day before, we sweep, scrape, mop, wipe and polish everything, and put vases of flowers in most of the rooms. Our cups are thick and white with what look like grains of black sand, and many are chipped, so we're embarrassed to use them when we have visitors, and Amelia and I ask Mum if we can use her good tea set.

"Well... I know you shouldn't have things you don't use, but I'd hate to break something."

She finds a chair and positions it below the high shelf where she keeps the set, and begins to tell the story we've heard several times before of how she won it in a raffle at a tennis match at Ellerston when she was sixteen, beginning with how she and her brother, Geoff, had to get up before daylight and saddled their horses by the light of a lantern before they set off on the fourteen mile journey.

She hands a cup and saucer and the milk jug and teapot down to us, and we put these on the middle of the table. After she's climbed down, we all stand admiring the china, which is white on the outside, pink on the inside, and edged with gold.

"Can we use it when they come?" Amelia asks again.

Mum takes a deep breath, and sighs, "I spose a person could."

She returns to her story. "I'd never have been allowed to keep it if the minister had had his way. Everyone wanted that set, and when they announced that I'd won it, I heard him say—she arranges her mouth to imitate his upper-class accent—'What a pity it's going up to that wild place!'"

"Well, Miss Hay—the postmistress at Moonan, happened to hear him. 'There's no reason why Gwen can't have nice things up there, the same as anywhere else,' she said. That shut him up."

Carefully, I pick up the cup. Its shape reminds me of the bodice of a wasp-waisted woman of former times, from the fullness of her bosom to the waist, the base like the beginning of a skirt.

"It's bone china," Mum says as if she's telling us for the first time.

"Do they use real bones?" I ask, as I always do, trying not to think of the bones clattering into my plate with the soup she makes.

"Oh yes," she says, nodding her head. "The bone is what makes it so white."

"How do they get the bones into it?"

"Oh, I don't know!" she says irritably. "Grind them up, I spose." She frowns at me. "Why can't you ever accept anything a person says?"

She lifts a saucer, and looks from Amelia to me. "Do you know how you can tell it's bone china?" She positions the saucer between us and the window, her fingers behind it. "See the shadows of my fingers through it?"

She's shown us this before, more than once. "Can we use the set when Jenny comes?" I ask again.

"Never mind that. Do you see what I'm showing you?"

"Yeah."

She puts the saucer back on the table.

"But can't we use the set tomorrow, Mum?" I insist.

"The other cups have chips," Amelia adds.

Mum looks at her, then me, then back at the china. Her words come out in puffs. "I wonder if a person should?" Hands on her hips, she stares at the china. "I ought to use it. I hate the idea of things just sitting in cupboards."

Amelia clasps and twists her hands in front of her. "It's so beautiful; it'd be lovely to use it."

Mum smiles as if she's imagining us and the visitors drinking tea out of the cups. She lifts the teapot with both hands, and gazes at it. Then the smile leaves her face. "Oh I don't know," she says. "A person'd hate to break something." And she puts the pieces back into the cupboard.

***

The visitors look just as uninteresting as I remember. I watch to see if they hate our old cups, but they handle them as if they *are* Mum's good set. Everything about Jenny is grey—her dress, her eyes, the roll of hair around her head. And she and Dave and the kids are all very neat. They all have their hair parted on the left, and strands lie across Dave's bald patch. The adults talk in low voices as if they're trying not to wake someone, and the children just smile. I can't imagine any of them ever having a good laugh the way Auntie and Polly do.

"Milk or orange juice?" Jenny asks the children—she's brought both. Mum's already told us how old they are—Amy's nine, Darlene's twelve, like me, and Rick's thirteen. I can't believe that kids their age drink orange juice and milk instead of tea—which I've drunk since I was six. They drink slowly, putting the glass down after every sip.

Mum says, "You've got good kids, Jenny. Very obedient."

She loves the word "obedient." It's as if she's talking about dogs.

Jenny smiles. "Oh, they have their moments, like any healthy kids, believe me."

After a while, they begin to fidget; then Amy walks over to her mother's chair and, in a whining little voice like she's three years old asks if they can go outside and play!

"Would it be alright if Leila shows them round, Gwen?" Jenny asks.

Mum nods. "Yes, I spose so."

Jenny turns her soft face towards me. "Would you, Leila?"

She raises an eyebrow—my face must have shown that I don't want to. "If you don't mind?"

How can I get out of this? I don't usually go off with people's kids.

Jenny is smiling at me. "It won't be that bad. You might even enjoy yourself!" She pauses, and looks at Laurence. "Maybe you'd like to go with them, too, Laurence?"

He says he would, and gets up.

"Go on Leila—it won't hurt you," says Mum.

I scrape my chair out from the table, and walk to the door where Laurence and the stupid city slicker kids are waiting for me. I glance back at Amelia, who's sitting up very straight and talking in her sensible voice like an adult, and is staying inside with the women. I throw her an angry look, but she pretends not to notice. It's funny, she's only sixteen, but she actually looks as if she belongs with the women.

Laurence and the other kids follow me like chicks. *Anyway, I don't have to talk to them.*

But Darlene, comes alongside of me. "Sorry you got saddled with us."

I look up quickly, and our eyes meet. I can't believe that she's saying something out loud that shows she understands that I don't want to be with them—and is apologizing. Nobody in my family would do that; something unpleasant could be going on right in front of us, but nobody would mention it unless you had to because someone was about to die. And a little warmth passes between us. "It's OK," I tell her, because that's what you say. But the weirdest thing is, once the words are out of my mouth, I mean them.

"Lets do the quick tour," she says. "That way, it'll be over sooner. Quick tour, gang," she calls over her shoulder to the others. "Repeat after me." She nods towards the shed, her shiny brown hair moving in one mass. "Shed."

"Shed," echo the others.

"You've got to do whatever I do," says Darlene. She starts walking in a funny, jerky way, and soon everyone, including Laurence and I, are doing the same thing.

"I know—let's make a conga line," Rick says.

We line up, our hands on the waist of the person in front; mine are on Darlene's. As we move off, suddenly, I feel light and happy, and say to her, "I like showing you round."

She smiles at me, and then calls to the others, "Let's go!" and we all move off. "Cow," she calls, nodding towards Nancy, on the other side of the fence.

"Cow," say the others, giggling.

"Nancy's her name," I say.

"Sorry—Nancy's her name," Darlene echoes. "Sorry Nancy's her name," giggle the others. And soon we're all laughing.

We're heading for an electric fence that's just been put up. "Stop!" I say, holding up my arm. "Electric fence! If you touch it, you'll get a shock."

"Stop! Shocking electric Fence!" yells Darlene, the line breaks up and we all fall onto the ground, roll around laughing and then sit for a while. "I'm not going near the thing," Darling says. She hops up and runs in the opposite direction, the rest of us following.

I never run unless I have to—that's for kids. But before I know it, I'm running everywhere with them, and it feels great. I point to things, and we shriek and giggle. Then, feeling peppery all over and very thirsty, I tell the others to come inside for something to drink, and start off running. Then I think how silly I must look, and slow to a walk.

Amelia is in the loungeroom talking with Mum and Jenny—the men have gone off somewhere—and pays no attention to us. We're all puffing. I've never run around like this, even when I was small—and it feels peculiar, but also really good. I know a couple of girls my age—I see Jenny MacLaughlin and her cousin in town sometimes, or if we go to a rodeo or something, and that's nice, but we walk, and talk quietly.

Mum always says that playing is a waste of time. I keep expecting that she'll say this now, or complain about the noise we're making, but she does neither. Jenny says, "You all seem to be having a good time."

And I realize that our playing seems normal to her. "Amelia was just telling me she hopes to go nursing. What do you want to do when you grow up, Leila?"

"I want to get a job in the city when I'm old enough." I'd decided that years ago, when Auntie first talked to us about working there, but I've never talked to Mum about it, and I'm telling her as well. "I might go nursing, too," I add. But no surprise shows on Mum's face. Jenny's always seemed so... dry... but now she says with a quirky grin I find myself liking, "Is that so?"

"And I want to live in a two-story house with a hedge," I say, making it up as I go. "Near a river with a swimming hole."

Jenny looks at Mum. "Wait till she has kids, eh Gwen? She'll soon find out she can't have everything she wants."

Then I hear myself say, "I'm never going to have kids." *That should shut them up.*

She, Mum and Amelia all laugh. "You'll change your mind," says Jenny. "They usually come along whether you want them or not—don't they Gwen?"

Mum looks uncomfortable and shifts in her seat.

"Well, I'm not going to have any," I say. Darlene and the others have already gone outside again, and now I follow them.

We come inside for lunch and later for afternoon tea, but the rest of the time, we continue to run around.

The sun is setting when our visitors say goodbye, but the happy feeling stays with me as their car disappears over the hill. It's growing dark, but I linger outside, our screeches and giggles still in the air. As the yellow fades from the sky, I walk towards the house, the lovely day settling into smoothness and quiet in my body.

***

The Tilley lamp's light glares as I go into the loungeroom where my parents, Claude and Amelia are, and I think how stiff they look.

As I walk past Amelia, she sniffs, then screws up her face and waves her arms in the air between us. "Pooh! You've got B.O. You'd better go and give yourself a good scrub."

I don't know what she means. "B.O.?"

"B.O.?" Mum screeches. "She's too young to have B.O." She gestures for me to come over to her. The happiness draining out of me, I stand there while she lifts one of my arms and sniffs my armpit. "Thew!" she says, drawing back and coughing. "That's B.O. alright." She stares at me.

I feel like crying. All the while I've been feeling so happy, my body has been getting stinkier... I look from Amelia to Mum. "What's B.O.?"

Amelia's voice is like sandpaper. "Body odour. It's what you get when you sweat."

"Perspire, Amelia. *Perspire."* Mum turns to me. "It's something that happens when you... reach... a certain age."

I sniff my own underarms, and get a whiff of something like cut onions. But I say, "I can't smell anything much."

"That doesn't mean a thing," Amelia says. "You never can smell your own BO." She turns to Mum. "You'll have to buy her some deodorant."

"Why on earth would she have B.O. at her age?" Mum asks Amelia, as if I'm not there.

Amelia looks at me. "It's no wonder—running around all day like a mad thing! You're too old for those capers."

Mum says again, "She's too young to have B.O."

"Well, she has it anyway," Amelia snaps. "Running around like that." To me she says again, "You'd better go and wash yourself before dinner."

It's as if I've turned into someone like Mervin, a man who lives in Moonan everyone laughs about because he never washes and smells terrible.

I boil up the kettle, pour it into a dish, add cold water, go to the bathroom, and soap and rinse myself. A few times when we've met Mervin in the street—because he saw us before we saw him—he lifted a trouser leg to show us his "war wound," as he calls it, and his leg was filthy with what looked like mud. My parents are always polite to him, though they stand as far away from him as possible.

From the loungeroom, I hear Mum saying yet again that she can't believe I have B.O. *God, won't she ever stop?*

Then I hear Amelia ask, in a low voice, "Have you told her about..." I can't hear the rest, but I Mum replies, "No—not yet. I suppose it's about time."

" *The B.O. must be something to do with the bleeding Mum hasn't told me about yet. I wonder what other nasty surprises are in store?*

When I come back to where they are, Mum hands me a small pot of white cream. "If you rub that under your arms, it'll stop the BO. Make sure you use it when you go to town."

Chapter Forty-six

EVERYTHING IS CHANGING

Usually, if a crop grows particularly well one year, all the other crops of the same type in that area also do, driving the price down. But in 1956, potatoes bring the record price of ten pounds[1] a bag, suggesting that many crops failed and ours didn't. I don't know why, but maybe this was because Dad saved for seed most of the potatoes that survived the blight when we lost almost the whole crop—making his potatoes resistant to the disease, whereas those of the other farmers weren't. We end up with, for us, the incredible amount of a thousand pounds in the bank.

Dad buys a bulldozer, and once he and Claude have taught themselves to drive it, they start clearing our valley. First, they plan to cut down the big, dead trees, starting with the ones near the house. Dad says they can make them fall wherever they want them to, and it's safe to stay inside, but Amelia and I, who are friends again after the BO business, don't trust the process, and go for a walk. We cross the valley, and climb half-way up the hill on the other side, where, about a mile and a half away, we sit under a bottle brush[2] tree to watch.

A few moments later, we hear Mum screaming at Laurence, every word clear. Then there's rhythmic yelling from her, and wails, and we know she's hitting him. It's embarrassing to know that the neighbours in the white house, and even anybody who happens to be riding by, could hear. We're also surprised, as she seldom hits him. Lately, though, after dinner, when the rest of us have left the table, she and Dad have been staying there with him, and telling him to eat his vegetables. Usually, at some

---

[1] The pound was a unit of currency before Australia adopted the decimal system in 1966.

[2] One of the Callistemon or Melaleuca genus of shrubs endemic to Australia, although the ones near the farm were more like trees, being about fifteen feet, or five metres, high. Its flowers are shaped like the bottle brushes used for washing dishes.

point, they start yelling at him, Mum bursts into tears, and Dad says, "Now look what you've done! You've upset your mother." Then things become quiet, and Laurence starts eating.

After the wailing stops, we hear chopping, and, one by one, the huge trees around the house crash to the ground. None hits it, and we go home. When we get there, the bulldozer is pushing the fallen trees and old logs that have lain around forever into piles, and Mum is cooking in the kitchen. We're getting ourselves a cup of tea when Laurence appears, his face red from crying, and goes and stands in front of her. "Look," he says, showing her red marks criss-crossing his legs. She squats and peers at them, looking puzzled, and then stares up at him and asks, "What happened?"

"You did that with the switch," he says.

Strangely, her eyes widen. She looks at his legs again. "*I* did that?" she asks, as if she can't believe she did. We wonder what's wrong with her memory.

***

A few days later, Laurence and I explore the piles of logs and dead trees on the flat. In one, a log is so huge that it's like a wall next to us, and in it is a square, oven-like depression. It feels as if we're in a little house, and we gather chips and twigs, put them in the depression, and light them. But the fire has hardly started burning when we hear Mum yelling, "Get out of there, you two!" I climb out, and she goes in and drags Laurence out, then throws handfuls of dirt into our "oven" and puts the fire out. "What the hell do you kids think you're doing? Trying to burn yourselves up?"

One afternoon, Dad and Claude set all the piles alight, and that night, there are huge blazes all over the flat. It's cool, but the fires make the air so warm that Amelia and I race bare-armed from one to the other. But suddenly, something rips into my right arm and the pain is terrible. In the dark, I've collided with a newly-erected barbed-wire fence.

Sobbing, and blood running down my arm, Amelia helps me home. Mum disinfects and dresses the gashes, while I struggle to keep still, tears running down my face.

***

Mum receives a letter from Ruby, her brother Geoff's wife, who's just had her first baby and is ill; she and Uncle Geoff live with Nan and Grandfather, who now have a poultry farm and orange orchard near Gosford, not far from Sydney and about a hundred and fifty miles from us. She asks whether Mum could "spare Amelia for a few months to help out."

Mum and Dad want to say yes, and that night they talk with Amelia about going. She's still in school, but hasn't needed Mum to supervise her schoolwork for years, so they think she could continue with it at Nan and Grandfather's. She herself seems to see helping out as a bit of an adventure, so it's decided that she'll go.

When I say goodbye to her before she catches the train, I feel sad, but we don't always get along well these days, and I'll be glad to have the bedroom to myself.

***

Dad hasn't had a drink for so long that I've stopped worrying about going places in the lorry alone with him, and one hot afternoon, he says he's going to Moonan and Ellerston and asks me if I'd like to come.

We drive down the mountain, and he pulls up at Dry Creek, the tiny place where he and his family lived long ago, and asks if I'd like some lollies.[3]

I say I would, and he points to a house nearby with a large tin door. "If you knock on that door, the old woman inside will sell you some."

I have to knock twice before I hear footsteps and the door being unbolted. It opens a few inches, and an old woman's face appears, blinking at the light. She lets me in when I tell her I want to buy some lollies.

I hardly ever buy or eat sweets, so I don't know the ones in the jars, and point to some at random. As if she thinks I might steal something— or maybe it's just part of how peculiar she is—her eyes never leave my face as she slowly unscrews the lid and reaches in, rattling the hard lollies against the glass as she gathers them in a hand. She pops one into her mouth, and sucks away, then takes a white packet, opens it, lets the small avalanche fall in, and twists the top shut.

I'm looking forward to a sweet as I climb up into the cab of the lorry.

Dad is staring ahead and doesn't start the engine. "Did she get them out with her hands?"

"Yeah." *Why's he asking?*

"How do you know she'd washed them?"

My mouth goes dry. "Why did you ask me if I wanted lollies, then?" I'm surprised by my own cheekiness, but he doesn't seem to notice.

---

[3]Candies.

"Well, how was I to know she'd get them out with her hands?"

None of this makes sense. I shove the lollies into the glovebox, knowing I'll never eat them now, and we continue to Moonan. There he buys a couple of loaves of bread, and then we go to Ellerston, where someone gives him a box of tomatoes.

It's late in the afternoon when we get back to Dicky Dan's Crossing on the way home. Just after we cross, the engine conks out. While Dad tries to get it started again, I wander along the river bank, which is covered in rocks, and I slip on them now and then, but the beautiful song of the frogs is loud in my ears. I get back as he's closing the hood. "It's a warm night and we have plenty of corn bags on the back of the lorry to sleep under. I reckon we might as well camp here."

It's still hot, so we decide to have a swim in a waterhole nearby. Wearing just our underpants, we wade in. For a few moments, he splashes at me awkwardly, as if he's trying to play, though he's never really played with me, even when I was small. Then he points out, on the cliff on the other side of the river, funnel-shaped lumps of mud with holes in them. "Fairy martin's nests," he says. "They're a kind of swallow."

Back on the bank, we let the air dry us before we dress, and when it's nearly dark, we break pieces of bread off the loaves we bought and eat them with some of the tomatoes. I shine a torch for him to find the bags on the back of the lorry. He lays two for each of us side-by-side on the still-warm sand—one for a blanket. And when we lie down, I drift towards sleep with the heavenly sound of frogs popping, clinking and making their clacking sound, which is like rocks hitting one another under water. I wish I could go on hearing them forever.

The lorry starts easily the next morning. When we get home, Mum eyes Dad suspiciously, wondering if he's been drinking, I think. He explains that we broke-down, and it's soon obvious that he hasn't been.

But I wonder if we really broke down; perhaps he just wanted to spend some time relaxing with me.

***

Dad builds a room next to the kitchen, and, off it, a large bedroom and an inside toilet, for which he puts in a septic system. And, next to the back verandah, he builds a laundry and a bathroom.

We've never had electricity in any of our houses, including the one we're in now—it's still not available this far from Scone. We haven't had water laid on in any of the houses we've lived in, including the current one, either; our water has always been collected from the roof during rain, and stored in a corrugated iron tank. The one here holds a thousand gallons, and mostly it rains a lot, so there's been enough; but sometimes, in dry spells, we've almost run out, and have had to use water sparingly and keep checking the level in the tank by listening to the sound when we banged on it with a stick.

But now Dad and Claude dig a trench about half a mile long and halfway to the house from the stream that runs into the swamp at the far end of the valley. Then they run the water into piping which brings it the rest of the distance to the house, and we have cold water laid on.

Always, till now, if we wanted hot water, we've had to heat it on the stove, but now Dad and Claude figure out how we can have it from the tap. Dad buys what's called a "slow combustion" stove, which burns wood like the old one but extracts the heat more efficiently, and he and Claude secure pipes carrying cold water around it, so that we have hot water in the kitchen, laundry and bathroom. Claude saves up the small wages Dad pays him and buys a double sink as a present for my parents, and when it's installed, we say goodbye to the old tin dish.

Then Claude and Dad go to Scone and come home with a new bath. It's wrapped in cardboard and paper like a huge, square present, and grunting and puffing, they and Trevor, who's helping out briefly, get it into the new bathroom. In one place, the wrapping has torn away, through which I see its green surface gleaming with cleanliness; I'm so looking forward to being able to bathe in it instead of the greasy old tin bath I've always hated.

But when they unwrap it, I see a crack in the bottom. I show them, saying they'll have to return it. "Oh that's nothing," says Dad. "That don't make no difference. It doesn't leak, and the bloke knocked the price down."

Claude is standing in the doorway. "You don't want to let a little thing like that worry you. There's nothing wrong with that bath."

Why can't we ever have something that's new and perfect? I can't believe they bought it like that.

But despite the crack, once it's installed, I have a nice deep bath and pretend it's a swimming hole, and that the walls—though Mum has painted them pink—are a rock cliff, like the one next to the swimming hole in Dicky Dan's Crossing.

***

I've just finished sixth class, and am about to start highschool. I wish I could go to a real school. A while back, when Mum would become angry, she'd threaten to send me to boarding school, though I knew she never would. So I started responding with, "That'd be good. I'd like to go to a real school instead of doing correspondence." And I asked her if I could sit for a bursary that would pay for me to go to a boarding school.

"Oh you wouldn't be able to get a bursary; they'd say we earn too much. I know we don't have a lot of money, but that's what they'd say. We pay a terrible lot of tax." I so wish I could go to a real school; I think the Government should give special consideration to country children. And I wonder if Mum has it right about the bursary—I don't think she's really checked. But I have no idea how to find out what the truth is, so plan to continue with correspondence for highschool.

She helps me choose my subjects for first year, and I end up with needlework, art, history and geography. "What about mathematics?" I ask.

"Oh you'd never be able to do mathematics," she says.

I don't know why she thinks this because I've always done quite well in Maths—at least when she wasn't standing over me with the strap, frightening me so badly that I couldn't think. But not liking the subject much, and knowing that I can sit for a test in English and Arithmetic to get into nursing once I'm old enough, I don't argue.

Needing to get away from Mum's anger, I tell her that I want to supervise myself from now on. Again, she's negative. "I don't think you could work alone like that."

"Well, Amelia did."

"But you're not like her. She's always been very responsible."

I ignore the last bit. "I know I can do it. It'll be better for you if you don't have to supervise me."

She eventually agrees to let me, pleased to be free of one burden, at least—she still has to supervise Laurence.

***

I don't know why, but things between Mum and me have been better since Amelia left, and I'm pleased when my parents decide that just they and I should spend a week with Grandma and Grandfather at Warners Bay. Claude is to keep an eye on the property, and they send Laurence in the mail truck to Polly's, where he'll stay till we get back.

Before we leave, Mum takes me to her wardrobe. "You'd better start wearing one of these," she says, picking up a pink bra and opening it out. "You're very well-developed for twelve." She looks away. "It's not nice when people can see too much through your clothes."

I know she means nipples; in Scone once, seeing a woman walking down the street in a cotton t-shirt, her nipples like wobbling sink plugs, she said, "She looks as if she's nude."

A miriad of long threads of pink cotton, from the places where the whirlpool stitching has broken, wave like thin worms from the old bra's cups and inside each is a large tuck. I know she'll never get me a new one without a lot of persuasion, and although I hate the idea of wearing her old bra, I can't wait to try it on. And when I do, Hey presto! my breasts are transformed into two hard mounds.

We arrive at my grandparents' house in the early evening. Grandfather out somewhere, Grandma takes thick, coloured cups from the kitchen cabinet, and we sit drinking tea in the front room and admiring the flowered bone china in a glass-fronted cabinet. She's small, unlike the rest of us, who are tall and sturdy. When she leaves the room for something, I say how lovely her face is.

Mum smiles. "It's her bones."

Images of Mum's bone china tea set come into my mind. Even though she's old, her face looks as delicate as bone china. "Her bones?"

"Her high cheek bones."

Grandfather still hasn't come home by the time we go to bed, but the next morning, a breathy whistling wakes me, and when I go to the kitchen, he's making breakfast. He smiles when I come in, and later, as we eat, he talks about the "dorgs"—greyhound races—he was at the day before, and offers to take Dad to the "ponies"—horse races—that afternoon. After breakfast, Mum, Dad and I decide to go swimming in the bay, and Grandma appears in a bathing suit of matted green wool with a scattering of moth holes, and announces that she's coming, too. As she splashes about in the shallow water, I think how wonderful it is that she doesn't care about people seeing her skinny legs and the folds of flesh hanging from her thighs.

That night, Grandfather doesn't say much at dinner, but Grandma tells stories about how the people where she and her family lived one time were afraid that a group of Aborigines known as the "Breelong Blacks" would break in and murder them. Everyone's quiet for a while, and then Grandfather says, "All the same, what people done to them black people wasn't right."

When we leave a few days later, I'm sad to say goodbye to Grandma; I feel I hardly know grandfather.

We take the coast road, which I've never been on before, and near a town called Forster, we pass a collection of huts, rough houses and water tanks surrounded by a high fence. Inside, black people wander around, or stare at the passing traffic, hands spread on the netting as if they're prisoners.

I crane my neck to look back, then ask what I've just seen.

Mum sighs. "An Aboriginal reserve, that's what that was."

"A *reserve?*" I'm puzzled. The only reserve I know is the piece of land near ours set aside for cattle being driven to market to rest in. "A reserve for *people?*"

"I know. I know. That's what they call these places. They're for Aborigines. They used to wander all over the countryside, but now the authorities have put them in these reserves. It must be awful for them."

"But why do they call them reserves? Reserves are for animals."

"How am I supposed to know?" she snaps.

We continue in silence, images of the faces and hands behind the wire strong in my mind. In my history lessons, I've read about trouble between the aborigines and the early settlers, and Mum has told me that Australia was their land first. In the district where we live, there is an Aboriginal woman married to a white man who have several little boys, and these are the only Aboriginal people I've seen previously.

Part III

GROWN UP

Chapter Forty-seven

I'M A WOMAN NOW

On the way to Scone one day, I find myself feeling slightly nauseous, lay a hand on my belly and close my eyes.

Beside me, Mum asks, "What's the matter with you?" She's looking at me strangely.

"I feel sick."

She lowers her eyes. "It might be your age." She throws a look at Dad, but he's concentrating on his driving and doesn't notice. "I think I'd better give you a book to read when we get home."

Claude told me about periods in his ugly way years ago, and I remember Amelia and him giggling at the diagrams of nude people in a book they found in my parents' wardrobe, and reading aloud things about sex. I'll have to pretend it's new information.

We don't get back till late that night, and the next day, she hands me a booklet with a paper cover. "Here's that book I said I'd give you." On the cover is a sketch of a young woman on a chair absorbed in a booklet the same as the one in my hand, and behind her, an older woman gazes lovingly down at her. It's entitled, "Becoming a Woman." Mum hesitates as if she wants to say something else, then turns and goes outside.

I sit on my bed and look through the booklet. The square-shouldered dresses in the illustrations were fashionable when Mum was young—she used to make clothes with shoulders like that for Amelia and me till we convinced her that they were out-of-date (which took some doing). *Oh God! This must be the booklet her mother gave her!* It's obviously put out by the company that sells menstrual products, and whose name is on the cover—strange, considering how my parents hate capitalism.

Mention is made of the "new responsibilities" that menstruation brings, such as being able to get pregnant—though the authors don't explain how

Figure 47.1: Me at thirteen with bush in background.

this can happen. When the booklet was put out, people probably thought that young ladies didn't need such information. The booklet claims that, with their brand of pads and belts—the clips lie flat against the body so that there are "no telltale outlines"—you can wear "sheer and fashionable clothing, and even swimwear" when you're menstruating. As long as you don't go in the water, I guess. I like the sketch of the mother handing the daughter a packet of white, disposable pads, and an image flashes into my mind of the disgusting bits of old towels writhing on the clothes line. The booklet says that menstruation represents "the beginning of womanhood," and makes it sound like something to celebrate.

Such positivity is foreign to me. I'm used to Claude and my parents warning about, and fearing, so many things. Whenever we go to Scone, Dad reminds us not to sit down on public toilets because we might catch a disease, and to wash our hands after handling money—which he calls "the filthiest thing on God's earth." To my parents, kissing is "filthy," and they shudder at the thought of New Year's Eve parties. And they're always talking as if "the American Imperialists" might start another war at any moment. The booklet shows me a new way of looking at life.

Later that afternoon, I hand it back to Mum.

She looks surprised. "Did you read it?"

I wish she'd stop. "Yes."

"Is there anything you want to ask me about?"

"No."

A few days later, I happen to be near Mum as she's pegging clothes on the line. "Men don't respect you if you give in to them, you know," she says. *Why would she think I'd know what she's talking about—I certainly wouldn't from reading the booklet!*

"Oh?" I murmur.

Some months later, I find a little V of blood on my panties. *It's happened—my periods have come!* I stand in front of the loungeroom window, looking out. The valley, under blue-black clouds, is the most vivid green I've ever seen it. "I'm a woman," I murmur. "I'm a woman." And joy floods through me.

Reluctantly, I make my way to Mum in the garden. She straightens up, and looks at me. It's hard to speak. "I think my period's come," I finally manage in a raspy voice. She looks at me as if she's taking me all in, and a strange look of pleasure comes onto her face.

After she's washed her hands, she takes me into her and Dad's bedroom and opens the big drawer at the bottom of the wardrobe—where I imagine

Figure 47.2: My mother's beautiful flower garden.

she's keeping the pads for me. She pulls out a bulky harness in grubby-looking unbleached calico, and dangles it in front of me. A big white button on a stalk—obviously part of the clasp—swings back and forth, and attached to two tabs of material are large safety pins. I half listen to her explaining how to put it on, revulsion rising in me at the thought that she must have worn it.

But she's holding it out. "Take it," she says cheerfully, as if I'm too dense to know what it is. "It's a belt—I made it myself."

I still don't take it.

"Don't you remember reading about them in the book I gave you?"

The last thing I want is to talk with her about what's in the booklet. "I know," I say, forcing myself to take the thing with the tips of my fingers.

Mum laughs. "It won't bite."

I lay it on the corner of the bed, and search for something to say; but she's looking in the drawer again—for the bought pads, I hope. Instead, her hand emerges holding some of the oblongs of threadbare toweling she's stitched together. An image of similar ones floating in a dish of ruby water one day when I came back from the potato field to get something flashes in my mind.

"But I thought—" I begin. Puzzled, she eyes me in a kindly way. *But she must have some bought pads in the drawer for me.* "I thought... er... you'd give me a packet of the pads they talk about in the booklet..."

Suddenly, her face clears. *Now she'll get them.*

"Oh! I see!'" she says, then adds in a strong voice, "Oh no! These are just as good. I make them, and they cost nothing." she pauses. "Those bought ones are too expensive." She holds them out. "Now, you'd better go and put one of these on." She pauses. "Do you know how to pin it on?" She puts the toweling wads under her left arm, and picks up the belt to demonstrate. Horrified, I blot her out as she goes through the procedure.

I am dense. The grubby belt and toweling wads are all she has. "OK," I say, taking them, and escaping to my room.

Before I put on one of the toweling monstrosities, I remember that the booklet said to be careful of hygiene, and mentioned "frequent showers." We don't have a shower, but we do have the cracked green bath, and I hope the warm water will soothe the strange heaviness in my belly.

Lying in the bath, my happiness returns. "I'm a woman," I tell myself, over and over. And I make a resolution: "I'll never let Mum hit me again."

I wrap myself in a towel and go back to my room. Everything seems pleasantly fuzzy. I catch a whiff of a stale smell from the horrid old belt as I button it on, and resolve to buy one and some pads the next time I'm in town. The toweling thing feels rough on my tender parts. I put on slacks, and examine myself in the mirror. Sure enough, you can see the bulkiness, and the lump where the button is looks like a boil on my bum. If anyone knew I was having my period, I think I'd die. I find a long sweater to wear over the slacks.

Later, I overhear Mum telling Dad the news, so casually that she might be talking about one of the heifers "springing," meaning that slimy mucous is coming out of her, indicating that she's close to calving. And his response sounds less interested than if I *were* such a heifer. I know she's told him because it's a kind of milestone, but his knowing embarrasses me. I don't intend to discuss my periods with her ever again, and don't tell her that I've decided to buy pads. I'll have enough money; Dad always gives me money when we go to town, and nobody asks what I spend it on.

***

On the way to Scone the next time we go, we call on Polly and Charlie, who have just moved to Dry Creek, and offer to get them anything they need, and they give us a list. As we continue on our way, I silently practice asking for pads and a belt.

But I have to walk around with Mum and Laurence and wait for a chance to slip off to what we call "the chemist" where you can buy such things. It closes at five o'clock, and as the afternoon wears on, I start to worry. Then we meet Dad on the street, and he tells us we'll be heading home after some tea at the Vogue Cafe, and the chemist is right across the road from there, so I'll have my chance. I add a lot of milk to my tea, drink it quickly, and say, "I just remembered! There's something I forgot to buy." I get up quickly and leave before anybody can question me."

I stroll past the chemist shop, looking in through the window. *Nobody I know is in there.* Mr. Jackson, the silver-haired Pharmacist, is in the booth where he makes up the prescriptions, and Marge, his young, curly-haired assistant, is at the till. I scan the street in both directions. *Nobody I know is coming.* I look back inside, take a deep breath, and go in.

"Have you got any—" my voice is a squeak. "I mean, I'd like—some... pads... a packet... please. And a b-b-belt."

"Pins or clips?"

I stare at her, not quite understanding.

"On the belt."

"Oh—yes." An image of those huge safety pins on the contraption Mum gave me flashes. "Clips, please."

"Pink or white?"

Through the display window, I see a sheep farmer we know coming up the street. I look back at Marge, who's grinning to herself as if she knows what's going on and finds it funny.

"W-what?"

"Pink or white?"

"Um—white."

She finds the pads and belt and puts these on the counter.

Pink would have been better. The farmer is hesitating in front of the shop, but I say, "Um—can I have pink instead? I'm sorry."

"Certainly." She exchanges a pink for the white. A telephone rings. *Thank goodness it's the one next to Mr. Jackson.* He answers as, back at the till, Marge tears a piece of brown paper from the roll, lays the items on its shiny side, and is about to start ringing them up when Mr. Jackson calls, "It's for you, Marge." Marge takes the call. The pads and things in front of me, I stand there squeezing my hands together, checking the street and wishing she'd hurry back. *Good. The farmer has gone, and nobody else is coming. Oh God, please make her hurry.* But she's talking and laughing as if she has all day. "Well you can pick me up here at 5.30... No, but if I go to your place... Well I know, but he won't be in... "

Then I see a woman with slitty eyes I know, walking towards the shop. *Please God, let her walk by.* A cough brings my eyes back to the counter. "Will that be all?" Mr. Jackson's silver head is before me, his hands hovering over the items on the brown paper.

I nod, very embarrassed, as Mr. Jackson tots them up on the cash register. His back straight and his mouth clamped shut, he carefully folds the corners of the paper into triangles, wraps everything up, and snaps the parcel shut with sticky tape, just as slitty-eyes walks in. *Thank you, God. I'm safe.*

Our lorry is parked near the Vogue, and realizing that if I carry the parcel in with me, Mum will want to know what's in it, I push it between some boxes where nobody will notice it, planning to sneak it out when we get home.

Only Polly is home when we get to her and Charlie's place, and Laurence and I go into the kitchen with her, leaving Dad, Mum and Claude to bring the things we bought for her and Charlie inside. Polly asks me about my school work, how Amelia is doing, and whether we're going to an upcoming rodeo. Then I hear loud voices coming from outside. "Well whose could it be then?" Mum screeches. Dad sounds annoyed, too. "How should I know?" *I wish they wouldn't argue when other people can hear.*

Polly throws me a glance and gives a short laugh. "Looks like there's trouble at the OK Corral. Well, just as long as they don't get off with my things, I don't mind."

I hear Claude say, "It feels like wool."

Oh no! My parcel! The thought of Claude knowing what I've bought makes me feel sick.

Polly says, "Would you excuse me a minute, Lov? I've got a couple of things to do in the other room."

I consider going out there and saying, "That's mine." But they'd ask questions, and I don't move.

Dad echoes Claude. "It feels like wool."

Mum says irritably, "I told you. I didn't buy any wool."

"Well, did you buy some for Polly?"

"No I didn't! Give it to me so I can feel it." There's a silence which seems to stretch on and on. "What on earth could it be?"

There's still time. I could walk out there and say quietly, "That parcel's mine," take it and leave.

Dad's voice again. "Are you sure you didn't buy any wool?"

"Sure? Of course I'm sure. Don't be so damn stupid! Do you think a person's a fool?"

She pauses. "Are you sure you don't know what's in it, Claude?"

"Haven't got a clue. But it feels like wool."

Oh God. Will this never end?

"How can it be wool? I haven't bought any!" Mum shouts.

"Well, there's one sure way of finding out what's in it." Claude says.

I hear snaps as the sticky tape is broken. The rattle of the brown paper. A long silence, followed by Claude's guffaw.

Yuk!

Mum says, "Oh for heaven's sake!"

"What?" Dad asks—as he looks, no doubt. There's a pause, and then his soft laugh. The paper rattles again as the parcel is re-wrapped.

Soon they troop in with Polly's things, slight smiles on their faces as if they're trying not to laugh. They don't mention the parcel, and I keep my eyes averted from them all.

***

Mum says nothing to me about the pads. But a couple of months later, she asks why I haven't been "doing any washing."

'I wash my clothes every week," I say.

"No. I mean of those things I gave you," she says. "For your periods."

"I don't have any to wash."

"Why not?"

"I use bought ones."

"We can't afford them. They cost too much. I've never bought any, so why should you waste money on damn luxuries like that?"

"I buy them with my own money." I stand up tall, and stare back at her.

"Your *own* money! Don't you dare speak to me like that. What gives you the idea it's your money?"

I'm close to tears, and yet, inside, I feel stronger than I've ever felt in my whole life. "It *is* my money."

Her face ugly now, her hands become fists and begin to lift. I grab them. "Stop it!" I say, the loudness of my voice surprising me. "I'm a woman now, and I'm not going to let you hit me ever again!"

"We'll see about that!" she shouts, but her attempt to extricate her fists is half-hearted. I eventually let them go and step back. She throws punches at my body and one hits me on the arm. Then she almost loses her balance, and, for a moment, I feel sorry for her. She hesitates, starts to walk past me, then suddenly turns, and lands a painful uppercut under my tailbone. She glares at me for a moment, but I see in her eyes a recognition that I'm no longer her victim. And then she's gone.

Elated, but shaking all over, and my arm and tailbone hurting from her punches, I go to my room. I can scarcely believe how easy it was. *Could I have stopped her years ago?* But I'm sure if I'd stood up to her when I was smaller, she'd have grabbed me and given me a worse beating than ever. And I know that she could feel the strength of my conviction just now, and that was not there before.

Chapter Forty-eight

AMELIA RETURNS

I'm thirteen when my father hears that Scone Council is calling for tenders to build a road some ten miles long to avoid Dicky Dan's Crossing, and it's to be near Dry Creek where Polly and Charlie live. The contract is worth a lot of money, he says, and, being the owner of a bulldozer which Claude usually drives now, he decides to put in a bid. The lowest bid from someone who looks as if he can do the job, will win, he tells us, adding that the bids are kept secret till the decision is made. When I ask him how he can make the lowest bid without knowing what the other bids are, he just grins.

When we hear that he's won, we're all very excited. One day, Claude tells me what may explain his success. He'd discovered that one of the biggest expenses in building any road is related to the size of the outcrops of rock where it's to go, and that potential bidders drill into any outcrops on a proposed route with an instrument called a corer to estimate this cost. The corer is hollow and produces pieces of rock showing the depth of the stone deposits, and he and Claude obtained one. The outcrops where the road was to go proved to be fairly thin, and they took these cores away and hid them. Then they searched the district and beyond, till they found very thick deposits of the same type of rock and obtained cores from these, which they took back to the site of the proposed road, placing them next to the holes they'd already drilled. The idea was that, seeing these, other potential bidders would assume that they represented the true thickness of the rock deposits, and submit high quotes. I can scarcely believe my father's cunning.

The first thing he and Claude do is to build a bark hut near where the road is to be, for themselves and whoever they employ to live in while they're working there. And the family will also be able to stay in it, say, if the road home is slippery or boggy. The hut is on the bank of a river close to a waterhole about thirteen feet deep, with big rocks to jump off. It's summer and the water is warm, and we love swimming there, as well as sitting on the bank late in the day listening to the loud sounds of the frogs. Soon we're spending a lot of time at the hut, and visiting Polly and Charlie more often as well.

***

We receive a letter from Amelia to say that she's coming home, as Aunt Ruby no longer needs her. The train she's supposed to arrive on is very late, and we wait on the platform of the station. I remember Amelia's slimness, her straight, brown hair, and the way she clasps her hands together in front of her when she's anxious. But I haven't seen her for something like a year, and I can no longer get a clear image of her.

Finally, the train appears in the distance, looking like a toy, then rushes in, looms, and stops. I have to look past the girl with bushy fair hair— me in a reflecting window—to the doors opening along the train's length. A sophisticated-looking woman in a black sheath dress with a white lace collar emerges and walks, a little uncertainly, towards us. I wonder if she was always as pretty, and I didn't notice.

After she's hugged the others, she says hello to me with a catch in her voice, and a secret look passes between us. She let's me go before I've finished hugging her—which is familiar. As we move through the station to the lorry, Dad carrying her suitcase, she says things like, "Everything looks the same," and her hands make quick movements, as if they don't quite know what to do with themselves. I wish she and I could ride on the back of the lorry together so we could talk, but someone so ladylike obviously must ride in the front. I just hope she won't think she'll always be riding there from now on!

On the way home, we stop briefly to show her the new bark hut. By the time we get to the Black Cutting, it's cold and misty, and at the house, Dad lights the fire in the loungeroom, Mum gets the stove going to cook dinner, and I follow Amelia into our bedroom.

She flips up the locks of her new suitcase like a seasoned traveler, and while she's hanging her clothes in the wardrobe, I tell her there's a rodeo at Moonan in a month's time, and we talk about going to the dance afterwards. She says she'll wear her strapless—which she hasn't worn since Warren's party. I mention that Mum has taught me to sew, and that I have a red dress I made, but I've worn it to a dance before, and

Figure 48.1: The road my father built around Dicky Dan's Crossing.

I'd like something new. She says I could cut a pattern from the one she's wearing, and make myself a sheath dress. But I'm not sure Mum would let me wear it, and I want something that's more fun.

I mention a couple of rodeos and boring dances I've been to while she's been away. Mum made me sit next to her, so I didn't get any boys asking me to dance. "As if it's not enough to have a six-foot-four father with a reputation as a boxer!" I add.

Amelia looks at me. "She'll want us to sit with her at this one, too— let's see if we can figure out a way not to."

We talk about whether we should change in the hut for the dance after walking around in the sun at the rodeo all day. "But it's miles away," I say, "and Polly might know someone who lives at Moonan where we could go."

Then she says, "Hey! You'll never guess what the gossip around the district is. Polly wrote to me, and apparently the old biddies are saying that I went away not to help Aunt Ruby, but to have a baby."

"My God! I've never heard anyone say that."

"Well, they wouldn't, in front of you, would they? Or in front of any of us."

"That's awful."

"I wasn't surprised—they're always saying some girl's having a baby. Maybe there wasn't anyone else to gossip about at the time."

She seems so much more confident than she used to be. "I wish I'd had the chance to be at Aunt Ruby's for a year," I say.

"Believe me, it wasn't any picnic. I worked like a slave picking beans and oranges and cooking and scrubbing floors—and I had to fit my school work in, too. Most of the time, it took me a fortnight instead of a week to finish a set of work. The only time I had off was a week when Ruby took me to Sydney and showed me round. That was great. And they bought me this outfit."

After we've helped Mum with dinner and done the washing-up, we hurry back to our room to talk some more. Amelia keeps searching in her suitcase and saying, "Damn," and she finally tells me that her period has started and she can't find her pads, so I lend her some.

While she's behind the wardrobe door putting one on, I say, "I want to try those tampon things."

"I do, too."

"They reckon you can even go swimming with them in."

"Yeah I know. Wouldn't that be great?"

Remembering "the booklet" Mum gave me—which doubtless she also gave to Amelia—I say, *"No tell-tale outlines."* We both laugh.

"Did Mum try to get you to use those horrible toweling things?" she asks.

"God yes." I shudder. "I bought some pads the next time I went to town after my periods started." I tell the story of how they found the packet of pads when they were looking for the things they'd bought for Polly, and we laugh and laugh. And I also tell her how, a few months later, Mum wanted to know why I hadn't been "doing any washing," and of my putting a stop to her hitting me.

When we're silent again, Amelia says, "One good thing about being at Ruby's was I didn't have those sorts of problems. I had a lot more freedom in some ways. Every time one of us pauses, the other thinks of something else to share. I've never felt so close to another person in my life. The wonderful thing is, despite the experiences she's had that I haven't, we feel the same about almost everything that comes up. We exchanged letters while she was away, but the words on the sheets of paper told us as much about what was happening to each other as the bark that curls off a tree tells about its life.

We talk a lot about boys. She didn't have a chance to meet any while she was away, and I've never met one who liked me, or that I liked. But maybe I'll meet someone at the rodeo dance...

Since she's been gone, I've stuck pictures of the singers I like above my bed—mainly Sal Mineo and Elvis, and one of Pat Boone.

I point to Sal. "Isn't he great?"

"I can take him or leave him." She taps the one of Pat Boone. "I like *him*, though. Maybe I'll put a nice one of him above my bed."

She's brought some *Women's Weeklies* and movie magazines, and in the next days, we devour everything we can about makeup, hairstyles, clothes, singers and movie stars. She loves Marilyn Monroe, who has a bit of a funny way of walking, but everyone says her wiggle is sexy. Amelia herself walks in kind of an odd way. Claude used to say she walked "like a duck," and that hurt her, but maybe her walk could look sexy, too. I think it was Marilyn who answered, when someone asked her what she wore to bed, "Chanel No. 5," and Amelia has a little bottle of it, and gives me some to try.

I say I like Sabrina because she has the biggest bust. We compare our measurements. Mine are 36-24-34. She says her bust is 38, but I think maybe she had her finger under the tape, or took a really big breath.

It's about one in the morning when we finally drift off to sleep, and I feel really happy.

The next time we go to Scone, we buy some more movie magazines; I like reading about how famous actresses are "discovered" when they're waitressing, walking down the street, or sitting in a cafe. It's as if it could happen to anyone—us included. One day you're living this boring life, and the next you're famous and your picture is everywhere.

Every week, we listen to the *Top-40* songs, and find out what the singers are up to. When Dad, Mum or Claude comes in and finds us listening, whoever it is yells something like, *What's that damn noise on for?* and turns it off. Neither of us says anything—we've agreed that there's no point in getting into fights with them. We seem to like all the things Dad, Mum and Claude hate.

***

One day, Amelia mentions the old trunk to Mum, and we go through it. More or less the same routine as always, except that we no longer follow the script in terms of asking questions we know the answers to, and I finally ask why I'm the only one without a baby dress in there. "Oh, yours all wore out," she snaps.

The next time Amelia and I are alone with Polly, I ask her if she knows why there's no dress for me in the trunk. She rubs her chin. "No, I don't," she says. "But I can tell you one thing. I know your mother wanted you because she lost the baby before you, and she was real upset about that, she was." She pauses.

That's something I didn't know. Could this have affected her feelings for me, the next baby?

"I dunno," Polly says again. "But when you were born, she had the most Godawful layette for you. Little dresses and jackets and a floppy hat—but I couldn't believe it—she'd made them all out of that horrible material. What's it called? Oh yes, *unbleached calico.*"

"*Unbleached calico?*"

"Yeah—the whole lot. I hate the damn stuff, myself. She'd made every last thing out of it.

The cheapest cloth you can buy. It looks as if it was once white but fell into muddy water; and it's dotted with black bits like fly spots and even occasional grass husks—probably from the field where the cotton grew. Mum still keeps a bolt of it on hand, and any time one of us says we need a petticoat or panties or something, she tells us to use it. I think of Claude's, Amelia's and Laurence's baby dresses in the trunk, made of fine, white material, and embroidered or smocked.

"I wonder why the relatives didn't give her any baby clothes when I was born?"

Polly shakes her head. "I dunno. But that layette was the ugliest damn thing I ever did see."

Then the absurdity of it strikes us, we start giggling, and soon we're roaring with laughter.

A few weeks later, I happen to read in a magazine that at the end of the war, baby clothes, as well as the materials they were usually made from, were not available in Australia. I don't know why neither Polly nor Mum mentioned this.

Chapter Forty-nine

ROMANCE AT THE RODEO DANCE

Amelia and I talk constantly about the upcoming rodeo dance, and one day when she and I and Mum are visiting Polly, I mention that I don't have anything to wear to it.

Mum sighs, "I've told you—wear your red dress!"

She's said the same thing so many times that I can't be bothered reminding her that I've already worn it and it's red, so nobody's going to forget they've seen me in it.

Polly smiles at me. "You know what, Lov? I've got some materials you might like; they've been in my sewing box for years, and *I'll* never use them."

I smile. "Yeah?" She leaves the room and comes back with several yards of mauve taffeta and the same amount of matching net. We find a mirror, and I hold them up together in front of me; the colour suits me, so I thank her and put them aside to take home.

Amelia looks at Mum and then at Polly. "Mum's upset because we want to sit on our own at the dance." To Mum she adds, gently, "It's not that we don't want to sit with you, Mum. It's just that no boys will ask us to dance if we do."

"What utter nonsense!" she snaps. "Why on earth wouldn't boys ask you to dance just because you're sitting next to your mother?"

"Boys— " Amelia begins.

"Boys! What boy worth his salt wouldn't ask you to dance because I'm there? That's just a lot of damn hooey!"

Amelia says quietly, "Mum, they're just shy."

Mum has tears in her eyes. "Oh I don't know what's wrong with you two! Any other girls would be proud to sit with their mother!" She sniffles and blows her nose.

Polly says very gently, "I know how you feel, Gwen." She pauses. "But I can understand them wanting to sit on their own, too. I tell you what! If these two think they're too good to sit with you, why don't you and I just ignore them and sit together?"

Polly to the rescue for the umpteenth time! And she's managed to make Mum feel better, too. Mum leaves to take something to Dad in the bark hut, and the three of us sit around the table drinking tea. I mention that up to now, we've always left the dances before supper.

"You've never stayed for supper? Oh, that's the best part! There are all kinds of lovely things to eat—the women bring cakes and sandwiches— and it's all set up on long tables. All the girls hope that some nice fellow will ask to take them to supper. And, usually, if someone's interested enough to do that, the next thing he does is ask if he can see you home."

"The twenty miles up the mountain from Moonan? He'd have to be mad with love!" Amelia quips, and we all laugh.

After a silence, elbows on the table and chin in her hands, Polly says, "An awful lot of drinking goes on outside those dances, you know. Some of the men drink gin—it's got a kind of sweet smell, so they think women won't know what it is on their breaths." She moves in her chair. "And talking of smells. If you girls smell your fingers after you've danced with a few blokes, you'll be surprised. The thing is, men have to *touch themselves* when they pee, and they don't always wash afterwards."

"And talking of whatsits. I don't know what you two know about men and how they work," she goes on. "But when a man is excited by a woman, his whatsit gets stiff and sticks out. When I was a teenager, someone told me that men tie their thing to their leg so it won't embarrass them if it gets excited by the girl he's dancing with."

We all giggle for a while, and then she says, "Yep, it's wild outside them dances. As I said, that's where all the drinking goes on. And necking." We know what that is from reading *True Romances.* "And more."

She looks hard at us before she continues, and talking quickly, to be sure to finish before Mum gets back, she tells us about what Mrs. Bowen did outside a dance a while back. We've met her on the street when we've been with Mum lots of times. *Black rimmed glasses and permed hair. Very proper-looking.*

"She was very drunk that night," Polly says. "Very drunk. And they reckon she was calling out, 'Fill my hole, boys. Fill my hole.' And they did, apparently, one after another. Car lights on them, and the rest of the men yelling and cheering."

God! Fancy Mrs. Bowen!

"Drunk," Polly says again. "Very drunk."

The following week, Mum says that if we're going to the dance, we'd better learn how to waltz and do the foxtrot. "You, too, Claude." She finds a book that teaches dancing; in it are removable sheets of paper with outlines of men's and women's shoes on them, which she cuts out. And after dinner for many nights, she lays these the floor, and takes turns dancing with each of us and teaching us the steps.

I spend most of my free time sewing my dress, but before I know it, the dance is the next day and I still haven't finished it. Mum offers to help, and for once she's relaxed, and doing something with her is a treat. About nine o'clock that night, we finish it.

On the big day, there isn't room in the front of the lorry for both Amelia and me, and although riding on the back embarrasses us—we never see other girls arriving at events on the backs of lorries—we decide we'll both ride up there. A couple of hundred yards from the sports ground where the rodeo is being held, Dad stops to buy something from the shop in Moonan, and we jump down and say we'll walk the rest of the way.

We decide that, instead of walking around with Mum, we'll try to stay by ourselves at the sports ground; then we won't have to be polite to the boring women she always talks to for hours. And, who knows? We might meet some boys.

As we get nearer, we hear the nasal voice of the commentator coming over the loudspeaker, and it's nearly deafening once we're there. Mum's talking to some women, and we wander off. The events are boring—we're here for the dance. But every now and then, a good-looking young man in the tight moleskins[1] they wear riding just about make me swoon.

We get hotter and hotter in the sun and the blaring loudspeaker nearly drives us mad, so we wander out of the sports ground and back along the road. We find a cool spot under a tree and talk till late in the afternoon, then go to find the others.

Polly has arranged for us to change at the house of a friend of hers. When I put my new dress on, she says, "You've done a real good job on

---

[1] Trousers usually worn by men for riding, with tapered legs so that they are often very tight, and made from heavy cream-coloured cotton.

Figure 49.1: Me at thirteen on Barrington Tops, in front of a trig station erected during the war.

that dress, Leila. You look real nice." She turns to Mum. "I just wonder, though, Gwen, if a touch of lipstick might kind of set it off?"

"But she's only thirteen!"

"Yes, I know, Gwen. But she looks seventeen. And girls her age do wear a little bit of make-up these days. Specially in the evenings. Just a touch. Don't you think? It'd go so nice with her dress."

"Well, I suppose so. Just a little bit, though."

Amelia, beautiful in her dark blue *strapless*, holds out her tube of lipstick. "This would go well with mauve, too."

I put some on—lightly, as ordered. Polly looks at me, and then Mum. "Very nice, don't you agree, Gwen? But maybe just a very light touch of that blue eye shadow I saw Amelia putting on. What do you think, Gwen?"

Mum hesitates, frowning, but then nods, and, again, Polly admires the effect. Smiling, she says, "And perhaps the tiniest, teeniest hint of mascara—but only if your mother agrees, mind."

Looking slightly suspicious by now, Mum sighs. "Well, alright. Only a tiny bit, though."

The last thing is perfume; Amelia lets me wear some of her Chanel No. 5, even though the bottle is so tiny and less than half-full.

The four of us walk to the dance in the dark, carrying torches—Amelia and I ahead in our cloud of perfume.

The wooden hall comes into view, and, faintly, we hear fiddle music. We're almost there! But suddenly, one of my shoes slides towards what looks like a small pool of water shining in the moonlight. I manage to regain my balance, and as I look more closely I see that the water is in a pool of mud from recent rain. I warn Mum and Polly.

We climb the steps of the hall, and push our way through the crowd of men around the entrance.

Will I meet the one who'll love me hugely and forever?

As usual in these halls, a seat runs all the way around the wall, and Polly sits with Mum not far from the front door, while Amelia and I find a place at the other end near the stage where the musicians play. Soon, the music starts, and people begin to dance. The Red Ant Man asks me, and I'm pleased to find myself doing the steps OK as we waltz around, him giggling every now and then; but, remembering the kind thing he did when he took the keys so Dad couldn't drive drunk, I feel fond of him.

He also asks Amelia, and then a scrawny-looking fellow with a big Adams apple asks her and Dad asks me.

But a few dances later, this nice-looking young man I've never seen before asks me, and as I'm accepting, I notice that someone who looks just as nice is asking Amelia.

My dance partner is Roland, and when we sit down after the dance, I find out that hers was Russ; they're New Zealanders who are working on a big property near Ellerston. I can hardly believe it when they ask us again! And again! And then they sit with us while we're waiting for the next dance. And—get this—what Polly said could happen, does—they ask us to supper! I deliberately don't look at any of the other young women, but I'm sure they're full of jealousy. On the long table where we sit, are vases of jonquils. And Roland, or Roley as he likes to be called, removes one and gives it to me! They want to know all about us, and we try to explain where we live and what our lives are like. Of course, I don't tell Roley that I'm only thirteen—the subject of age doesn't come up. And, anyway, since I'm a good girl, why would it matter? Amelia and I agree that, while necking is alright, we'd never go "all the way." Pregnancy is a great black bird waiting to pounce and destroy our lives. In the stories in the *True Romances*, some girl is always going for an innocent walk at night with a fellow, and the next line reads, "And then there was only—Doug, or Alan, or Brad—and me..."

As the end of the dance draws near, I nearly die when they ask if they can take us home. We tell them we'll have to ask Mum and Dad, and just then Dad comes over. The boys stand up and introduce themselves, and Roley says, "If it would be alright, Sir, we'd be honoured to accompany your daughters home."

Dad says he supposes they could take us as far as "the turnoff" to where they live, a few miles away.

They've come in Russ's car, and he drives with one arm around Amelia. Roley's arms are soon around me in the back seat. The lorry with my parents, Claude and Laurence in it follows us, its lights glaring through the back window, but Roley and I slide down to where it's darker and kiss and kiss.

Back at home, I press the spray of jonquils in a book, and, in the days that follow, Amelia and I talk endlessly about Russ and Roley.

When we next visit Polly, we talk and laugh about the evening once the three of us are alone, and she tells us that one of the old biddies told Roley he'd be had up for cradle-snatching if he wasn't careful because I'm only thirteen. I'm upset because he won't want to be my boyfriend now, and I'm also angry because, since I'm a good girl, so my age doesn't

Figure 49.2: Me, thirteen, and Amelia, seventeen.

matter. Russ does call Amelia, and invites her to go horse-riding with him. When she asks my parents, Mum—who's told us that you should never get in a car with, or kiss, a boy till you've known him for at least six months—snaps, "No. He could pull you off your horse or anything!" So poor Amelia has to tell him she can't go.

At the next dance we go to, Russ dances with her quite a few times, but Roley asks me only once, and we don't talk about my age.

Roley is constantly in my thoughts and daydreams, and when I hear, a few months later, that he and Russ have gone back to New Zealand, I'm sad. I tell myself he'll come back for me when I'm older, and sing "Now is the Hour" over and over.

> "Now is the hour for me to say goodbye
> Soon you'll be sailing far across the sea
> While you're away, oh please remember me.
> When you return, you'll find me waiting here."

Chapter Fifty

HOLIDAYING IN THE CITY

One day, a letter comes from Auntie addressed to me and Amelia; we're home by ourselves, and she opens it. "She's been in hospital... something to do with her asthma... But she's OK and home again, now."

"Does she say if she's coming up? She hasn't been here for a holiday for years."

Amelia grins. "No. But guess what good thing *is* in her letter.."

I squirm. "I don't know... She's getting married again?"

"Married!" She pulls a face in mock disgust. "Don't be mad. She hates men." I grab for the letter, but she twists away, keeping it out of my reach. I groan. "Come on. Tell me what it is."

"W-e-l-l. Alright. She wants us—you and me—to come down to Newcastle for a holiday in a month's time." She hands me the letter.

Auntie says we can stay with Jan and Doug, Jan's husband; we've met them both but hardly know them. Apparently, they've just finishing having their house built, and it's big, and right near the lake.

"Wouldn't it be great if we could go? I'd so love to see her!" I say.

"Did you notice she says she isn't well enough to show us round, and that Jan wouldn't have time—she and Doug both work long hours in a cotton mill—but she'd tell us where things are, and show us what buses to catch. We'd have to look after ourselves, pretty much."

Auntie has written a note on a separate sheet of paper, "Let's hope I can get together with you two scallywags soon, then. I don't think your Mum and Dad will like my idea, though. I'll have to leave it to you two to talk them into it; I'm sure you're up to the job."

After a silence, Amelia says, "She's right. They'll never let us go if we just ask. But you know what? I'm determined to go. It'd be sooo good."

"How can we get them to let us go? You've only just got home from being away."

"Maybe we can... persuade them, without them knowing it."

"Trick them into it, you mean?"

"Well, there's a lot in the way you ask people for things."

"What do you mean?"

"She stands up, raises her eyebrows and, chin in the air, says in an exaggerated accent, "We ought to go down and see Auntie. She's not getting any younger, you know." We're both quiet for a while and then she points to me. "And you need a holiday after being the only one here helping Mum while I was away, and working so hard on your school work at the same time."

"That's a great idea. I am tired, you know."

"Anyway, we can come up with all kinds of reasons that we need to go. We just have to figure out the right ones to feed them. The right bait. We'll bloody well trick them into it."

I feel a rush of excitement and power. "I bet we can do it. We'll figure out what will work."

She shoves the letter back in its envelope and puts it in her pocket, and burns the note. "Anyway, let's not tell them about her invitation until we've prepared them for it. We have to think everything through carefully. It doesn't do any good to meet people head on. I learned that with Grandfather. God! All his rules... And if you didn't do exactly what he wanted, when he wanted it, he'd get snaky. He had to have lunch every day right on twelve—not a minute before or after. One day, I changed the clock to see if he'd notice, and gave it to him early. Of course he didn't know. I changed it back later when he was having his nap. He couldn't believe how early it was when he got up. He gave me a suspicious look, but I smiled and looked innocent."

That night after we go to bed, we laugh and giggle our way through all kinds of crazy ideas, but by the time the first birds are squeaking, we have a plan.

The next morning, Amelia says, "I've just thought of something that might help." She puts some powder on my face, then blackens the end of a forefinger with her eyebrow pencil and rubs it under my eyes. "Now you really do look tired."

"Let me put some under your eyes, too."

"No. It'd look too suspicious if we both had circles." After breakfast, when she and I are clearing the kitchen table and Mum is sweeping, Amelia tilts her head, and looks hard at my face. "I cant believe how tired you look, Leila," she says. She turns to Mum. "Don't you think she looks tired?"

Mum glances at me and keeps sweeping. "What do you mean?"

"Can't you see how pale she is? She was never like that before. And—" She comes close to me and inspects my face. "There are dark circles under your eyes," she says to me. "You must've worked hard to do as well as you did on your exams."

Mum stops sweeping, comes over and looks, then frowns and walks away.

For the next few days, I wear the powder and circles, and whenever Mum is around, Amelia either says how tired I look and that I need a holiday, or sighs and says how tired she feels and lists all the things she had to do at Ruby's, and it's my turn to say *she* needs a holiday. We re-seal the letter from Auntie with some glue, and Amelia slips it in with the next lot of mail as she empties the bag onto the table. She looks convincingly surprised to see it, and as she pretends to read it. "Auntie's inviting us down to Newcastle for a holiday," she announces in a high voice. We have no trouble at all convincing Mum to let us go.

We write to Auntie telling her when to expect us. The next time we go to Scone, we buy new pyjamas, and materials to make ourselves a few things, and start sewing as soon as we get home.

***

Jan, Doug and Auntie are waiting at Broadmeadow, the station at New-castle, when we arrive. Auntie takes my right hand and Amelia's left, and we each kiss a cheek. As her face touches mine, I get a whiff of the scent of her powder, and my love for her rises up. She holds us both at arms length and looks into our faces. "I hope you two are still pure."

We struggle to find a witty answer, but can't; the corners of Auntie's mouth twitch, puffs of giggles start escaping from her, and then she's swaying with laughter.

Jan laughs briefly, and then clucks. "What a thing to say to them, Mum!"

Doug, who's tall, picks up our big suitcase as if it weighs nothing, and we set off down the street. After a few blocks, Auntie pecks each of us on a cheek again. "I'm going to leave you with Jan and Doug now. I have some shopping to do. You're going to have a fantastic time." She walks a few yards, then calls back, "And don't be in a rush to come and see me. Get used to the place, and have some fun first."

Doug stops next to a big, luxurious-looking green car—to admire it, I think. But he puts the suitcases down, and opens the boot. *My God. It can't be theirs. Only rich people have cars like that. These people are related to us?*

Doug grins. "Ever been in a Jaguar before?"

Amelia says, "I have.... er, once." A flash of jealousy goes through me in case she isn't making it up.

"When?" I challenge her, but she doesn't answer.

As the car growls into life, a slight squeaking makes me look up to see a section of the roof sliding back. Jan turns and looks at Amelia. "You were saying?" With a scarf tied under her chin, and cats' eyes sunglasses, she looks like a movie star. Amelia mutters something about her supposed Jaguar ride.

In Scone, the streets are always almost empty, but here people of all ages, shapes and sizes swarm along the sidewalks and over the crossings, including gorgeous boys in leather with hair like Elvis. And every time we pause at lights, everyone is talking and laughing, rock 'n' roll blasts from car radios, and on a corner, a man plays a trumpet.

The shops go on for miles and miles, and Doug calls out the names of the places we're passing through; I wonder how he can tell where one ends and the next begins. And we pass restaurants like the ones in the magazines, with white tablecloths, candles and flowers, men in suits and ties, women in glittery dresses, and waiters in black.

Jan and Doug's house is big, like Auntie said. The floors are cement, and some of the walls have no lining yet and you can see the wooden beams, but being in it feels exciting. We have a nice big bed, and drift off to sleep with the wonderful sound of city traffic.

In the morning, before they leave for the factory where they work, they give us a set of keys, and show us how to lock up, and where the food is. They tell us where the bus stop for the city is, and which buses to catch, jotting notes on a piece of paper they give us. They suggest we look in the Newcastle Herald to see what's on. "There are often concerts at the Stadium where your father had his big boxing match," Jan says. "Don't worry how late you get home, and you can sleep in in the morning; we'll be up early to go to work, but you two can get up when you feel like it."

We decide to wear the white pedal pushers we made ourselves, with iridescent pink socks. But what to wear on top? I find a blouse, but

Amelia slips on her new blue knitted pyjama top, and asks me what I think.

"You look great. No one'll ever know what it is."

We find the bus stop after a bit of a search, and I catch my first bus ever. We get off at a milk bar in Newcastle, drink Cokes and look in the Herald. Wow! That very night, there's to be a concert at the stadium with Johnny O'Keefe—"the Wild One," as they call him—whose music we love, and we decide to go.

Feeling fantastic, we wander around the city all day, looking at all the great clothes, trying food we've never eaten before, like hamburgers, and drinking more Cokes. We sit on the beach for a while, and look for the nurses' home Auntie said was there, but can't tell which building it is.

In the Stadium, Johnny is belting out the last of a song, and everyone's dancing. As he finishes, girls scream out his name, and people have to stop them from rushing onto the stage—just like we've heard about on the radio! The girls don't throw their panties, but it's *really, really* exciting. When the next song begins, we jive with everyone else—instead of having to do boring steps, you just move with the music. And you don't have to wait for some fellow to ask you to dance, either. When the song ends, I want to scream, too, but somehow I don't, and Amelia doesn't either. On a break in the music, we're walking past some people and—God It's awful—one of the girls points at Amelia and and I hear her say, in a really catty way, "She's wearing a *pyjama* top." Amelia blushes; I wish I hadn't said it looked OK.

But, a bit later, a thin fellow with an Adam's apple says G'day, and we stop to talk. Then a kind-of plump friend of his comes over. The tall one, who seems to like Amelia, is Cliff and his friend is Peter. When they start asking us about ourselves, we struggle with our complicated story. They've never heard of Barrington Tops, and we can't seem to make them understand where it is, or what our life is like so far from shops and milk bars.

"What do you do for fun there?" one of them asks.

We think for a while. "Go to the milk bar in Scone," we say. And then there's school to explain.

"Correspondence? What's that?" they ask.

Even though they still don't really get it, we end up feeling like we've told them more about ourselves and our families than we wanted to.

The boys aren't that exciting, but they *are* boys, and we jive with them for the rest of the evening. When Johnny sings "Party Doll," the girls scream louder than ever, and I'm so excited I just about die. After the concert ends, Peter puts his arms around me, and they ask if they can take us home. We don't know the way, but they say *they* do, and we all climb into Cliff's old car, me in the back seat with Peter.

The next thing we know, we're parked on a hill with the lights of Newcastle below, and Cliff's kissing Amelia. At first, Peter just squeezes me, but then he starts kissing me. Lets just say he's not Roley, and pretty soon Amelia and I say we'd better be getting home. They're really nice and start the car right away, but it's one o'clock by the time we get back to Jan and Doug's.

Chapter Fifty-one

SAYING GOODBYE

Next morning, we don't even hear Jan and Doug leave. When we finally get up, I find the pink satin bra with the waving worms and the dark pink triangles where I let out the big tucks that were in it when Mum gave it to me, and put it on. "It makes my breasts look like they need a shave," I say.

"My bra's lost its uplift," says Amelia. We decide to go bra shopping.

We have Cokes and hamburgers in the city, and then find a department store. There's a weird moving metal staircase thing called an escalator to Women's Underwear. Madam Amelia jumps onto it without hesitating. "Just step on, Leila!" she keeps saying as she moves up on it. I reach out the toe of one shoe, but the thing's going too fast, and I pull back. I keep having to stand aside so other people can get on, and my face is hot. Then Amelia appears alongside of me—she's caught the other one back down. She takes my arm, guides me onto the first step, rides along with me, and helps me get off.

"You'll get the hang of it," she says. "I've been on one in Sydney a few times."

We wander through miles of satin and lace and silky-looking underwear, searching for the bras with the "whirlpool" stitching the ads say give the best uplift. When we find them, each of us takes a few and goes to a cubicle with an assistant. Mine's an old biddy who purses her lips in disgust as she watches me take my horrible one off.

We emerge dressed at the same time, our breasts in our new bras sticking out as never before. A red patch on either cheek, Amelia looks excited and embarrassed at the same time. Before we catch the bus home, we buy tampons, and it's great not to have to worry about who's serving, or who might see.

When we get home, Jan and Doug aren't back from work yet, and with the house to ourselves, we decide to try the tampons, even though neither of us is having a period. We read the instructions, insert them and ask each other if we can feel anything. We can't. But soon I want to wee. "Damn!" I say. "I'll have to take it out again—I have to wee. Guess that's the only disadvantage."

Amelia stares at me. "You don't have to take it out to wee."

"How do you do it, then?"

She hesitates, embarrassed, and says "Well..." a couple of times, and then blurts out, "You have two holes."

I'm embarrassed. "Yeah?"

She gets the box. "Look at the diagram."

"God! I didn't know. That's great. That would have been a problem."

Soon afterwards, Jan arrives home. "How do you like our new bras?" Amelia asks. We both stand up straight, suck our tummies in, and show her our lines.

She raises her eyebrows and smiles. "Wow!" She leaves the room and comes back with two knitted cotton sweaters, one striped in green and white and the other in blue and white. "Knitted them myself—they give you a great line. Try them on."

We do, admiring our profiles in the mirror.

"You both look great! "Jan says. "They're yours to keep."

"To keep?" we echo.

"Yeah. I've got plenty. I knit all the time."

We're still thanking her and jumping around in excitement when Doug comes in and whistles. "You two want to come for a spin?"

Jan smiles at us. "Go ahead—it'll do you good. He won't bite. I've got to iron some things for work."

As the car races around Warners Bay with the sun roof open, we see a crowd of boys about to cross the road up ahead.

"Wave, why don't you?" Doug says. "You're safe."

Slipping our shoes off, we stand on the seats, and lean out of the sunroof, waving our arms wildly. We can scarcely stop giggling, but we manage to yell "Gooday," and the boys wave back.

Doug makes the car screech round the corners, and as we pass another boy, we yell, "Want to come for a ride?" He's older than us and stares angrily as if he's trying to fix our faces in his mind. But in seconds, he shrinks and disappears.

The next time we see a boy, I yell, "Want to come for a ride, Handsome?" And he waves.

But soon Doug has to drive us home—he and Jan are starting on night shift.

After they've left, we pose in front of the mirror, pretending we're being photographed for a movie magazine. "My bust's just as big as yours now," I say.

"No it isn't. Mine's bigger."

"OK, Smarty. What are your measurements then?" They always give the star's measurements in the stories about them.

"Thirty-eight, twenty-four, thirty-six. What are yours?"

"That's *in* your bra. They don't measure with the bra on... I don't think."

"Course they do."

"OK, then. Bra's on. Let's see." We find a tape in Jan's sewing box, and Amelia watches me measure. "The waist first." I hold my tummy in a bit, hoping she won't notice. The magazines say that the bust should be at least ten inches bigger than the waist, but I reckon the smaller the waist and the bigger the bust, the better. I measure. "Twenty-three." A cross look comes onto her face. The hips are supposed to be about the same as the bust, or a bit smaller. "I measure mine. "Thirty-four."

"Come on then. Your bust."

I put the tape round, pushing my breasts out as much as I can without her noticing. "Thirty-seven."

Then she measures hers. "Thirty-eight. Told you I was bigger!" she says. But seeing the look on my face, she adds, "Not a lot, though."

We lie back on the bed. "You know the man we yelled at? That looked kind of cranky?" I ask.

"Yeah."

"Maybe yelling at him was a bit mad. What if he was someone from Scone? People from there come down here."

"I bet he lives here."

"I hope so. But I feel awful thinking about the way he looked at us."

After a silence, Amelia says, "I do feel a bit mad. Like a dog that's been tied up for a long time and just let off the chain."

"I guess yelling at boys is OK, I say. "As long as we stay pure, like Auntie says." We both laugh. "When'll we go and see her?"

"I dunno," Amelia says. "She doesn't have a phone, so we can't call. And how do we get there?"

"We'll have to ask Jan."

"We can ask her tomorrow. Auntie said not to be in a rush to go and see her, remember? She wants us to have a good time. She's always telling us to enjoy ourselves."

When we ask Jan, she says there are two buses to catch. "You won't remember if I tell you now. Ask me just before you're going."

But there are films and the beach, and shops, and more drives with Doug. And before we know it, it's late in the afternoon of the day before we're booked to go home.

We've been out all day, and Jan greets us and then says, "You two are going home tomorrow, aren't you? Mum phoned from a phone box, asking when you're going over to see her. She sounded upset."

Amelia says, "We don't know how to get there."

"But I told you to ask."

"I guess we never thought of it when you were here."

"You could have asked a bus driver."

I feel bad, and I think Amelia does, too. But Jan says, "Don't worry. Why don't you go tomorrow morning? Your train doesn't leave till the afternoon."

But packing takes longer than we expected, and on the way to Auntie's, the taxi keeps stopping because of heavy traffic. The house where Auntie lives is weatherboard with peeling paint, and in a driveway at the side is a rusty old car with no wheels. We lug our suitcase up the front steps; the door is ajar, and we walk along a gloomy hallway looking for the door Jan told us is hers. I'm pleased we've had a great time like she always said we should, and can't wait to tell her all about it. And I'm waiting, too, for her *Are you still pure?* And the way her mouth twitches till she breaks into laughter.

The door opens suddenly as Amelia is knocking. Auntie stares at us for a moment, before stepping aside to let us in. She says nothing, and doesn't touch us. She takes her time closing the door, then sits in silence in an old armchair on one side of the fireplace. I sit on the other side of it, and Amelia takes a chair nearby. Still, Auntie says nothing, and I start to feel jumpy. She's thinner than I remember, and, one hand on her tummy, she looks sad.

But I tell myself I'm imagining things, and decide to dive in. "We've had a great time, Auntie."

Her voice is loud. "You girls have been here two weeks and you haven't come to see me once. Here I am all alone in this God-forsaken room. The least you could have done was come to take me out somewhere."

I stare at her, then lower my eyes to the floor.

"We didn't know what bus to catch," Amelia murmurs.

"Jan would have told you—*if* you'd asked."

Suddenly, I feel that I'm horrible. *Now even Auntie, who said she loved me, and whose spirit has watched over me since I was six, thinks I am.*

After a silence, Auntie says, "How much time do we have now? Half an hour?"

Amelia looks at her watch. "Three-quarters."

"Not much better. Well— " she pauses, and in a stronger, more cheerful voice, says, "Well, now that you're here, you'd better tell me what you've been up to."

Amelia gets up and puts her arms around Auntie, and tells her we're sorry and that we love her, and I do the same. And then we all have a bit of a cry. After that,we tell her about the dance and meeting Cliff and Peter, and driving around in the Jaguar with Doug. But everything seems flat.

Why, Oh why didn't we come sooner? How could we have been so selfish and stupid?

Too soon it's time to call the taxi to take us to the station, and next thing we're hugging her goodbye. But, as she's holding me, she says, as she did so long ago, "Remember, Pet, wherever you are, I'll be watching over you."

Tears are dribbling onto my face as we lug our suitcase down the front steps. When we get to the footpath, we turn and wave—she's standing in the doorway. As soon as we're in the taxi, I'm crying.

But Amelia sounds irritated. "Well, she's the one who's always told us to spend time with people our own age, and to have a good time. But when we do, she gets annoyed." Then she looks at me, and pats my hand. "We should have come earlier, though."

***

After I've turned fourteen, a few months after our holiday, Mum gets a phone call, and I can tell by how she's talking it's bad news. When she puts the receiver down, she sighs. "That was Bill. Your Auntie Charlotte's died."

I leave the house and cross a paddock that's ploughed up; I need to walk where it's difficult. I don't cry, but I feel empty and very sad.

Chapter Fifty-two

AMELIA MAKES HER ESCAPE

When Amelia is eighteen, she sits for the Royal Prince Alfred Nursing Arithmetic and English test and receives a letter back telling her that she's been accepted into their program, starting in a few months. But a week goes by and she still hasn't told Mum.

It's cold, and she, Mum and I are by the fire in the loungeroom. Amelia stands with her back to it, eyes bright, and one hand in the pocket where I know she has the letter. She's finally gathered up her courage. Mum is in the chair next to mine, absorbed in her crocheting, but I see Amelia's eyes fix on her, and she's just drawn the letter out when there's the sound of a motor. Mum stands up, lays her crocheting on her chair, and looks out the window. "That mail's early—I'll go and get it," she says as she starts for the door.

As the door closes behind her, Amelia lets herself fall into an armchair. "I was just about to show it to her." She passes a hand across her face. "God I wish she was an easier person. I just know this is going to be hell."

"Well, you've already told her you're going."

"But I don't think she really took it in. She's still got it in her head that I'm going to marry some yokel and settle down in this valley."

"She thinks we're all going to do that," I say, turning on the radio. I struggle to tune past the whistles and static for some rock 'n' roll.

"Don't put that on now—it'll just make her cranky."

"You're right. I'll see if I can find something she likes to quieten her down."

Elvis's voice. *She thinks this one is nice.* But it finishes as we hear her step on the back verandah, and Johnny O'Keefe comes on.

"Why do we have to listen to that damn noise?" She switches it off. "It hurts my ears."

"There was one you like on before that one," I say.

"Well, that one wasn't nice."

She tips the mail onto the table and starts going through it. "Bills, bills and more bills." She gathers them up and puts them in a drawer, then sits down and starts crocheting again. She looks from me to Amelia with soft eyes. "You two will never guess what I saw over in the paddock when I was outside. Topsy has a lovely little calf."

Amelia sounds bored. "Has she?"

Crocheting away, Mum smiles. "I'll have to go over and see it a bit later. She's a wonderful cow. She's already given us two heifers. They're such lovely little things when they're first born."

"Well, that's another one for the butcher later on," Amelia quips.

Mum's hands stop moving, and, sounding like a child, she says, "Why do you have to say such things, Amelia? Don't you like little calves? *I* think they're lovely."

"Well, it's the truth, isn't it? Sending them to the butcher is what it's all about."

Mum crochets wildly. "You don't have to *say* such things." She pauses. "I wish you'd take more of an interest in the cattle."

"Well, there's not much point since I'm going nursing."

"Why you'd want to leave here, I don't know." Her eyes look watery. "It's such a beautiful place. How could you leave it?"

"I want to be a nurse."

"A nurse! You can't stand the sight of blood."

Amelia groans. "Not that again. That was when I was about six."

"Now, it wasn't just the once. If you got a cut, you'd get all woozy. I remember two times quite clearly, and I know there were others. Ask Claude—he remembers."

"I don't want to ask Claude. He's always saying I can't do things. He thinks *he's* so clever."

"There's no call to throw off at your brother!"

"But that was then, Mum. And now's now."

"Well, anyway." Mum is quiet for a moment. "I don't think you'd be able to stand the strain, either, my girl. You were always delicate."

She stands up tall. "Do I *look* delicate?"

I look at her strong body and rosy cheeks, but Mum just keeps crocheting.

"There's nothing delicate about me," Amelia continues. "Remember how I looked after you when you had the flu last year?"

"Well, I *was* in bed for a few days... I got up as soon as I could. You didn't have that much to do. It's not the same thing, you know. I'm your mother."

"Well, anyway, I *am* going to go nursing, and Royal Prince Alfred is probably the best nursing school in the country."

"If you're so bent on going, what's wrong with the hospital in Scone? It has a very good reputation."

Amelia's voice is a wail. "We've been through this already. I want to go to the city." She takes a breath. "Scone is only a little country place. I want to see things, and do things, and meet people."

Mum lays her crocheting on the table. "It was that Charlotte that put these ideas into your head, wasn't it? *She* couldn't wait to get to that damn city. Why anybody would want to go to a horrible place like that is beyond me. I hate the city. All those crowds. And it's dangerous. You only have to listen to the news. Murders, every damn day. You *think* you'd like it. It's all a fantasy—a daydream. You have *no idea* how *awful* it is in those cities. It won't be like you think. And Scone does have a good hospital. If you must go nursing, you can meet plenty of people there. And you'd be close enough to come home on weekends." She thinks for a moment. "And what you don't realize is that nursing is damn hard work."

"I want to get married. I'll never meet anybody here."

"I grew up here, and I got married."

"Well, you were lucky. I can't even go out with anyone here, it's so far away. And when someone wants to take me out, you and Dad won't let me go."

"Won't let you? Of course we will."

"What about Russ? You wouldn't let me go riding with him."

"That was last year. You were just a kid. Still are, for that matter." She shifts irritably in her seat, and they stare past one another for a while.

I catch Amelia's eye, and send her a tiny nod. Her hand goes to her pocket, and again draws the letter out. Suddenly Mum stands up. "Anyway, I have more important things to do than to sit around here arguing with you. I have to go and check up on that calf." And she stomps out the door.

Amelia starts crying.

"Tell her as soon as she comes back," I say. "Come on. You can do it. I tell you what. I'll be Mum. Tell *me*."

She hesitates, then takes a deep breath. "Mum, I've been accepted to start training at Prince Alfred Hospital. In the next intake. In—in November."

"See? You can do it."

When Mum comes back an hour or so later, she goes to the kitchen and starts banging pots about.

"Get her to come in here," I whisper. She takes a deep breath, waits a minute, and then goes to the doorway to the kitchen. "Mum, she says. Please come in here. There's something I have to tell you."

Mum comes in, looking lost, and sits down.

The letter trembles in Amelia's hand.

Mum looks suspicious. "What's this?"

"It's the letter of acceptance from Prince Alfred."

Mum hesitates as if she doesn't want to take it, but then does, and reads it. The hand holding it drifts to her side. She stares at Amelia. "How long have you known about this?"

"It came last week." She pauses. "I didn't know how to tell you. I knew you'd be upset."

"Upset! Course it upsets me." She starts crying. "How... can... you... leave... just like that... So selfish! How... can... you... leave... your... *mother*?" She cries for a while longer, then takes a breath. "How will I manage? And who'll look after me when I'm... I'm old?" She starts sobbing again.

Amelia and I exchange a look, and then she says to our mother, "I'm sorry. I–I *have* to go. They've accepted me. And it's what I want."

Mum covers her face and sobs more loudly.

Amelia's voice is steady. "I'll be able to come home on long weekends. And for holidays."

At last she knows. And is crying, just as we thought she would. We are quiet for a while, and then I stand up, and, making as little noise as possible, we both go outside, bound off, and don't stop running till we're in the bush. We dance and whoop—but not loudly enough for Mum to hear, then, breathless, sit on a log.

"I told you she hadn't heard me. I knew she'd go on like that." She pauses. "I know she really *is* upset, but why does it always look as if she's putting it on?"

"I know. Did she really think you were going to stay here waiting for her to get old so you could look after her? I can't believe she was serious."

"I hope *I won't* be that clingy when I have kids."

"God yes. Well, you did it! You'll be gone soon." And, thinking of being without her, an ache starts inside me. I'll miss her terribly. But I'm excited for her—and if she can go, so can I.

For a while, neither of us speaks. Then she says, "You'll be alright."

I glance quickly at her. "Yeah, I know. I'll go too, as soon as I'm seventeen."

We leave it to Mum to tell Dad. And the next morning at breakfast, he says to Amelia, "Your mother tells me you've been accepted into nursing school. Congratulations. Nursing is a good thing to do, if that's what you want. I wish you weren't going so far away; but you're grown up now, and I suppose you've got to make your own life."

Amelia looks into his eyes, thanks him evenly, then bursts into tears. She stands up to leave the table, but Dad puts his arms around her. "It's alright, Lov," he says.

***

The hospital has sent a list of things Amelia will need, most of which she has to buy, but she's also going to make some new clothes to take with her. After about a week, Mum seems to have accepted that she's going, and helps her with the sewing. And the funny thing is she looks really pleased as she tells everyone she meets that Amelia is going nursing at Royal Prince Alfred. I enjoy watching the shocked looks of the old biddies when they hear the news; most of the people in the district hate the city as much as my parents, and almost nobody ever leaves to do anything interesting.

***

We're all on the platform at Scone station again, this time waiting for Amelia to leave. Nobody seems to know what to say. When the train glides in, there are only three minutes before it takes off again. We all hug her, and there are tears in my parents' eyes. "Goodbye, Girl," Mum says, her voice catching.

We don't talk much on the journey home. I've lost my best friend, and when we get back to the house, it feels empty.

The next morning, when I go to the kitchen, Dad is cooking breakfast as usual. "Will you set the table for me, Pet?" he asks casually, then adds, "I can't bring myself to set only five places."

I go into our bedroom—now *my* bedroom—and think about how to change things there. Now I have all the wardrobe space, so I spread my things out. Amelia's bed will stay where it is for when she comes home to visit, and there's a desk I can do my school work on. Although I feel lonely, it's nice to have the space to myself again.

Chapter Fifty-three

HIGH SCHOOL AND SCHOLARSHIP EXAMS

Even though I've always said I'm going to the city when I'm old enough, all my parents seem to see me as doing in life is marrying and having children, and they've never paid much attention to my school exams. But this year, the end of the third year of high school, when I'm fifteen, I have to sit for an examination if I want to obtain an Intermediate Certificate. And, because I've always done well in art—sometimes coming second or third out of ninety students—I decide to sit for a scholarship to study commercial art—which, as far as I know, is the only way to earn a living in this field.

Until now, I've liked the challenge of the end-of-year exams, and although I've done them all at home without supervision, I've never studied for them—nobody has ever suggested I should—and I've never even thought of cheating. But the Intermediate examination has to be taken in a real school, and I'm to sit at Moonan Flat Public School for everything except Home Economics. I have to sit for this last subject at the main highschool in Scone, where I'm also going to sit for the scholarship to study Commercial Art. I'm excited at the prospect of being among other students for the first time in my life.

The Moonan Flat school is a pleasant-looking cream building not far from the town, and the next few times we pass it, I crane my neck to try to catch a glimpse of the children, but never see any. "Where are all the kids?" I ask Mum.

"Oh, they'd be inside, doing their lessons."

The exam at Moonan school is to take two days, and because of the bad roads, my parents say I'll need to stay nearby. "She can probably stay with the Williams's," Dad says to Mum. "They haven't got much, and they'd probably be glad to have her if we take them a bag of potatoes."

This kind of makes me feel that my worth is a bag of potatoes. And although I thought I knew, or knew of, pretty well everyone in the district, I've never heard of the Williams's; I hope they're not too peculiar.

"What are they like?" I ask.

"She's really nice," says Mum, as if the husband doesn't exist. "Really nice."

Mrs. Williams agrees to have me stay, and Mum telephones the teacher—the only one in the school—who is to supervise my exam; he says to be at his house, next to the school, at 8.30 a.m. on the days I'm to sit.

The afternoon before the first exam, my parents drop me off at the Williams's house; they're old, and she's bulky while he's thin, like the Roses. I like being there from the beginning—they're kind to me, they speak respectfully to one another, and their house is pleasant and tidy.

The next morning, Mrs. Williams wakes me, gives me breakfast, hands me a packed lunch as I'm leaving, and wishes me luck. I imagine that this is how she treated her own children. I'm so excited at the thought of being with other kids that the mile or so I have to walk to the school seems like nothing.

I arrive early, and the teacher says, "I think we'll put you in here," shows me into his loungeroom, and points at a formica table. That's when I realize I'm not going to be in the classroom after all, but I smile and sit at the table. There's plenty of light, and a vase of fragrant sweet peas next to me.

Needlework is my first exam; I have to draft a pattern, and begin by drawing small, carefully-measured pencil lines. Every now and then, I pause and listen, but can't hear the children on the other side of the wall. Then, around 11 a.m., faint voices tell me they're outside on a break. It hurts to be alone when I know they're so close.

The pattern almost finished, I lay several sheets of tissue paper under it, take the little tool with its red handle and wheel with sharp points, and, as always, run it along the marks I've drawn. I lift up the paper. Damn! The wheel has cut a line of dashes in the Formica table.

When the teacher comes to collect my morning's work, I consider telling him about the marks; but thinking he might never notice, I don't.

I eat my lunch in the garden, and stand on tiptoe, trying to see into the playground, but a wooden fence and shrubs block my view. I can't hear the children, either; they must be in the classroom. If only my breaks coincided with theirs. I see no kids when I leave.

Mrs. Williams is in the kitchen frying fish for dinner when I get back. She asks how I did and I tell her that I think I did OK.

Half-way to the school on the second morning, I notice a girl who looks a couple of years younger than me up ahead, also on her way there. I walk faster, trying to catch up with her, but she gets there before me, turns briefly to close the gate but doesn't notice me, and disappears inside. I finish the Intermediate exam at the end of that day without having spoken to one other student.

***

The day before the scholarship exam in Scone, I'm mopping the floor with my dress hitched up, and I notice that my legs have become red and are scattered with large, itchy white wheals. Polly calls in and says I must be very nervous about the exam. But by the next morning, my skin has returned to normal.

Knowing that the Scone highschool uniform is made of checked material, Mum has made me a similarly patterned dress in red to wear, but when I arrive for the exam, the rest of the students' uniforms are blue-checked. A teacher leads me into a room and sits me in front of a vase of flowers with a swathe of cloth in front of it, which turns out to be a still life I have to draw. Everything goes well, and, seeing my drawing, the teacher's eyes widen; she picks it up and looks at it carefully, holds it at arm's length, looks some more, and smiles. "That's very good indeed."

I spend the lunch hour in the school grounds with the other students, and talk to some of them, but, as usual, it's too hard to explain about my school situation, and I don't find them all that interesting after all.

After lunch, I'm dismayed to read that I have to paint a group of people at a "barbecue." I'm pretty sure this is like a picnic where meat is cooked over a fire, but it's a word nobody I know uses. Although we've recently had electricity connected to our place, we've never had a TV, or gone to films. We sometimes cook chops or freshly caught trout over a fire, but have never thought of it as a "barbecue." Most importantly, though, whereas I can draw portraits quite well, and even a whole person, I've never drawn or painted a group of people. As I struggle with the painting, I begin to feel light-headed. It doesn't turn out well, and I write something to this effect on the paper. The same teacher says nothing when she collects my work.

Next, I have to write an essay, on any topic I choose. I'm good at English and writing, but have trouble focusing and have to read the instructions over and over. I write a story about a lost child stumbling through a dark forest—a place I recognize from nightmares—who becomes more and more tired and frightened. A part of me knows that the story is melodramatic, but I can't seem to get it off the track it's on. And another part of me doesn't want to, because it's saying something about myself.

The Home Economics exam is easy and boring.

***

Some weeks after the Intermediate exam, a letter arrives from Blackfriars telling me I've passed, but adding that they can't give me the actual Intermediate Certificate because I've completed only six months of the final year's work. I've been supervising myself, and hadn't realized that I was working so slowly that I was submitting only a week's work every two weeks. The school had never drawn my attention to this, or warned me about the possibility of not getting the Certificate.

Blackfriars does allow me to go on to fourth year, nevertheless, and I take the same subjects as in third year—geography, history, art and English. I suspect that I've failed the Art Scholarship exam, but receive no result. My parents don't seem to notice, and I don't discuss it with them, so the question of writing to find out whether I passed never comes up.

I see Mrs. Williams in the distance at Moonan one day, and say hello when she's close enough; she smiles and says "How are you?" as if she doesn't expect an answer and continues walking. I'm disappointed, though not really surprised, and decide that to her I *was* just a bag of potatoes.

***

The road contract over, Dad and Claude build several dams where the swamp is, planning to stock them with trout and put caravans nearby so people can rent them for fishing holidays. My old dream of having a swimming hole returns, but weeks go by while I wait for them to finish the work, and then for the dams to fill with water. The first hot day after this, I get into my swim suit, and wade in, only to see the mud boiling up around my legs as it always has. And where it's deep enough to swim, there are large areas of warm water, and others which are very cold, and the two don't seem to mix, so it's not pleasant.

Figure 53.1: Our little valley after the dams were built.

Figure 53.2: Me at Fifteen about to try swimming in the water of one of the newly-built dams.

Figure 53.3: Laurence at seven or eight playing in the water of one of the dams.

Chapter Fifty-four

CANNIBAL

After many years of being sober, Dad goes to town on his own, and returns home very late and very drunk. Afterwards, he again vows to give up alcohol, but I don't think anyone believes that he will. A few months later, he goes to Muswellbrook, fifteen miles from Scone, for a couple of days to buy some machinery, and is to stay overnight with an old friend, Harry. He doesn't come back when he'd said he would, and we spend yet another night full of fear.

He arrives home, sober, the next morning as we're having breakfast. As he eats his cornflakes, he tells us that he went into a pub for one drink the first night he was away, and couldn't stop, and that the next day, Harry took him to an Alcoholics Anonymous meeting, and he also saw a doctor. "Alcoholism's a disease," he says. "Part of what causes it is a shortage of Vitamin B." The doctor had given him a bottle of the vitamin, as well as some barbiturates, I'm not sure why. I'm very grateful to Harry, and I think that maybe he really will give up this time.

***

I become friends with Nathalie Crosson—her husband, Balfour, is managing the property called the station not far away—the same place that my grandfather managed when Mum was in her teens. Nathalie turns out to be Mrs. Rose's niece and is very sweet and kind, and I often ride Mum's mare Locket to their place to see her.

One afternoon when she and Balfour drop by, I overhear Dad arranging to sell Nancy, the cow who's given us milk since I was little, to them for meat.

After the visitors leave, I lie on my bed. *All that milk! All those mornings of intimate murmurings as I milked her!* Into my mind come

Dad's words when I was six, "She can be your cow if you learn to milk her." I did learn, and milked her for a time, but haven't for years. I continued to pat her and talk to her every now and then, though, and always kind of thought of her as mine. After I began riding the teenage roller-coaster, she became just part of the scene on the farm, but deep down, I remained very fond of her. She must be too old to calve and produce milk, and that's why he's selling her. I know that my parents don't have a lot of money, that he couldn't bear to kill her himself, and that selling her for meat is simply a practical solution. *Does what's about to happen to her hurt me? It doesn't seem to, really. It feels like there's nothing I can do about it, anyway. I'll just have to put it out of my mind, be a "man" about it.*

One morning, many months later, Nathalie telephones, inviting me to visit, and I saddle Locket and ride over. Around midday, I say I'd better be getting home, but they urge me to stay for lunch. We're at the table about to begin, when Balfour turns to me. "Nice bit of brisket[1] there. That's that old cow your father sold us. Corned up nicely."

I'm shocked. I'd expected all her meat to be long gone. *Brisket... Oh my God! Brisket is what they call the dewlap–the curtain-like thing that hung from her neck... All that's left of her... It's too late to say "No."* I cut the meat into small pieces, load it on my fork with lots of vegetables. Chat. Chew and swallow... Drink lots of tea... Till it's all gone...

I arrive home in the middle of the afternoon to find Dad snoozing in one of the big chairs in the sunlight coming through the loungeroom window. He begins a slow, luxurious stretch. Sees me. Sits up. Glares. "You stayed for lunch. What meat did you eat?"

I struggle to answer.

"You cannibal!"

How did he know? Horrified, and deeply ashamed, I wander away.

For weeks, I avert my eyes whenever I'm around him, and we don't talk to one another. But, late one afternoon, he comes into the loungeroom where I'm sitting on the couch and stands silently in front of me till I glance his way.

"I was wondering if you'd like to come up the paddock with me." He pauses. "I've got something to show you."

I don't want to go, and don't answer.

He shifts on his feet. "Aw, come on."

---

[1] However, the definition of this cut of meat varies, and is not necessarily the one I knew then and give subsequently.

I'm drawn to the possibility of a reconciliation. "OK," I say, getting up and following him out the door and onto the verandah. When he takes the rifle from it's hook and slings it over his shoulder, I fear he's going to shoot some poor animal, and wish I hadn't said I'd go, but I continue to follow him.

Without speaking, we walk a long way into the bush. Every now and then, he pauses, looks all around, and then continues, and I wonder what he's up to. Finally, we stop at the edge of a small clearing, around which are white-trunked eucalyptus trees. "I reckon this'll do," he says, sitting on a log facing the clearing, and propping the gun against the log next to him. He pats the place on his other side. "Sit yourself down, mate."

Out of the pocket of his jacket, he draws something flat and shiny, and grins at me. "This is a whistle I made." He pauses. "Now, don't move a muscle till I give you a bit of a nod. Then, if you look around the clearing, you'll see something you've never in your life seen before. But you have to stay completely still, and move only your eyes when you look. OK?"

He puts the whistle in his mouth and blows, and a trembling squeal emerges, swelling and fading, swelling and fading. I'm getting bored when his head nods very slightly towards the other side of the clearing.

Moving only my eyes as instructed, I see, peering around a tree trunk, a triangular orange face full of curiosity. A fox! And, as the sound continues, one by one, foxy faces appear at the sides of most of the other tree trunks, until we're surrounded by them, watching us. I've never seen anything as beautiful in my whole life, and suddenly I'm filled with breathless happiness.

When he stops blowing, the orange faces disappear one by one, without so much as a rustle. Surrounded by the tree trunks, now luminous in the late afternoon light, Dad and I don't move or speak for some moments. Then I sigh, and ask if I can try the whistle. Face shining, he hands it to me. "Made it out of a strip of tin," he says. "Sounds like a rabbit caught in a trap."

I hadn't realized till now that the sound was like the cries I'd heard at the rabbiting camp when I was little. It's an oblong piece of flat tin bent in half so it's about the size of my palm, with, near where it's bent, a hole punched through both sides.

"Poor fullahs were expecting a bit of dinner," he says. "Have a go. But we shouldn't torture them too much longer."

Not wanting the sound to be loud, I don't blow very hard, and a weaker sound than the one he made emerges. I give it back to him. One big hand on my shoulder, he looks at me lovingly. "Are you alright now?"

I nod.

As he picks up the rifle, I realize that he'd never even thought of using it, and that it had been propped against the log the whole time, as useless as a dead stick.

We set off through the darkening bush. At the edge of the hill with the lights of our house below us, we pause. His voice seems to come from the sky, where stars are beginning to appear. " A man doesn't like shooting the poor things, but they're such villains. Bloke out at Niangla told me he caught a silver one in a trap once. And old Andy Wilson reckons he saw a snow white one, down on the Pigna Barney.[2]"

---

[2] A river on the Gloucester side of the Barrington plateau, and which merges with the Manning River.

Chapter Fifty-five

THE MOTHER LODE

I'm still fifteen when the bulldozer has a very dramatic effect on our lives. Dad and Claude have been building a dam on a property owned by the same Pod Taylor whose house we shared when I was three, and one day they arrive home much earlier than usual, come into the kitchen where Mum and I are working, and stand just inside the door, grinning.

"You two will never believe what we've got to show you," Dad says.

Mum looks from one to the other. "Well, what is it, then?" she snaps. "Why don't you tell a person what you're talking about, instead of standing there like a couple of ninnies[1]?" They still don't move, and she sighs loudly. "Oh I haven't got all day to stand around waiting—I'm trying to get tea."

Dad takes something from his pocket, but keeps it covered with his other hand. He looks hard at Mum. "Didn't I always tell you that one day I'd find the mother lode?"

He slowly lifts the covering hand, and in his outstretched palm is a piece of quartz studded with corn-kernel-sized gold nuggets.

Mum and I stare. She takes it from his hand. "Where did you get this?"

"Ahh, that's the question. Where did we get it, Claude?"

Claude laughs. "We got it from a gold reef. On Pod's place."

"On Pod's place?" She looks at Dad. "Is this some kind of joke?"

Dad glances at Claude. "Told you she wouldn't believe us!" He turns back to Mum. "Well, it's true, believe it or not. It's from a reef right alongside of where we built the dam."

---

[1] In Australian slang, weak or stupid people.

I take the piece of rock from Mum, and as I look at it, Dad explains something we already know—that, in Australia, anyone who discovers gold, regardless of whose property it's on, can take out a Miner's Right granting ownership of the minerals in a small, specified area. "The problem is, right now we have no idea how far the reef extends, or how deep it goes," he says. "So the first thing we *all* have to do—and quickly—is to take out Miner's Rights so we own the gold. Between us, we should have a large enough holding. He looks from Mum to me, his face serious. "And, until we've had a chance to assess how much gold is there, we have to keep the whole thing absolutely secret from everyone outside of the family. We can't say a word—*not one* single word—about it to *anyone*—even people we think we can totally trust. Believe me, if some other bugger finds out about it, and we haven't got it secured under Miner's Rights, we'll end up with nothing." He pauses.

"And, even after we've got the Miner's Rights, we still have to find out how much is there so we can decide whether to sell it or mine it ourselves. So, until we've had a chance to assess it properly, we have to continue to keep it secret."

I lay the specimen in the middle of the table, and everyone keeps picking it up, and examining it again. I feel giddy and breathless, and can hardly believe what's happening.

Dad tells us that although no gold-bearing ore was on the surface, he'd suspected that there was a reef in that place ever since he was in his teens, and tramping around the countryside with his brothers Bill and Sid, taking whatever work they could get. His suspicions came from his knowledge of geology, a subject he'd learned about early in life from his father, who'd worked in goldmines, as well as from old prospectors he happened to meet. Later he'd read as much as he could on the subject as well.

He explains that to find the location of the suspected reef, they'd had to wash many dishes of dirt from parallel lines below where they thought it was, and that finding gold in particular dishes told them for sure.

Dad has taught us all how to pan for gold—the first time I saw him "wash a dish" was when I was four. A prospecting dish—metal and about twenty-two inches across and six deep—is filled with what is, hopefully, gold-bearing dirt. Then, water is poured in, and this and the dirt are swirled vigorously to make the heavier gold sink to the bottom, after which the dish is tilted and the water carefully poured off, as the fingers of one hand sweep away the topmost, and lightest, layer of dirt and pebbles. For each dish of dirt, many similar washes are required, until all that remains in the dish are any lumps or specks of gold that were in the dirt, and, usually, a little heavy black sand as well.

What had prevented him from finding the reef until now, he said, was that this process required a considerable quantity of water, but the nearest creek was many miles away, at the bottom of an escarpment of several thousand feet. Even after the track to Pod's place became a road, and Dad had a vehicle instead of a horse, the problem persisted.

"Every few years," he tells us now, "I'd go back to that place." He turns to Claude. "I even took you there a couple of times, didn't I? And we went back there again recently. We were standing on the very place where the reef is, when I said to Claude that if only Pod would get us to build a dam nearby, we'd at last be able to find out if what I suspected was true.

"Well, the good Lord must have been listening." He takes a breath. "Not five minutes later, who should ride up but Pod. We had a bit of a yarn,[2] and then, damned if he didn't say, 'I've been wondering if you blokes could build me a dam.' And then we heard the words that were music to our ears. 'I don't care where you put it, as long as it's close to here.'

"So, as soon as we could, we built the dam exactly where we wanted it. And soon after it was finished, there was a good fall of rain, and it filled right up. The first chance we got, we started on the test washes. That's how we found where the reef is, and then we dug down to it."

***

Once we all have Miner's Rights, Dad and Claude, twenty-two, now, form a syndicate with Uncles Bill and Sid—someone I haven't seen much of till now. Being on a Returned Serviceman's Pension, Uncle Bill has no money to invest, Uncle Sid is only just getting by, and Dad has no spare cash either—in fact, things were looking so grim, he now tells us, that he'd thought that he might have had to sell our property. So, they have to see if the reef is rich enough to warrant borrowing the money to mine it. As soon as they can, they start crushing samples of the ore, and measuring the percentage of gold.

***

---

[2] A talk.

Months later, one evening at dinner, they tell us that they've decided to sell the mine. The next day, we go to Scone, and to the Vogue Cafe for lunch. We usually take the first vacant table, but today Dad leads us to the one in front of the big front window.

Almost as soon as we're seated, he takes a lump of quartz studded with gold nuggets the size of match heads from his pocket, gazes at it for a while, and then says to Mum in a loud voice, "Once we get the gold mine going, you'll be pulling up outside of here in a chauffeur-driven Rolls."

Mum's cluck of exasperation turns to a giggle, but she keeps her voice low. "Yeah. I'm sure I will."

Holding the specimen at arms length now, and gazing at it with narrowed eyes, Dad doesn't seem to notice Andy, the middle-aged Greek owner of the restaurant we've known for years, arrive with the menus. "Nice bit of gold there," he says, nodding his head. "Plenty more where that came from, too." Then he pretends to notice Andy standing next to him, staring. With a flourish, he hands him the specimen. "Take a look at the gold in that, Andy."

Andy takes the specimen and stares at it, his eyes large. "From your er—place?"

"Well, not exactly," Dad booms. "It's from a property a few miles from ours. But we've taken out Miners' Rights, so it's the same as if it was on ours. Anyone who finds gold in this country can take out a Miner's Right and mine it, no matter whose property it's on."

Andy searches Dad's face. "This—this is—" he pauses. *"Real? Real gold?"*

Dad nods. "Certainly is."

"And—and you own the place where it came from?"

"Yeah. Well, as good as."

Andy looks as if he's in a trance. "Real gold!" He jiggles his head. "Real gold."

"Well, if you like that one, take a look at this." Dad reaches into his pocket, and brings out another quartz specimen with even larger nuggets.

Andy hands the first specimen back, and takes the second. Laughing like a little boy, he turns it over and over. *"Real gold.* I never thought I'd ever have a piece of real gold like this in my hand. *Real gold!* And you are the owner of the place where it came from!"

"Yeah. That's right. Me and me brothers have Miners' Rights—and me eldest son." He doesn't mention that, to tie up as much of the land around the reef as possible, Mum, Amelia, Laurence and I also have Miners' Rights.

Dan, a fellow we know, walks into the cafe. Seeing us, he lifts an arm in greeting in the casual way the local men do, watches us for a minute or two, then comes over, eyebrows raised in curiosity.

Dad nods to him, and says to Andy, "Let Dan have a look at that specimen." When Andy hands it to him, he says to Dan, "That's gold from up on the Tops."

Once Dan realizes the gold is real and from a reef Dad owns, he becomes as dazed as Andy. And, before long, we're surrounded by people who've come in to eat, passing the specimens around, gasping, and asking questions in high voices.

Now Dad fishes in his shirt pocket and produces a solitary nugget bigger than any of those in the specimens. "This came out of another piece of quartz." Sunlight is now flooding through the window, making the specimen gleam.

Chapter Fifty-six

GOLD POTATOES

Before long, the first reporters find their way up the rough road to our property as well as to the goldmine, to interview and photograph Dad, Claude and Uncles Bill and Sid—who are at our place most of the time, now.

"We'll need plenty of strong tea," the reporters tell Mum one day, as if she's a servant; they never ask her, me, or Laurence how we feel about the gold find.

Mum huffs and puffs, but does as she's told, filling and refilling our foot-high enamel teapot as the reporters question and photograph, guzzling cup after cup, and eating from the table loaded with homemade cakes and cookies, bread, butter, jam, cheese and tomatoes.

I'm casting around for a career, and when I see a young man only a few years older than I am sitting on the front steps writing in his notebook, I ask him what it's like to be a reporter.

He stares at me. "Alright, I suppose. Why?"

"I want to go to the city and get a job when I'm seventeen, and I was wondering if I could be one."

"*You?*"

"Yes, I haven't decided what to do yet."

"Well, you have to study it, and do all kinds of annoying things for a while."

***

One afternoon, some men from ABC (the Australian Broadcasting Corporation) Television arrive at our house on foot, and tell us that they couldn't get up the last hill because the road was too boggy. I go over to

Figure 56.1: Left to right: unidentified man and my father at the gold mine.

where Claude is working and tell him, and he pulls their van up the hill with the tractor.

The reporters say they want to photograph Dad leaving for the mine. Whereas every morning he gathers up whatever he's taking, throws a comment over his shoulder about when he'll be back, leaves the house and drives off, the television people have their own ideas. They make us rehearse, having Dad, Mum, Laurence, and I walking with our arms linked from the house to the lorry. Then Dad is to drive off, waving, and the rest of us are to stand waving back. My parents have always said that a lot of the news is lies, and this shows us something about the manipulation that goes on.

But as we're going through all this, a brilliant idea comes to me. Having read so many stories about how young women are "discovered" and end up being famous actresses, I realize that an opportunity for a screen test has fallen into my lap.

During the rehearsal, we all follow the cameraman's instructions.

"That's good," he yells. "Now, can you all do that again, just like before? OK? Ready? The same as last time, but this time it's for real. Wait for me to say, Go."

Two cameramen stand in the yard, each with a large TV camera on his shoulder..

"Go," I hear, and arm-in-arm, we walk towards the lorry; as I pass the first cameraman, I turn towards him, and give the broadest—and what I hope is the most beautiful—smile of my life, even twisting around after we've passed to make the moment last.

When the cameramen stop filming, the first one shouts to the second, "Did you see that?"

He sounds excited, and hoping he's going to say how nice I looked, I lower my eyes.

But instead, he sneers, "She hammed it! Wouldn't you know? There's always one!"

Shame floods me. Boy, that was a stupid thing to do!

The film is to be broadcast on the ABC news, but, having no television, and not knowing anybody who does have one, we don't see it.

***

Telegrams making offers for the mine begin arriving, and one day I answer the phone and the postmistress says she has a telegram for us. Sounding as if she's almost choking, she reads, "Offer one hundred and fifty thousand pounds for gold mine."

By this time, the syndicate has already checked out several potential buyers, and when Mum reads the telegram to Dad, he says, "Hmmm... More likely ten thousand pounds and a hundred and forty thousand of worthless shares."

Some potential buyers arrive in person, without warning. It's raining heavily one afternoon, when I see the mail truck coming down the hill, and put on a raincoat and hat to go and collect the mail. The truck has already left when I get outside, but standing in the yard is an elderly man in a suit with rain pouring over him, clutching the mailbag to his chest and staring at the house. On the ground at his side is his briefcase, sitting in a drain running with several inches of water, and moving back and forth, about to take off. I grab it, and seeing me, the man explains gravely that he's here to make Dad an offer for the gold mine.

I take him inside, and give him a towel to dry himself, and Mum and I make him a pot of tea and a snack. He says he's already sent a telegram, though we haven't received one from him. When Dad gets home, he listens politely to what he has to say, but refuses his offer. The mail truck has already passed on its journey back down the mountain, so the man has no way of leaving, and we have to invite him to stay for the night. The next day, he catches a lift to Scone with someone who happens to call.

Another day, two Scotsmen from Sydney arrive unannounced in a small car. They continually make puns and jokes which aren't very funny. And they clink their cups when we're drinking tea, lift them high, and say, Cheers. Dad refuses their offer, also, but they stay three days, turning their visit into a mini-holiday, and talk of coming again. I happen to mention that my sister is a nurse at Royal Prince Alfred Hospital, and I hear one say to the other that they might be able to give her a lift up for the long weekend that's coming up.

After they leave, I tell my parents what I overheard, and they look worried. Years before in Australia, a boy named Graham Thorn, whose parents had won a major prize in the lottery, was kidnapped for a large ransom and murdered, and with all the talk of our supposed wealth, they've begun to fear for our safety. Amelia is due home for the long weekend, and they send her a telegram saying, "Do not accept a lift home with anyone. Come home on the train."

After she arrives—by train—they explain why they sent the telegram, and she tells us that the matron at the hospital had looked at her suspiciously as she handed her the telegram, doubtless thinking she had some wayward plan of which her parents didn't approve.

Mum and Dad also worry about Laurence, too. He is eleven, boards in Scone and attends school there. He mentions that he's suddenly become popular with girls who've never paid him any attention before, and who ask about the gold find. My parents warn him to be careful, and not to discuss the possible value of the mine with anyone.

It's not long before our mailbag is bulging with begging letters. One is from a man Dad knew years ago, and remembers as dishonest and a user, telling of poverty, sickness, and the need for money to buy a washing machine. Dad prints, "NO GO," on the man's letter, signs it, Joe, and returns it to him. Knowing something about the person behind this letter influences us in not taking any of the others seriously, and we burn them after reading them.

The mine eventually does sell—for how much, I don't know—and one

Figure 56.2: The gold reef.

afternoon we are in the garden when the lorry carrying the first gold-bearing ore passes our house on its way to the city. It looks like a load of potatoes, the ore having been packed in the same kind of bags used to transport them; I think this must be a ploy to forestall potential robbers.

But I fantasize that word has got out, and imagine masked gunmen on strong horses galloping out of the bush, surrounding the truck and yelling, "Stick-em-up!" like the bushrangers of the old days. For me, seeing the strange cargo moving down the road, and knowing its secret, is an exhilarating moment.

I never hear how much each of the syndicate members receives from the sale, but I get the impression that it's a considerable sum, and I understand that money from gold is tax free. Uncle Bill takes a world trip, Uncle Sid buys a small property on the coast, and Claude goes on a trip to Russia, very excited to think that at last he'll be seeing their "advanced society." But when he comes back, he says it wasn't quite what he expected, and that they still have "a way to go."

My parents aren't the kind who celebrate things, and we don't even have a party to mark the sale of the mine, but I think I'm the only person in the family who sees this as strange. I also think it's peculiar that no consideration is given to further education for Laurence or me, and none of the women in the family gets as much as a new dress out of it; but I keep these thoughts to myself.

Figure 56.3: My father, Uncle Sid, Uncle Bill and Geoff Wright, my father's nephew, in a Melbourne street around the time the gold mine sold.

Chapter Fifty-seven

I FINALLY ESCAPE

I've thought of a number of different careers. When I was three, and living in the rabbiting camp with my family, I'd asked Uncle Bill if I could be a doctor; having a pleasant singing voice, I'd imagined being an opera singer; I'd thought of being a visual artist; I'd thought of being a nurse, and I'd wondered briefly if I could be a reporter. But lately, I've been thinking of becoming a teacher, and keep imagining walking up the steps of one of the lovely old buildings of Sydney University I've seen in photographs. I write to one of my teachers at Blackfriars about the teaching idea, and her reply is as follows:

"You ask about the possibility of going to university to be a teacher. I am afraid I cannot be encouraging. Many hundreds were turned away from the universities this year, and there is every indication that things will be even worse in the future. In any case, you would require mathematics for university entrance."

In other words, "You might as well forget it, kid."

I've been enjoying my schooling—and doing well in Art, Geography, History and English, but after the teacher's note, I realize that these subjects are pretty useless as far as my future is concerned, and begin to think of leaving school. Amelia likes nursing, so I decide I'll also apply to Prince Alfred. All I have to do is to pass the entrance exam in English and Arithmetic, which she found easy.

I'm sixteen and a half now, and even though I haven't done any arithmetic for a long time, again, I don't think of studying it for the test, and although I am to do this one at home, I don't think of cheating, either. The English is no problem, but I find some of the Arithmetic hard, and get increasingly anxious.

Eventually, a letter arrives telling me I've failed the Arithmetic. There's nobody at home I can tell, and I go to my room and cry. Now I do feel stupid; and I'm really disappointed that I won't be going nursing with Amelia. She comes home the next weekend, and once we're alone, I show her the letter, and start crying again. She brings me hot tea with sugar in it, though I don't usually take any, and I gulp it down between crying spells.

"The weird part is," I say, "I know it wasn't that hard. Oh why couldn't I have passed the bloody thing? You passed it."

"It helped that I did Maths in highschool—you haven't done any for many years."

"Yeah, maybe that's what made the difference. And after I had trouble with one bit, I just couldn't think properly. That's what's so annoying."

We're quiet for a few minutes, and then we hear Claude's loud voice coming from the loungeroom next door. "I see that old roan cow up the paddock," he announces. "One of her eyes is all bunged up. Out to here."

"The roan cow?" Mum squeaks. There's a pause. "Milly?" Another pause. "Oh no! Not Milly!"

"Yeah, the roan one. Milly—that's the one. Out to here, I tell you. There's got to be something in there."

"Something *in there?* What on earth could be *in there?* Are you sure it was Milly?"

"Yeah, it was her alright."

"*She* was the one that had the blight a while back."

"Blight? That ain't no blight! There's something in there, I tell you. She must've run into something."

"Son, she had the blight. That's what it must be."

He says loudly. "The blight doesn't give you an eye that size. It's out to here." He pauses. "Bloke ought to stick a knife in it."

What's he talking about? He's always saying something weird and ugly. I hope he wouldn't really stick a knife in the poor cow's eye—but who the hell knows?

Amelia rolls her eyes, and I break into sobs again. "God I hate it here! I can't stand much more. I have to get away."

"Well, you'll just have to do something else," Amelia says sensibly. "There are jobs other than nursing."

For stupid people, I think. "What could I do? I don't even have the Intermediate Certificate, remember?"

What sort of job will I be able to get? And where will I live? Going nursing would have solved that problem, too, because I'd have been able to live in the hospital. I talk to her about whether I should leave school, and she says I'm probably doing a lot of work for nothing.

I decide to tell Dad I'm leaving before she goes back to Sydney. Although he's mostly kind, he can be sharp and make me feel terrible. Several times, I think the right moment has arrived, only to be put off by something. But, late the next afternoon, he's sitting at his desk doing accounts and his face looks so peaceful that I go to him and blurt it out.

"After I bought all those books for you?" he snaps.

"But don't you get the cost of them off your taxes?"

"I still have to pay for them.' He pauses, and then says angrily, "I buy you the books and then you decide to leave!"

"Well, I don't think the subjects will... fit me for anything. The teacher said I can't go to university unless I have Mathematics."

I'm crying again when I get back to Amelia in our room. She puts her arms around me, and I gradually feel alright again.

After she goes home, Dad says that, since I've left school, he'll pay me a small wage to do the housework and cooking I've done forever. I know he's trying to help me, but with Mum still being really mean a lot of the time, it makes me feel like a servant.

A few months later, after I've turned seventeen, cousins who live in Sydney I've never met before come for a visit—Harold, Beth and their three children. Mum and Dad have always spoken fondly of Harold; he lived and worked with them in their first bark hut at Kangaroo Creek when they were gold-panning, and after Amelia went to Sydney, she got to know and like them. They're really nice, especially Beth, who has a lovely smile. Harold has worked in the general post office as a mail sorter for decades, and when he hears that I want to work in Sydney but can't go nursing, he says he'll look into getting me a job as a telephone operator at the main Sydney Exchange. And I'm thrilled when he and Beth invite me to live with them till I find a place of my own.

A few weeks after they've gone back to Sydney, I receive a letter from Harold saying that I can have a job if I want it in the next intake for the Exchange, which is coming up soon.

I'm sad to leave Dad and Laurence, and strangely enough, Mum as well. Despite her current crankiness, things have been better between us since I put a stop to the beatings when I was twelve. Even so, when she's not yelling, there's a kind of ghost-like quality to her. She was nice to to me when I was little, before we moved to the farm, but, now, looking back, I think that, even then, she was a bit whispy.

At least I didn't have to go through the painful business of breaking the news of my leaving to her like Amelia did—she was right there when Harold said he'd get me the job. Amelia says she paved the way for my escape by leaving first, but it's pretty obvious to me that Mum just doesn't care about me as much as she does about her, and isn't nearly as upset about my leaving.

I'm also sad to leave Rahnee, my mare till Dad bought her from me. When Amelia went nursing, he gave her money for her horse, and, once he knew I was leaving, he gave me thirty pounds for Rahnee, to see me through till I get paid. Ever since we moved to the property, my parents have had our mare Dolly "serviced," as it's called, by a stallion every couple of years. Her first foal was Claude's, the second Amelia's, and then it was my turn. I've loved Rahnee ever since I first saw her one crystal clear spring day, newly born and shadowing Dolly, her tail crimped from the womb. Mum gave me the idea of calling her Rahnee, meaning "Hindu queen." I managed to get close to her and stroke her that first day, and I've taught her to come to a whistle. She's just been broken in by Balfour, but I haven't ridden her—Mum says she's a bit too frisky for me yet.

I telephone the train station and book a seat on the Express to Sydney in a couple of weeks. Then I get my clothes together, and make myself a new green sheath dress to wear the day I leave. Finally, I pack one small suitcase, and Mum drives me to the station. Neither she nor anybody else cries when I say goodbye.

I do cry, but not until I'm on the train moving away from Scone. A kindly grey-haired woman sitting next to me asks what's wrong, and I explain that I'm leaving home for the city. She doesn't live in Sydney, but she writes her telephone number on a piece of paper which she gives me, saying to call if I ever need help.

Despite that bit of sadness, I'm full of excitement about my real life finally beginning.

Figure 57.1: Me at seventeen with my mother in Scone, the day I left home.

Part IV

AFTERWORD

AFTERWORD

Surviving my first seventeen years and escaping from the farm remain the hardest things I've ever had to do, but my first years in Sydney presented challenges, too.

For instance, city dwellers are constantly aware of, and driven by, time, which was a new concept for me—on Barrington Tops, though we followed a routine of sorts, we paid far less attention to the time things were done. And if someone Dad expected didn't turn up, he'd shrug and say he supposed that he or she would be along the following day. Then there was budgeting—which I have to admit I still haven't fully mastered. On the farm, my parents automatically provided food, housing and transport. Whenever we went to town, Dad gave me a small amount of money, and if I'd spent this by the next time we went there, he'd give me some more. I'd never had a bank account, or learned how to save. My wages in the city were low in the early years, and several times I had to ask my parents for small sums of money.

I read books about manners, and also learned by trial and error how to socialize and make friends. Amelia, who was of course already in Sydney, was very supportive when I was first there. Through her, I met a cousin who generously invited me to many dinners and parties.

For about a year, I lived with Harold and Beth and worked as what was known in those days as a "trunk-line operator," which meant that I sat at a desk in the middle of a room with hundreds of other women at similar desks, and connected callers to distant numbers within Australia. After this, I took an office job where I learned to type and take shorthand, and later enjoyed working as a private secretary for the managing directors of several companies.

After being with Harold and Beth, who were always very kind, I lived with various people in different suburbs, and then in a boarding house in Neutral Bay. There I met Andrew. Polish born and twenty years my senior, he'd been in the British army in World War II, after which he'd studied science at London University. He worked as a chemist, and was very intelligent and interested in many things.

When I was twenty, he wrote asking my parents' permission to marry me, and we were both astonished to receive a response from Mum saying, yet again, that I'd been a problem since the day I was born—as if she thought he should change his mind. Ignoring this, we were married in 1965 when I was twenty-one. He saw me as capable of much more than my current secretarial occupation, and I'll always be grateful to him for his encouragement and support.

With the idea of eventually matriculating so that I could study at university, I began taking evening courses in high school mathematics and science, which I'd never studied. Then I attended a day college for adults, studying highschool subjects full-time.

The psychologist at the college decided to give all the students an IQ test. I arrived slightly late for it, and was so anxious that I could not think clearly. Later, we were all called into his office for our results, and he gave me the bad news that I had an IQ of 108. Even if I succeeded in getting into university, he said, I'd never be able to complete studies at this level.

Part of me felt ashamed, but a stronger part continued to believe in myself and my intelligence well enough to decide to study medicine. My end-of-year exam results secured me a place in Science only, so I repeated the year at a different college. At that time, prospective medical students were not interviewed, and entry into the program depended on matriculation marks alone. At the end of my repeat year, my marks being in the top four percent in the State, I secured a place in medical school. I didn't have to worry about paying university fees, as I'd also won a scholarship; and, in any case, soon afterwards the newly-elected Labour government abolished such fees altogether.

Medicine was a six-year course, and I began my studies in 1971 when I was twenty-seven. One morning several years later, I happened to meet the psychologist who'd given me the IQ test on a railway station, and, as you can imagine, I delighted in telling him that I was in third-year medicine.

Towards the end of my studies, my marriage disintegrated and I moved into residence at the university; Andrew and I subsequently divorced.

Graduation gave me an M.B., B.S., a bachelor's degree in medicine and in surgery, and equivalent to the North American M.D. Registration to practice required the completion of a year's internship, which I completed at Royal Prince Alfred Hospital, where Amelia had nursed, although she was no longer working there by this time.

After a holiday of several months traveling alone in Asia in 1978, I worked for some eleven months as a resident at Gosford District Hospital, about a hundred miles north of Sydney. There I met many interesting people, some of whom are still friends.

Doctors won the right to be paid overtime around then, and I received a cheque for some $20,000 in back pay, which I used to travel in Europe for most of 1979. On a train in Germany, I decided to study psychiatry—the only medical specialty that interested me intellectually, and I loved the idea of talking to people from diverse backgrounds, and, as I imagined, learning about the "nitty gritty" of their lives. Later, in Italy, I met and traveled with several people from Canada, and decided to investigate the possibility of studying psychiatry in this country.

I was accepted into the four-year psychiatry program at the University of British Columbia in Vancouver, but first had to write the Canadian final medical exams—which, fortunately, were not very difficult—and I began my studies in 1980.

Not long before I completed the psychiatry program, I met Dennis, an artist, who was very intelligent with a delightful sense of humour. We married in 1983, and I became step-mother to his twelve-year-old son, Paul. Dennis and I traveled to many countries, visiting galleries wherever we went, and I especially enjoyed Mexico and Spain, and learned some Spanish.

After graduation, I started working in private practice and treating, mainly with psychotherapy, people with childhood trauma—the population with whom I continued to work for more than three decades before I retired at the end of July 2018.

In the nineteen-nineties, I studied English part-time at UBC, and enjoyed this very much. I graduated with a first class Honours Degree for my original work on the influence of Virginia Woolf's childhood trauma on her writings. Subsequently, Dennis helped me apply for a two-year MA program in creative writing at the University of Technology in Sydney. I won a scholarship, and enjoyed something like a year of studying there while I lived with friends, but I found the program insufficiently stimulating, and abandoned it.

After being together for decades, Dennis and I separated amicably and divorced in the early twenty-first century. I am glad to say that we remain friends and I am very close to his son, his son's wife and their two delightful children.

In 2011, I married my husband Newell on Pender Island, and we live in Victoria, BC. Brilliant and gregarious, and passionate about the natural world, he has a graduate degree in psychology but has worked mainly as a business consultant. He is unfailingly supportive, and has worked extremely hard assisting me in the publication of this manuscript.

I write—poetry, fiction, non-fiction and creative non-fiction—and frequently read my work at gatherings of writers. And Newell and I enjoy time with our many friends, as well as traveling.

***

I completed some two years of psychoanalysis with a pleasant psychiatrist from New Zealand in the nineteen-eighties, and found this very helpful. However, I didn't realize that I myself was suffering from Posttraumatic Stress Disorder (PTSD) until I had been working with others with this condition for a considerable time, and had attended many conferences on the subject.

A common symptom of PTSD is "blanking out," or Dissociation, precipitated by anxiety, in which, as a result of the brain being flooded with natural opioids, thought, and, at times, even movement, is severely limited or impossible. Some people can appear to be relatively normal during such episodes, even though they later have no memory of what happened during them. As far back as when I was studying for my matriculation, I realized that, when I became anxious, I suffered from cognitive difficulties—though without subsequent memory lapses.

This problem might well have prevented me from succeeding at all had I not discovered a non-addictive medication with the generic name of Propranolol, which performers, such as singers, use, and which blocks adrenaline and prevents dissociation; I took it subsequently whenever I was anxious and before writing exams.

For a short time, I also saw a psychologist for Eye Movement Desensitization and Reprocessing (EMDR), one of the most effective treatments for PTSD, and in the course of learning various psychotherapies over the years I have completed, with colleagues, a considerable number of hours of various other types of psychological work on my early trauma.

Nevertheless, realizations continue to come. Only in 2012, did I fully recognize my huge underlying longing for my mother's love after she began to rage. Also, although it's difficult to see an enraged person as the victim of an illness, I now believe that Mum herself suffered from PTSD, which surfaced as rage after we settled on the same mountain where she'd grown up.

It seems that she suffered from Dissociation: on one occasion (described in my memoir), after she beat Laurence, she subsequently appeared to have no memory of having done so. I now think that, although I always found her mother to be extremely kind, Mum had experienced her own early maternal deprivation due to her mother's physical illnesses, depressions, and absence for months at one point. Mum always denied having been beaten, saying that she was too well-behaved to need such punishment, but she was probably also traumatized by seeing her father beat her younger brother—sometimes with a horsewhip, according to what others have told me.

After realizing that she had been ill, one day I went to Emergency with chest pain, fearing that I might die. The pain eventually turned out to be due to a gall-bladder problem, rather than a heart attack, but that day, I had the thought that Mum's illness should have been treated. In reality, the usual treatment being psychotherapy, even had this been available, she possessed so little insight that she would have been unlikely to accept such treatment.

All my life until recently, I have struggled with unpleasant body sensations, an over-active startle reflex, annoying gastrointestinal problems, an intermittent negative sense of self, and the unquenchable thirst for maternal love. But whereas many people traumatized in early life—especially if they have not dealt with their trauma in psychotherapy—find their symptoms worsening with the stresses involved in aging, I'm happy to say that my PTSD continues to resolve, leaving me with, mainly, an over-active startle reflex, occasional, and now mild, Dissociation, and a greatly diminished longing to be close to my mother.

My parents are no longer living, but, these days, they both appear in my dreams as quiet, respectful presences—rather like they were until I was five. They treat me like the adult I am, however, pointing out things I need to know, or quietly waiting for me to join them. And last year I dreamed that it was evening and I was in the bedroom I used to share with Amelia in the house on Barrington Tops, feeling very secure in the knowledge that they were in their room across the hallway.

I know now that one of the reasons I survived and eventually prospered despite my early abuse was that I had a good first five or so years, and those loving people in my life after this: Alan Sroufe's highly-respected prospective longitudinal Minnesota study found that a good first few years, and/or one loving person, protects from the worst consequences of later abuse.[1]

What I feel most about my parents now is admiration for their achievements, and sorrow for what those achievements cost them. I'm grateful to

---

[1] Sroufe, L. Alan et al. 2005. The Development of the Person: the Minnesota Study of Risk and Adaption from Birth to Adulthood. The Guildford Press, p. 225-229

them for those first years, the love of the natural world they, and especially my mother, awakened in me, for Dad's love, and that of Amelia and many others who were there for me when I needed them. And, wrongheaded as Dad's Communist ideas were, I'm pleased that he introduced me to intellectual thought and questions of ethics and justice early in life.

Like others who are knowledgeable about PTSD, I believe that the vast majority of human beings who have a loving childhood develop into empathetic adults, and that the problem behaviours of most dysfunctional people, including the worst criminals, are usually due to PTSD.

***

When I was living in Sydney, I visited the farm on long weekends and for holidays. Mum remained quick to anger, and rarely acted positively towards me, and I would almost always leave with unpleasant feelings. After I came to Canada in the nineteen-eighties, I continued to visit Australia and my parents, but less often, of course. I never succeeded in persuading them to come to Canada to see me—I'm not sure why.

On one visit during the time I was seeing my first psychotherapist in the nineteen-eighties, I told Mum that she'd made my early life a misery, and she murmured that she'd never meant to. I told Dad something of the horrors of dealing with him when he was drinking, too, and he said he wished things had been different. Now I'm sorry I didn't thank them for the good things they did do for me. Many years later, I also talked to Claude about the unpleasant things he'd done to me, and he apologized.

On a visit to the farm when I was in my forties, I was in my nightgown on my way to the bathroom next to the kitchen one morning, when Mum rushed out, grabbed me in her arms and, for the first and only time in my life, told me she loved me. She released me almost immediately and hurried back to getting breakfast.

From when they were first together, my parents had wanted to run Hereford cattle, and they succeeded in building up an impressive herd, for which they won a prize in the nineteen-eighties. In the photograph of them taken that day their faces are full of joy.

Mum died of Motor Neurone Disease in 1991, and I spent a week in Scone where she was hospitalized, visiting her every day. For most of this time, I was the only one of her children who was there. I was amazed to find that her anger had disappeared. I was still struggling to get the love I needed from her, but now I wish that I'd been able to be more loving and "motherly" towards her during that time.

Trevor Rose was in Scone hospital at this same time, and I had a pleasant conversation with him. He passed away several years later.

Polly remained a kind and loving friend; she spent the last years of her life in Maitland, a town some sixty kilometers south of Scone, and I called on her each time I visited my parents—except for when Mum was dying. I did have a pleasant conversation with her by telephone that time, but on the morning of the day Mum died, we received word that she'd had a stroke and was in hospital, and she died later that same day. Thus, I never formerly thanked her, either, and was unable to attend her funeral.

Dad remained on the farm after Mum's death, but eventually developed dementia to some degree, and was cared for in a Sydney nursing home. But he still knew who we were, and each time I visited, he told me that he loved me. He died in the home in 2002.

Before I left Australia, Uncle Bill, now in his sixties, married a lovely woman, and in the nineteen-nineties when I visited them near Brisbane, where they lived, I told him I loved him, and his face opened like a flower. I wish I'd thanked him, also, for all the wonderful things he did for me and Amelia. He died a few years later.

Claude married and lived with his family in a house he built close to that of my parents. He and his wife had three children. He died of Cancer in 1995, and his son now owns the property, but lives some miles away.

Amelia graduated from Nursing school in Royal Prince Alfred Hospital, and married not long after I went to live in Sydney; she later worked in a nursing home for many years. She and her husband had two delightful children, and I continue to enjoy friendships with them, as well as with their partners and children. Sadly, her husband—whom I'd come to love dearly—died in 1991, the same year as Mum. Amelia is now retired, lives in Sydney, spends most of her time writing creative non-fiction and poetry, and has published several books.

I have become very close to my brother Laurence. Unfortunately, my parents took him out of school years before he was due to matriculate. He was involved in acting and singing for a time, and was a video salesman; he did not marry. Retired now, he lives in a Sydney suburb, but suffers from many minor illnesses and considerable fatigue. He and Amelia have both visited me here in Canada.

I had an excellent friendship with Auntie's son until he died in 2018, and I continue to enjoy spending time with his wife, their adult children, and their partners and children, most of whom live near Newcastle. Several members of that family have visited me here, also.

GLOSSARY

adze A large implement with a sharp blade at a ninety degree angle to the handle, used for woodwork.

asphalt In Australia, a surfaced highway—also called bitumen.

cat's head The common name for the seed of a low-growing plant, *Emex australis,* which is shaped roughly like a cat's head; also called a "bindi."

billycan A tin can about six inches across and ten deep, with a handle, used for boiling water over a campfire and for making tea; also called a "billy."

biscuit The Australian word for what is known as a cookie in North America.

blight A disease which attacks potato plants, rotting the potatoes under the ground while the tops look healthy; it contributed significantly to the great Irish famine.

bloke Australian slang for a man.

blue heeler An Australian dog with bluish fur that is part dingo—a wild dog in Australia, but thought to be descended from domesticated dogs; they nip the heels of the cattle they are bred to herd.

brisket Though the definition varies, during childhood, I understood it to be a cut of beef from the beast's dewlap, a "curtain-like" piece of flesh that hangs between its front legs.

boot The storage space in a car, known as the "trunk" in North America.

bottle brush One of the Callistemon or Melaleuca genus of shrubs endemic to Australia, although the ones near the farm were more like trees, being about fifteen feet, or five metres, high. Its flowers are shaped like the bottle brushes used for washing dishes.

brolga Also known as a "native companion," a large grey-blue bird and member of the crane family, found in Australia and New Guinea.

buggy A horse-drawn vehicle.

camp As a verb, to stay in makeshift accommodation—usually a tent. Labourers formerly lived in such accommodation while they were working on the land. Used as a noun, it means such accommodation.

cat's head The common name for the seed, shaped roughly like a cat's head, of a low-growing plant, *Emex australis.*

chemist A pharmacy where medications are sold, and where other goods and services may also be offered.

chooks Fowls, or what North Americans call "chickens.

cicada A large flying insect, of which there are some 3,000 species, hatching and emerging from the ground at intervals of up to seventeen years; the males make a mating sound by vibrating a part of their body, which becomes very loud when many sing in trees in hot weather.

correspondence school Also called simply, "correspondence;" the means by which many children living in remote regions were educated, receiving their lessons by post from what was formerly Blackfriars Correspondence School in Sydney, and returning them by the same means; usually, a parent acted as "supervisor."

cradle A contraption used in the old gold panning days, which used the water pressure in a stream to trap gold.

coop A small building such as that where fowls sleep at night and, often, lay their eggs.

copper A large receptacle made of copper and, before electricity and washing machines, was arranged so that a fire could be lit under it, and used for boiling white linens.

cornbag A large bag, about two by three feet, made of heavy string.

cutting The word Australians use for a road cut around the side of a hill or mountain.

damper Australian bush "bread," formerly made from flour, baking powder, fat and water, but now made with butter, or sometimes cream, and this version uses beer instead of water. In former times, it was cooked in a cast iron casserole called a "camp oven" over the fire.

dingo A wild dog in Australia, which is hunted because it eats sheep etc.; thought to be descended from domesticated dogs.

dinner The midday meal in rural Australia in former times.

droving Cattle are usually taken to market by road transport these days, but in the past, they were driven in a mob by a person on horseback called a "drover," and this occupation was called "droving."

Echidna Also called a spiny anteater, belongs to the family Tachyglossidae in the monotreme order of egg-laying mammals. It eats ants and termites but is not related to the true anteaters of the Americas. It and the platypus are the only mammals that lay eggs.

Echo The name my sister Amelia was given in the Argonauts' club, and, in Greek mythology, a mountain nymph who loved the sound of her own voice.

eiderdown A bedcover, traditionally stuffed with down, and similar to a North American duvet.

flying possum Also called a "sugar glider," because of its taste for sweet substances, Petaurus breviceps is a small, omnivorous, arboreal, and nocturnal gliding possum belonging to the marsupial infraclass."

fullah The way "fellow" is often pronounced in Australia; the plural was probably originally used to mean just males, but, like "guys" in North America, it's now used for both males or females.

gaol Jail

gillbird A large grey bird, also called a wattlebird (Anthochaera carunculata), found in Australia, with red eyes and wattles; it eats honey and insects and makes a sound like coughing or barking.

greenhead An ant five to seven millimetres long with a green head, which gives a very painful, but harmless, bite; endemic to Australia, its scientific name is Rhytidoponera metallica.

grog Now Australian slang for any alcoholic drink, it originally meant a drink of rum and water.

grubbing Digging out the stumps and roots of trees that have been previously cut down.

Gooday An Australian greeting like "hello."

grub Australian slang for food.

gum tree What Australians call the eucalyptus tree, of which there are more than seven hundred species, most native to Australia.

ibis A long-legged wading bird with a curved beak; Threskiornis molucca, or the white ibis, is white with a black head and neck, and is found in northern and eastern Australia, while Threskiornis spinicollis, or the straw necked ibis, is black with a straw-coloured neck, and is found throughout Australia, as well as in Indonesia, New Guinea and Norfolk Island.

jimmyburn Native Australian bushes with thorns that cause a painful burning sensation.

jobby A word formerly used by children to describe faeces; to "do one's jobby" meant to have a bowel movement.

joey A baby kangaroo.

katydid A type of insect in the same family as grasshoppers but with longer antennae, sometimes very brightly coloured.

kookaburra Tree kingfishers of the genus Dacelo native to Australia and New Guinea, whose loud call sounds like human laughter.

lattice Criss-crossed slats of wood. When this material forms the outside wall of a veranda, Australians say it's "latticed in."

lollies Candies.

mattock A digging implement with a long handle, and, at right angles to this, a heavy, narrow blade.

meat ant A member of the genus Iridomyrmex (iridomyrmex purpureus) endemic to Australia, with a dark bluish body and red head and 6-7 mm. in length.

meat house Before refrigeration, a small building for storing meat on a farm.

meat safeA small metal cupboard perforated all over with tiny holes to allow air to circulate through it while keeping flies out; hung in a shady, cool place, it was used, when refrigeration was not available, to store corned meat and other food.

metho Methylated spirits or rubbing alcohol, which is a disinfectant when used in a concentration of seventy percent.

moleskins Trousers usually worn by men for riding, with tapered legs so that they are often very tight, and made from strong cream-coloured cotton.

ninny Australian slang for a weak or stupid person.

noxious weed In Australia, a plant declared so under an act of parliament because it is considered to have the potential to harm individuals and the community; land occupants have an obligation to control such plants.

nurse In Australia, to "nurse" someone, commonly means to have him or her sit on ones lap.

packing needle A thick needle about six inches long with a large eye; threaded with string, it is used to sew the tops of bags such as cornbags together.

paddock In country Australia, to go "out in the paddock or paddocks" usually means to visit the countryside somewhere on one's own property, but it can also refer to a space enclosed by a fence, and designated by an adjective such as "potato," or "back," and may refer to anybody's property.

passion fruit The purple Passiflora edulis edulis is a vine which thrives in many parts of Australia and produces edible purple fruit (genus Passiflora).

Pauson The name I was given as an Argonaut, and that of an artist in ancient Greece who depicted what was defective or repulsive in his subjects.

Phidias Named after a Greek sculptor, painter and architect, the man who spoke about art on the Argonaut's Club; in real life, he was Jeffrey Smart, who subsequently became a well-known artist.

Pigna Barney A river on the Gloucester side of the Barrington plateau, and which merges with the Manning River.

poddy calf An orphaned calf fed with bottled milk, and which often have a large belly.

port The word formerly used to mean a suitcase in Australia.

porcupine An Echidna, or spiny anteater, which belongs to the family Tachyglossidae in the monotreme order of egg-laying mammals. These animals eat ants and termites but are not related to the true anteaters of the Americas. They and the platypus are the only mammals that lay eggs.

pound A unit of currency before Australia adopted the decimal system in 1966.

property name Usually in Australia, large properties have names, whereas small ones do not, so those associated with a property without a name may be seen as lower class by class-conscious people.

quid Slang for the monetary amount of one pound; in Australia, the currency before the Amelial system was introduced in 1966 was pounds, shillings and pennies, or pence. It can also mean simply "money," e.g., to "make a decent quid" means "to make a decent amount of money."

redback A highly venomous Australian spider (Latrodectus hasseltii) found throughout the country.

ringbark To cut a strip of bark from the trunk of a tree all the way round, which kills the tree by preventing it from receiving nutrients from the ground. In the old days, "ringbarking" was the easiest way of allowing the sun to reach the ground so that grass and crops could grow. A tree killed in this way is said to have been "ringbarked."

setter A short-handled digging tool with a narrow blade and a top like a hammer.

snap A photograph.

Solyptol The brand name of a disinfectant with eucalyptus oil as its main ingredient.

spitfires The larvae of the sawfly wasp that does not sting.

springing When a young cow is about to calve for the first time, she loses thick, mucous from her vagina.

station The Australian word for a large landholding used for livestock production, and equivalent to a North American ranch, though the word originally referred to the homestead and outbuildings only. The owner is called a "grazier," or "pastoralist" rather than a rancher.

storeroom Pantry.

stringybark A type of eucalyptus with very thick bark, traditionally used for building huts in the bush.

tarp A tarpaulin.

tea The evening meal in Australia in former times.

Tilley lamp The brand name of a lamp which runs on kerosene pumped up with air to make it gaseous, and which has a mantle which glows and gives off a very bright light.

timber jinker A lorry with a long trailor used for carrying logs.

trunk call The old name for a long distance telephone call within Australia.

torch A flashlight.

trapline A line of rabbit traps.

tucker Australian slang for food.

tussock A plant of tussock grass or bunch grass, which is in the Poaceae family; each plant appears to be separate from the others, unlike in grass as we usually think of it. A tussock can be several feet tall.

up When my father used this word to describe a river, he meant that it was in flood.

Vegemite The brand name of a very popular vegetable extract Australians spread on bread and butter.

verandah Open to the air but protected from sun and rain by the main roof of the house, a pleasant place to sit, work, play or sleep in hot climates; frequently seen in houses in rural Australia.

wallaby A medium-sized kangaroo.

washing-up In the Australian bush in former times, to do the "washing-up" meant to wash the dishes, and the "washing-up dish" was the dish in which they were washed.

water bag A canvas bag formerly used to carry water in the bush.

wether A castrated male sheep.

Wild Wests Cowboy adventure stories.

wireless A radio.

witchetty grub The name given in Australia to the large, white, wood-eating larvae of several moths, and eaten by the indigenous people.

yarn A yarn is a "tall tale" in Australian slang, but to yarn, or have a yarn, usually simply means simply to talk with a person or people.